The Stress-Free Pregnancy Guide

The Stress-Free Pregnancy Guide

A Doctor Tells You What to *Really* Expect

Carol Livoti, M.D., OB/GYN
and Elizabeth Topp

New York • Atlanta • Brussels • Chicago
Mexico City • San Francisco • Shanghai • Tokyo • Toronto • Washington, D.C.

Special discounts on bulk quantities of AMACOM books are available to corporations, professional associations, and other organizations. For details, contact Special Sales Department, AMACOM, a division of American Management Association, 1601 Broadway, New York, NY 10019. Tel: 212-903-8316. Fax: 212-903-8083.
E-mail: specialsls@amanet.org
Website: www.amacombooks.org/go/specialsales
To view all AMACOM titles go to: www.amacombooks.org

This publication is designed to provide accurate and authoritative information in regard to the subject matter covered. It is sold with the understanding that the publisher is not engaged in rendering legal, accounting, or other professional service. If legal advice or other expert assistance is required, the services of a competent professional person should be sou

Library of Congress Cataloging-in-Pub

Livoti, Carol.
   The stress-free pregnancy guide : a
Livoti and Elizabeth Topp.
    p. cm.
   Includes index.
   ISBN-13: 978-0-8144-8055-7
   ISBN-10: 0-8144-8055-1
    1. Pregnancy. 2. Pregnancy—C(
health. 4. Pregnant women—He;
6. Childbirth. I. Topp, Elizabeth.

RG525.L5475   2009
618.2--dc22   2008024324

Printing number
10 9 8 7 6 5 4 3 2 1

Contents

Introduction

*O*ver the years my patients have shown me hundreds of pregnancy books, often so I could reassure them about something alarming they had read. The information was almost always exaggerated, misleading, or just plain wrong. I've seen books instill the worst fears in pregnant women; one alarmingly stated that it if the baby hiccups in utero, it could be a sign of a tangled umbilical cord. Often, these highly detailed manuals terrified women who could not live up to their precise specifications about everything from what they should eat to how they should sleep, when in most cases these behavioral adjustments can only hope to create marginally better outcomes.

My goal with this book is to remove the unnecessary anxiety and replace it with joy. All the information and recommendations in this book are drawn from the American College of Obstetrics and Gynecology (ACOG), as well as my own experience in over thirty years of clinical practice and teaching, and my own pregnancy, of course. Based on these resources, I am happy to assure you that when it comes to pregnancy, the odds are overwhelming that everything will go just fine. Approximately 90 percent of pregnant women will have a completely normal, alarm-free, healthy pregnancy, labor, and delivery.

That said, there are many good reasons to view pregnancy not only as the happiest thing that's ever happened to you but also as a significant medical undertaking. There *are* things to be concerned about in pregnancy; it's a risky proposition requiring a huge biological commitment from the future mother. It's difficult not to get really nervous about the whole thing, but remember, anxiety never helps! Do your best, for your physical and emotional well-being, to stay as calm as possible from before inception through the postpartum stage.

To that end, this book is divided into "normal" and "abnormal" chapters. All the information you will most likely need is in the normal chapters, and healthy readers may elect to skip the sections dealing with abnormalities. There's no reason to create more anxiety for yourself. However, you may need or simply desire to have all of the relevant facts, good and bad.

The information in this book is based on the premise that knowledge is power, so I've endeavored to explain the what, why, who, and how of every stage in a normal pregnancy. From common symptoms to fetal development, I'll tell you what to expect. Whenever possible, I'll also tell you why certain things happen in pregnancy, but remember that much of conception and pregnancy remains a mystery even to obstetricians. For example, nausea is a well-documented side effect of first trimester pregnancy, but no one really knows why it happens.

Since most pregnant women want to have as positive an impact as possible on their unborn children, I provide clear guidelines for optimizing your outcome, answering questions such as: How much exercise is too much? What should I eat every day? What tests should I consider? Again, these are only guidelines; don't get fanatical about following every suggestion precisely. For example, if you hate milk and it makes you gag to drink it, don't panic—talk to your doctor about potential alternatives.

Although your obstetrician is the ultimate resource for your pregnancy, I'll tell you what you can expect from her, too. I'll also address questions you might have about your medical care, such as: How often should I see my doctor? Why all the tests? How do they work? I'll describe and explain all the major medical landmarks of pregnancy, although you should keep in mind that your doctor's approach might differ from the protocols mentioned here. This way, you can be prepared with questions and review what your doctors said after your appointments, which can be short, fast, and over-whelming.

This book fills in the blanks, refreshes your memory of basic biology, and helps you navigate childbirth in the twenty-first century. The emphasis is first on good information, with the ultimate goal of reassuring you that this can be the most exciting and fun time of your life.

CHAPTER 1

Before Conception

*T*hese last fifty years mark the first time in human history that sexually active women have been able to choose whether or not to have a baby. In the past, women's options were celibacy or motherhood. Of course, it's liberating and exciting to be able to control our own reproduction, but these benefits come with responsibility: If it's possible to *plan* a pregnancy, it's worth trying to do so.

Even Unplanned Pregnancies Deserve Some Planning

More than 30 percent of babies born in this country are the result of unplanned pregnancies. Because no contraceptive device is 100 percent effective, there are a few things you should think about if you're a heterosexually active female, regardless of whether you're trying to get pregnant at this very moment.

First Step: Don't Panic!

If you are a perfectly healthy, addiction- and medication-free woman under the age of forty, and you do nothing at all about your prenatal health—and by nothing I mean you never see a physician, get tested for anything, or alter your diet or lifestyle—your chances of having a healthy baby at term are still over 90 percent. However, modern medicine has quite a lot to offer the pregnant woman in terms of her well-being and that of her child. To make informed decisions for your baby and yourself, you should know and understand the standard obstetrical process. I'm not saying that you must follow every suggestion offered by prenatal experts to have a healthy and happy pregnancy, but don't just guess at which guidelines to bend or rules to break. Therefore, if the condom breaks and you are at a place in your life where you would at least *consider* having a baby, think about cutting back on booze before you get your next period—embryos don't seem to handle their liquor well. It's also a good idea to take a multivitamin every day, especially one containing folic acid, which is known to prevent certain birth defects and is relatively easy to incorporate into your life. Smoking isn't good for anybody, mother or child, so consider dropping that out of your regimen. Talk to your doctor about any medications you might be taking. Some relatively common drugs, like the acne treatment Accutane, unnecessarily raise the risk of birth defects.

The point is that even an unplanned pregnancy should not be a completely haphazard affair. The minute you begin to suspect that you could be pregnant, start avoiding behaviors that could be harmful to the embryo.

Planned Pregnancies

Planning to have a child is a deeply personal process that often combines careful planning with soul-searching. For me, deciding to have a baby was at least in part the result of a strong desire to make myself a better person—someone less egocentric.

Not long before we decided to have children, my husband and I went to a dinner party. Our hosts, a professional couple, announced early in the meal that they were voluntarily childless. They were professors, and perhaps they fancied that they had intellectualized themselves out of a biological imperative. Yet during the course of dinner, the wife showed off her husband's PhD dissertation like a grandma with baby pictures, and the two of them cooed at their pet bird the whole night. Watching this couple dote on their academic accomplishments and their pets left me with a strong urge to have a baby immediately.

There's arguably a standard progression to the human experience, and those who disagree probably aren't reading this book. Having a baby should be an expansive experience in more ways than one. Instead of thinking about yourself all the time, you are supposed to think about someone else. If you believe that life is a continuous process of learning, expanding, knowing, loving, and maturing until the day you die, then having a child is one of the best ways to make yourself into a better person. Other good reasons to have a baby are that you want to give life to the world, you have a strong desire to love unconditionally, you have an interest in watching another person grow and mature under your thoughtful guidance, and you have an undeniable urge to carry your genetic dynasty forward.

There are some not-so-good reasons to have a baby, too. From the baby's side of things, it is nice to be planned and wanted, but just being planned doesn't necessarily make for a better situation. For example, it's not so nice to be wanted as an accessory or as a cure for a shaky marriage. It's also disheartening to see parents of girls try again and again, just hoping for a boy (or vice versa). It may seem obvious, but it bears repeating: All babies are human beings, and the birth of a child—boy or girl—will change your life indelibly and forever.

It's sad when babies are born for the wrong reasons. Teen mothers have achieved notoriety, perhaps unjustly, for saying, "I wanted

THIS SURE AIN'T CHINA

One of my patients who had four sons desperately wanted a girl. She sought out a special in vitro fertilization (IVF) procedure, whereby a few embryonic cells are tested to determine the sex before insertion. She requested that they use only females. These attempts failed several times. She subsequently became spontaneously pregnant, but when tests showed the embryo was a boy, she terminated the pregnancy. I can empathize. I wanted a girl more than anything, and I don't know how I would have felt if my daughter, Elizabeth, had been a boy. It's always difficult to observe parents eager for one sex over the other, because the disappointments are so frequent and unnecessary.

A BUNDLE OF JOY... AND SOME STRESS

I delivered the baby of a psychiatrist and his wife, and when I spoke to him several months after the baby was born, he said that he just couldn't believe that no one talks about how stressful and difficult it is for the marital relationship to have a newborn in the house. As a mental health professional, he was shocked that this was not more commonly understood.

someone to love me unconditionally." However, it is a rude awakening for all parents to learn that babies cannot love you right out of the womb. Instead, they need constant supervision—they need to be nurtured and kept warm and dry. For months, even years, those adorable little eyes will communicate a pretty constant message: "Feed me, love me, hold me, take care of me." And while they will certainly cling to you, they're mostly holding onto what is familiar to them. Becoming a good parent means being excited about your role as a giver rather than a receiver of love.

The good news is that it's a thrill when a four-year-old picks a flower and presents it to you. Or when she goes out to the local drugstore on Mother's Day and comes back with a five-dollar bottle of perfume. These are moments you don't forget, largely because you've been waiting for them for so long.

The logistics of getting pregnant may not be so important. Women who face their forties without a partner in sight get inseminated. Lesbian couples buy sperm, have a few romantic interludes with a turkey baster, and head into parenting as partners. Women whose marriages are on the rocks accidentally (or not so accidentally) get pregnant all the time. Regardless of how you get there, with the right attitude any pregnancy can have a magnificent outcome.

Of course, when you first decide, with your partner or on your own, that you want to get pregnant, it is the obstetrician's hope that you will then and there make an appointment for a *preconception consultation*. The advantage to this approach is that once you are pregnant you don't have any catching up to do. You won't have to hear your doctor say, "Wait a minute, let's think about this medication you're on. You may have to see a geneticist." Or "Let's look at that X-ray you had last week." The best conception plan starts with just having a plan, although this seldom happens in the real world.

Preexisting Health Conditions

At your preconception consultation, your obstetrician should investigate your underlying health. The vast majority of women who want to get pregnant have very little to talk about. However, if you suffer from any autoimmune disorders such as rheumatoid arthritis, lupus, or scleroderma or you have a significant, chronic medical problem such as high blood pressure, diabetes, kidney disease, epilepsy, multiple sclerosis, or bipolar disorder, you need to address these issues with your physician. If you've had any significant surgery or if you were born with a birth defect yourself, especially of your reproductive or urinary tract, your obstetrician must have all

EMOTIONAL HEALTH COUNTS

In this day and age, mental health issues are often as significant to pregnancy as physical ones. I had a patient with a very severe psychiatric illness. She had tried every FDA-approved psychotropic drug, as well as shock treatments, to no avail. Her psychiatrist had been treating her with medication from Switzerland, which he himself purchased abroad. This mysterious medication made it possible for her to function. When she became pregnant, I called her doctor and inquired about the risks to pregnancy associated with this unusual treatment. He told me that they use it in Switzerland all the time and don't have an increase in birth defects. On the one hand, his endorsement wasn't as good as a scientific study; on the other, she had to take this drug. Her only choice was to either have a baby and risk it with the medication or terminate the pregnancy. I'm happy to report that these things work out perfectly fine almost all the time, and she had a healthy baby.

of that information. She, possibly in concert with specialists, will try to proactively address how your particular medical situation will affect your pregnancy. There are so many different situations with infinite solutions that we will not attempt to address them all here—especially because less than 1 percent of pregnant women will have to deal with these problems.

Generally, if you are not perfectly healthy when you want to conceive, there are three things to consider:

1. How will your health problems impact the pregnancy? Will becoming pregnant threaten your health? Will your condition hurt the baby?

2. Could the treatment for your illness—medication, radiation, and so forth—affect the pregnancy? Could you switch to a safer therapy or suspend treatment for a year? Are there procedures that you can postpone?

3. Is your condition a genetic problem?

When the obstetrician is uncertain how your medical history might affect your pregnancy, your best resource is a geneticist. A geneticist is a doctor who specializes in counseling, diagnosing, and treating genetic problems. Geneticists rely on a huge body of infor-

WEIGHING THE RISKS

A patient with stable multiple sclerosis wanted to have a child. The strong medication she was on was dangerous to the pregnancy, but we had no way of knowing how suspending it would impact her lifestyle and health. During the period she was off the drugs, which included enough time for conception and potential miscarriages, we had to keep a close eye on any neurological changes. In the end, she was off her medication for two and a half years. She didn't feel great the whole time, but she didn't suffer any neurological damage, either. She successfully negotiated her pregnancy without doing any harm to herself or the baby, which we all considered a happy outcome.

mation that includes every recorded case of illness or problems due to medication in pregnancy. They can recommend specific tests, crunch the numbers, and give you odds. Geneticists also investigate the weaknesses of your particular ethnic background. For example, certain Jewish communities are statistically more likely to suffer cases of Tay-Sachs disease, whereas sickle-cell anemia disproportionately hits African Americans.

Things to Avoid

Of course, when you are pregnant it is ideal to maintain perfect health and steer clear of all medication. In particular, you should strive to avoid:

- Radiation
- Drugs
- Infection

Radiation

Actively dividing cells, such as those of an embryo, are most sensitive to radiation, which can dislodge part of a new cell, mutating or killing it. This is why we use radiation to treat cancer (characterized by rapid cell division) and why radiation is so bad for an early pregnancy. Every cell is extra important in a first-trimester fetus—a whole baby is going to grow out of that handful of cells. Radiation at this stage could damage a toenail cell or a brain cell, you never know. Either way, avoiding radiation during pregnancy, especially in the first trimester, is the only way to dodge the risk. The less you get, the less likely it is to damage something important.

Luckily, exposure to radiation is easy to prevent because you know where it is and can therefore make an effort to avoid it. Even in an emergency room, if you inform the hospital staff that you might be pregnant, they will find an alternative way to treat you.

For example, it may be that as few as 0.5 percent of head injuries in the emergency room turn out to include a skull fracture. The overwhelming majority of the time, a bump on the head is effectively treated with ice and Tylenol. But it's less likely to result in a lawsuit for the doctor to perform two hundred X-rays to detect the one person who has a significant injury. In fact, most of the X-rays you receive in emergent care are defensive, meaning that the doctors are defending themselves against litigation, as opposed to protecting you against harm. However, if you are pregnant, the physician might take the time to follow a less aggressive course of action, saying instead, "I don't think you have a skull fracture, but if you have trouble staying awake, if you get confused, if headaches persist for forty-eight hours or you have any symptoms whatsoever, come back and we'll give you an X-ray." That would save 199 people from unnecessary exposure to radiation, but it requires a brave doctor, a responsible patient, and a less costly legal system.

All X-ray technicians, radiologists, and emergency room personnel are supposed to ask whether you could be pregnant. But many women, especially when they're under the stress of an injury, quickly say, "Of course not!" Take a minute to think about it—you *could* be pregnant if you've had sex one time between your last period and now, even if you used a condom, the pill, and an intrauterine device (IUD).

The dangers of exposure to radiation during pregnancy start when the egg is fertilized, not beforehand. If you had a mammogram two years ago or a chest X-ray two weeks before you conceived, there's no reason to be concerned about your pregnancy. An egg still within the ovary is dormant (that is, not dividing) and so is relatively resistant to radiation. The amount of radiation that would be required to affect a dormant egg is a lot higher (such as the radia-

DON'T OVERLOOK THE OBVIOUS

Years ago there was a story in a medical journal about a poor woman who went to see her doctor because she was nauseated all the time. He sent her for a battery of tests, including many X-rays. It wasn't until her fourth dose of pelvic radiation that someone asked her, "When was your last period?"

DON'T GET HYSTERICAL

Radiation from computers became a hot topic in obstetrics after thousands of women logging above-average hours of computer use were surveyed, and the results revealed what seemed like a disproportionate number of miscarriages and birth defects. However, it's meaningless to calculate risk for something without a control group. In other words, once we compared the numbers attributed to computer users with those of women who were not computer users, we realized that they had roughly the same issues to deal with. Remember the women who went before Congress claiming their silicone breast implants led to a whole spectrum of diseases and vague conditions? The medical community kept saying, "Yes, but when you look at ten thousand women who *don't* have implants, you see the same incidence of these problems." You have to compare the numbers to a baseline in order to establish that there is any real risk.

tion level used to treat cancer) than that used to take a standard X-ray, for example.

Unfortunately, radiation is all around us; however, it's not something to go nuts over. Years ago, there was a big panic about computer monitors and pregnancy. Computer screens, like televisions, emit rays, but you tend to sit a lot closer to your computer than to your TV. Radiation from these screens becomes almost undetectable from more than three feet away, effectively nullifying the risk with televisions. Even so, there is still no evidence that computer use negatively affects fetuses.

Seek easy opportunities to avoid being exposed to radiation. For example, don't stand near the microwave while you're waiting for your popcorn. There's no need to rip your microwave out of the wall and toss it out the window because you're pregnant; just be a little more cautious.

Radiation is a legitimate, if hypothetical, concern when it comes to air travel. Some studies suggest that women should consider staying on the ground as much as possible during the early stages of pregnancy, though no specific guidelines or risks have been established. A general rule is that the longer the flight and the higher you go, the more radiation there is. A pregnant woman should avoid flights whose route is over the North Pole, where radiation levels are highest. U.S. government health agencies believe that the radiation risk from social traveling, meaning once or twice in the first trimester, is trivial. If you are planning on flying more than that, discuss it with your obstetrician. She might suggest moving a trip to the second trimester when the fetus is fully formed and less susceptible to environmental injury. Flying twice a week or more during the first trimester is considered too much radiation for a young fetus—if you are a flight attendant, consider a desk job for the first twelve weeks of pregnancy.

Medication

Among legal medications, there are those used to treat symptoms and those used to treat the illness. For example, strep throat is an illness that must be treated with antibiotics because it can quickly become a serious condition if untreated. However, a stuffy nose is merely a symptom of something else—such as a cold or allergies—and is unlikely to harm you; therefore, taking lots of Nyquil, Sudafed, or other over-the-counter medications is an unnecessary risk.

WHAT ABOUT THE PILL?

One of my patients was on the pill and wasn't getting her menstrual period. She kept telling her family doctor, "I didn't get my period this month." He accurately retorted, "That happens. Don't worry about it." She took the pill for another five months before she came to me and I diagnosed a five-month pregnancy. Even though this might seem perilous ("What if it's a boy, and I've been taking these female hormones?"), it's not uncommon for women to continue taking the pill for a cycle or two before realizing they are pregnant. Birth control pills have never been associated with any problems in pregnancy. The hormones in the pill are like a grain of sand on the beach compared to all the hormones involved in pregnancy.

When treating symptoms of illness in pregnancy, obstetricians try to keep things as simple as possible. Some studies have suggested an increase in birth defects associated with a multiplicity of drugs taken in the first trimester. So if you have a sore throat, gargle with saltwater. If you have a fever, take two Tylenol. If you have a stuffy nose, put menthol around your nostrils and chest, take a long steamy shower, and turn on the humidifier.

When it comes to addressing a real health issue, the rule of thumb in obstetrics is that if you have to treat it, treat it. It does no one any good if the mother gets really sick. Furthermore, we fortunately have a plethora of medical options. There are many antibiotics that are perfectly safe in pregnancy and are just as effective as more commonly prescribed drugs. While there are doctors who will give you the latest, newest, most exciting drug for any medical condition, obstetricians tend to stick with the classics. We like to use stuff that's been around for a while, that we know to be effective, and that has been used by hundreds of thousands of women during pregnancy without ill effects.

In the world of medications, only a handful have been proven 100 percent safe in every way during pregnancy. We call these *Class A* drugs, and their relative rarity may leave you with the erroneous impression that there are no drugs available to you while you are pregnant. Before designating a medication as a Class A drug, the Food and Drug Administration (FDA) requires a scientific study conducted specifically with pregnant women that evaluates their response to the drug versus a placebo. The study must show that the drug never causes birth defects. In reality, it's very expensive to do these studies and mostly unnecessary.

The majority of drugs have never been associated with birth defects, meaning that there has never been a recorded case of a pregnancy complication attributable to them. We call these *Class B* drugs and extrapolate that they almost definitely do not cause birth defects because they have never been known to do so. These drugs have not been tested specifically on pregnant women, so we technically do not know for sure, but many of them have been around for a long time and have been used during pregnancy without ill effects. Most obstetricians consider Class B drugs a fine choice for an expectant mother.

Any treatment with a medication riskier than a Class B drug must be justified by the medical need. Whether the condition warrants taking that risk is for you to decide with your doctor.

Recreational Drugs

It should come as no surprise that you should eliminate all illegal, recreational drugs. No one really knows the effects of party drugs on an early pregnancy—do you want to be the test case? When something is illegal, not only are its contents unknown, but the method of production is unregulated. You don't know what it was cut with or where it's coming from. So quit it.

Two legal drugs widely available in the United States are cigarettes and alcohol. Their availability makes them probably the most dangerous of all drugs, including the illegal ones. Even if you smoke only one cigarette a day, that's one too many during pregnancy.

Alcohol is also hazardous to the health of the embryo. Alcohol is a poison that the liver metabolizes, in the process producing an altered state that we commonly call being tipsy, drunk, or wasted. Because the fetus has an immature liver incapable of metabolizing any alcohol that reaches its circulatory system, a little bit of alcohol can swim around in the fetal bloodstream indefinitely. One of the most devastating effects of alcohol consumption on a developing baby is fetal alcohol syndrome, a set of birth defects, including mental deficit and characteristic facial features, that varies in intensity depending on how much alcohol is passed on to the fetus in utero.

AN OUNCE OF PREVENTION

I had a famous patient who was eight weeks' pregnant when she called in the middle of the night with a urinary tract infection. She said, "I've held out as long as I can, but the pain is unbearable." And I said, "This is silly. You've got a urinary tract infection. If you don't treat it, it will become a kidney infection. If you don't treat that, you'll get kidney damage, and then you'll need dialysis." I heard her turn to the husband and say, "The doctor says I need dialysis."

There are experts who believe that having one or two glasses of wine each week is safe in pregnancy. I believe it's not worth the risk, no matter how minimal. Many women find pleasure in alcohol, and that's okay (in moderation). But when you could be pregnant, you should not be drinking. It's simply not worth the risk, however slight, to have two glasses of wine a week. At that level of consumption, you're not addicted anyway, so quitting for nine months shouldn't be such a big deal. On the other hand, don't get upset if you eat an occasional slice of rum cake or a few chocolates filled with liqueur.

While you're still trying to get pregnant, you only need to give up alcohol in the week before you may (or may not) get your period. This is when the embryo has hooked up to your blood supply, and before that it doesn't really matter for a pregnancy what you ingest. If you give up alcohol one week each month and you end up pregnant, you're going to feel good about that. You should feel better than the glass of wine would have made you feel.

Infection

During pregnancy, the three most common and worrisome infections are rubella, toxoplasmosis, and listeriosis.

Toxoplasmosis is a parasite that lives in the intestinal tracts of cats, and in the early stages of pregnancy it can affect the baby's development. This has also been called the *kitty litter disease.* But don't just envision this bug hanging out in a cat's litter box; consider other places it might crop up. For instance, for cats on a farm, grass is a giant litter box. A cow on the farm eats the grass, and you eat the cow. Thus, rare or uncooked beef is unsafe for pregnant women, as it could still be infected. For the same reason, wash your hands after handling raw meat. Gardening is likewise a high-risk activity in pregnancy. If you're out on your hands and knees in your backyard, you could be digging around in cat droppings, so be cautious in the garden. If the dirt is dry and dusty, cover your mouth with a bandanna. Also, be sure to wear gloves when you garden. And definitely ask someone else to change the kitty litter.

These days, every child in the United States is vaccinated against rubella, also known as German measles. Chances are you were vaccinated as a child. However, if you weren't and you catch rubella in the first trimester, it can harm the baby. If you're not sure whether you've been vaccinated, there's a simple blood test that will tell you. This test should be done before you get pregnant, because you cannot receive the vaccine during pregnancy. Determining your immunity to rubella is another important reason to have a preconception consultation. If you are already pregnant and you are not immune, you will have to wait until you give birth to be vaccinated. This is frequently done in the hospital within a day of delivery, when a new pregnancy is highly unlikely.

Listeria are bacteria that seem to be inordinately attracted to pregnant women and can make both mother and baby very sick. Avoid unpasteurized cheeses and pressed deli meats, especially if they aren't fresh. *Listeria* have been found in processed meats, such as turkey roll, and in unpasteurized milk products, which are more popular in Europe than in the United States. Pay attention to food-related health advisories on the news; if authorities are recall-

PREGNANCY IS THE TIME TO BREAK BAD HABITS

A newly pregnant patient disclosed to me that she spent most of her weekends ingesting huge amounts of cocaine. I asked the husband to join us and said, "I think this is a big problem, and it's certainly not healthy." The husband said, "I think she just does cocaine because she's bored. She'll give it up once she has the baby to keep her busy." This isn't a good answer. Tremendous complications of pregnancy are a by-product of heavy cocaine use. Furthermore, this new mother might test positive for drugs at birth, which could get her reported to the authorities. I suggested we speak to a specialist or a psychiatrist about rehab. I never saw this couple again. I later found out who their obstetrician was, and when I inquired about the patient's drug problem, the other doctor told me, "Oh, I just don't ask those questions." So in case you have an unquestioning obstetrician, you heard it here: Stay off the drugs!

FISH TO KEEP OFF YOUR MENU

The U.S. Environmental Protection Agency (EPA) currently recommends pregnant women avoid these five fish:

1. Shark

2. Swordfish

3. Tile

4. Mackerel

5. Tuna

These precautions safeguard fetuses against mercury, high levels of which are present in large fish with long life expectancies (such as those listed here). But *do* eat fish. It contains very good protein and omega-3 fatty acids, which are great for the baby's brain development.

ing prepackaged egg salad, for example, make your own at home for a few weeks.

It's more important to be calm than vigilant in this crucial first stage and throughout the pregnancy. Yes, there's a lot of information about what to avoid and how to optimize your outcome, but think of these things as goals rather than threats. A piece of tuna or a glass of wine is unlikely to injure the fetus, and it's not worth fretting over. As Buddha advises, "Do your best"—and along the way, you might have the time of your life.

CHAPTER 2

Conception

Conception is the culmination of a complicated process full of biological checks and balances. It's that magical moment when a sperm pierces the outer defenses of the egg, gaining entry into the nucleus. There, the sperm's *haploid* (that is, half of the normal amount) chromosomes join with the egg's haploid chromosomes and become one with them. These newly fused strands of DNA have the genetic makeup of a unique person.

Typical Conception

A woman's ovaries contain thousands of follicles, each of which is like a little female reproductive bubble. Each contains an egg surrounded by cells that manufacture the female hormones estrogen and progesterone. At the start of the menstrual cycle, on the first day of your period, the pituitary gland hormonally signals the ovary, and the most responsive out of all the follicles (that is, the one that is at the optimal point in its development) grows and comes to the surface. Hormones continue to stimulate the follicle for about two weeks, until it ruptures and releases the egg in an event called *ovulation*. This egg heads for the fallopian tube, where it seeks a friendly sperm.

Each sperm is one contender out of one hundred million, all ejected into the vagina when the man ejaculates. This sperm has

THERE'S NO NEED FOR PILL DETOX

"I'm going off the pill now because I want to get pregnant in a year and I want my body to be clean," I've heard patients say. But think: If it took a year for the pill to clear your system, then you'd have to take the pill only once each year. Things you digest in the stomach tend not to linger in the body very long. Most women are fertile almost immediately after pill cessation. A very few get pregnant while they're still taking it. Don't make the mistake of assuming it takes six months of pill detox to get pregnant, only to find yourself pregnant before you were truly ready.

been created especially for this event and is therefore far younger than the egg it rushes to meet. While women are born with all (or, as some recent studies suggest, most) of the eggs they will ever have, men are capable of manufacturing sperm for their entire adult lives. Therefore, the egg is the same age as the woman, whereas the sperm are at most a few weeks old.

Hormones at this stage of the menstrual cycle create thin and salty cervical mucus to help the sperm swim into the uterine cavity. Even under these optimal circumstances, about half of the sperm will not make it past the cervix. So you're down to about fifty million sperm swimming around the uterus and up to a major fork in the road, where one fallopian tube heads left, the other right.

Half of the sperm go the wrong way. (The egg would have asked for directions.) So while the egg waits patiently on either the right or the left side, only about twenty-five million sperm start out toward it. The arduous day-or-so swim up the fallopian tube whittles the number of sperm to thousands. If the egg has been waiting for more than thirty-six hours, it may already be too late for fertilization to take place.

When sperm do make it on time, usually dozens arrive together. These sperm all hit on the egg (literally prodding and butting against it) until one breaks the outer shell, and the magic happens. Two sets of chromosomes join to become a totally new strand of DNA that immediately starts rapidly reproducing itself, in a process

> ## YOU CAN'T FEEL CONCEPTION HAPPEN
>
> Many women say they know exactly when they conceived. Either they claim to feel when it happened or, in retrospect, they pick the most special lovemaking session from approximately the right time. Of course, we now understand that at the time you make love, the sperm have just started a long journey and the egg may still be nestled in its follicle. Perhaps the same orchestra of hormones that ushers in pregnancy makes these women feel something noticeably different. But they're really not likely to be able to feel conception as it's happening.

called *mitosis*. This growing cell package, the *zygote*, has to swim back down the fallopian tube, which excretes certain fluids that aid in the journey and growth of the tiny embryo. It's important that the way is healthy, relatively straight, and not scarred by infections. This part of the process can take one to three days, unless the zygote gets waylaid in the tube, where it can implant and attempt to grow, creating a dangerous and unsustainable *ectopic* pregnancy (see Chapter 4).

In a successful conception, the tiny embryo makes it to the uterine cavity, where it implants itself in the wall of the uterus (called the *endometrium*), made ready by hormonal stimulation. The uterine lining is loaded with glycogen and arteries to keep nutrients and oxygen coming. The embryo burrows into its lush home and starts to grow.

Everything from start (ejaculation) to finish (implantation) happens one or two weeks before your next period is due. And if at any point something goes awry—the sperm are a little tired, the egg is a little old, the embryo doesn't implant itself properly—you get your next period as if nothing had happened.

One Obstetrician's Advice for Getting Pregnant

If you're young, healthy, and want to have a baby, the best advice is to just have lots of great sex. The more relaxed and patient you are, the better your odds of conceiving. Although there can be no guarantees, here are some tips that may give you an extra edge in your reproductive capability:

1. Have Sex *Before* You Ovulate

Make sure to have vaginal intercourse starting six days prior to ovulation and continuing at thirty-six- to forty-eight-hour intervals. If you wait until you're ovulating to grab your partner, those sperm won't make it to the egg in time. Ovulation predictor kits (see sidebar) generally predict ovulation about twelve to twenty-four hours ahead of time, which is not an optimal time frame.

2. Track Your Basal Temperature

Human females have a *biphasal* (that is, two-part) temperature curve that follows their menstrual cycle. Progesterone is *hyperthermic,* meaning that it raises the body's temperature, and is present in the female body only after a woman has ovulated. Therefore, a healthy, efficient ovulatory cycle reveals a rise in basal body temperature at ovulation that stays elevated and stable until the day before your next period, when you stop making progesterone.

To accurately measure your basal body temperature, keep a thermometer by your bed. First thing in the morning, before your feet hit the cold floor or you sip some hot coffee, take your temperature. It should be somewhere under ninety-eight degrees Fahren-

MAKING USE OF OVULATION PREDICTOR KITS

These are over-the-counter urine tests that measure the pituitary hormone that stimulates ovulation, called *luteinizing hormone,* or LH. This hormone indicates that there is a prime follicle at the ready. Some kits are more expensive (and perhaps also more accurate) than others, but in general they're all pretty reliable tools for planning ahead. For example, if you determine that you ovulated twelve days into your cycle this month, next month you can start having sex on day six.

heit for the first half of your cycle and then at least a degree higher from ovulation on.

This is not only a good way to keep track of when you're ovulating, but also a good way to tell how well you're ovulating. If your temperature drifts downward several days before your menstrual period, it may be that you aren't making adequate levels of progesterone. Conversely, if you see a clear, steady, consistent biphasal temperature pattern, you know with measured certainty that you're ovulating effectively.

3. Pay Attention to Your Discharge

In the first half of the menstrual cycle, a woman's body makes only estrogen, which produces perfect cervical discharge for sperm motility. It's got the right texture and concentrations of salt and acid. After ovulation, progesterone turns vaginal discharge thick, creamy, and less than ideal for swimming sperm. So if you notice that your discharge has changed, that cycle is pretty much over for conception.

Assuming you haven't ovulated, the more clear, watery discharge you have, the better. It's important to stay hydrated because water is a natural expectorant and keeps your cervical fluid nice and healthy. Some infertility experts recommend that patients improve the quality of their mucus by taking (orally!) over-the-counter expectorants

---

CONCEPTION REQUIRES INTERCOURSE

A young woman came to me for help with her infertility problem. Imagine my surprise at discovering that she was a virgin. When I said to her, "But...you haven't had sex," she replied, "I hoped you wouldn't notice." Every time her husband came near her, she would get nervous and cry, causing him to become nervous. Not wanting to hurt her, he'd tell her to relax and that they'd try another time. Six years had gone by this way. I advised her to use some lubrication and gently suggested that a glass of wine might help her relax. I also recommended that she get on top for a greater sense of control. She became pregnant within about four months, and (I think) she was also a little happier.

(such as Robitussin) to loosen secretions in the cervix. Your doctor might prescribe saturated solution of potassium iodide (SSKI)—some think this is more effective than over-the-counter options.

If you're just looking for some extra lubrication to keep you going through all the sex, choose wisely. Some oil-based lubricants may not be as good at helping sperm move as other, natural options that you probably already possess. A leading infertility specialist recommends raw egg whites. Saliva also works. Or you can buy any number of sperm-friendly lubricants at a pharmacy, online, or at your local sex boutique.

4. Have Sex Every Thirty-six Hours

Thirty-six hours constitute the perfect time interval between one group of sperm and the next. If you want to avoid the inconvenience and halitosis associated with morning sex, start at forty-eight-hour intervals. It's true, waiting for a long time (some couples try to go a week or more!) results in a high sperm count, but a lot of those sperm will be dead from overcrowding. Couples with specific, diagnosed fertility issues, such as a man with a low sperm count, might want to wait a little longer between rounds.

5. Have Sex for Fun

This might sound simple, but for many couples who struggle even the littlest bit to conceive, continuing to enjoy sex can become very difficult. Making love should not always be about reproduction. Most mental health experts suggest that couples who are trying hard to get pregnant have sex for fun (that is, after ovulation, when conception is highly unlikely) at least once in a while. Remember, you have a romantic relationship that is meant to last beyond conception and childbirth.

6. If You're Striving for a Boy or a Girl . . .

If you're hoping for a child of a particular gender, there are ways to influence your chances. The woman is all girl; that is, all her eggs are 100 percent X chromosomes. The man's sperm are half X and half Y, which means half will result in a female baby, the other half male. Research suggests that male sperm swim much faster than female sperm, and they seem to be healthier in an alkaline (less acidic) environment. They also die sooner. The female sperm, conversely, are slower swimmers, live longer, and seem to be happier in a relatively acidic environment.

For a Girl . . .

If you want to increase the odds of having a girl, give yourself a vinegar douche two or three days before you think you will ovulate. Then have sex in a position of shallow penetration—in the missionary position, for example, making sure to keep your hips on the mattress so the penis enters only two-thirds of the way. Once ejaculation happens, the sperm will have a lot of swimming to do in a relatively acidic environment. This weeds out the males, who burn out before they can get very far in hostile territory. The result is that the egg meets a bunch of female sperm.

For a Boy . . .

If you are desperate to have a boy, then you may want to make an exception to the six-day rule. In fact, you should avoid sex until two days before ovulation, because otherwise a leftover female sperm might still be hanging out in the tube when the egg shows up. The idea is to have sex closer to ovulation. An ovulation predictor kit can be helpful here. In addition, because male sperm prefer an alkaline

GENDER SELECTION IS NOT AN EXACT SCIENCE

A patient wanted to add a girl to her family of four, so I faithfully shared with her all of my best pointers for conceiving a girl. When she came in pregnant several months later, she told me that a friend of hers claimed all my instructions were wrong! My patient had defended me. Then she recounted how she dutifully followed all my instructions, and I realized that I had, in fact, told her the best way to conceive yet another boy. The sonogram was a real nail-biter, but despite following all my tips for having a boy, she had a girl.

AMERICANS PREFER FEMALES

Although gender selection is commonly practiced around the world, the United States is the only country where girls are more popular.

environment, when your at-home test comes back positive, make a sodium bicarbonate (baking soda) douche by dissolving a teaspoon of the powder in a cup of warm water and flushing the vagina with it. Finally, have sex in a position with deep penetration (such as placing your ankles on his shoulders) so he ejaculates right into the cervix. This way, the males will be ahead in the race to the egg, which just dropped into the tube.

These gender selection methods are not obstetrics' biggest success stories. With these at-home adjustments, you can affect your outcome by only 20 percent at most. Of course, specialists achieve much greater levels of accuracy. They can collect the man's sperm and then select the fast or slow ones to inseminate the mother. This is commonly called *sperm separation* and is about 70 percent accurate. Some doctors claim, and can probably deliver, higher efficacy rates. The procedure costs anywhere from a few hundred to several thousand dollars and is probably not covered by insurance.

Those who are absolutely determined to produce a particular gender opt for in vitro fertilization, whereby an infertility specialist extracts a few eggs, puts them together with some sperm, and grows a couple of embryos. Before implanting them back in the mother, the specialist teases out one cell (called an *embryonic biopsy*) and ascertains the gender so the parents can choose with 100 percent accuracy. This costs at least $5,000 and probably won't be covered by insurance if you don't have a real medical necessity.

The only people who have a medical reason to worry about their children's gender are those with a congenital sex-linked disease. For example, females don't get hemophilia, so a woman who carried this gene would tend to prefer a daughter because she would never suffer the symptoms of the disease, whereas a son could require significant medical care.

A WORD TO THE WISE

If you're reading this section because you are anticipating having a problem getting pregnant, I urge you to think positively. Many of my patients head into their first attempts at conception haunted by the belief that every woman they know has had so much trouble getting pregnant that they come in scared to death, for no reason. Don't fall into this trap. Have confidence in your body, have great sex, and don't anticipate bad news.

Dealing with Infertility

Eighty-five percent of women under age 30 conceive within four menstrual cycles' worth of trying. Ninety percent get pregnant within a year. If you are under 30, most fertility experts would encourage you to spend at least six months trying before seeking outside help.

What Causes Infertility?

When it comes to infertility, causation breaks down fairly evenly into problems with ovulation, problems with sperm, and structural issues. Rare problems, such as hormonal aberrations, infections, or

A SIMPLE REMEDY

A new patient came to see me when she was ten weeks' pregnant. The baby was coming along perfectly. This patient was in her midforties and had been married for a decade or more. I was so pleased for this woman because, of course, conception becomes more difficult as we get older. I wanted to be able to share the secret of her success with other patients, so I asked conspiratorially, "What did you do? Was it a tea? Acupuncture? What got you pregnant after ten years?" She replied, "We stopped using contraception."

poor-quality mucus, account for about 10 percent of problems with conception.

Bad Eggs

Women who struggle to conceive may receive a diagnosis of "poor egg quality." For these women, understandable anxiety is often compounded by the fact that this problem tends to be vague and poorly understood. Although defining it with precision is difficult, what this label typically means is that the woman's eggs just fail to be fertilized. Infertility specialists come to this conclusion based solely on observation and often in the absence of a clearer problem.

Because a woman's body doesn't make new eggs, the ones that are the healthiest, the most efficient, and the most responsive are the ones that also fertilize most easily. Because a woman's body is designed to have children at age 15 and then be dead by 30, if, like many women in the twenty-first century, you choose to wait until after 30, or even 40 or later, you're down at the bottom of your egg barrel, with a greater chance of poor egg quality. Sometimes all the numbers look good on paper, but the eggs simply fail to be fertilized. That said, it's impossible to predict which women's eggs will be poor quality.

EVOLUTION IS NOT FAIR ...

... and it's certainly not designed to keep up with social change. We evolved from primitive conditions in which women had no choice but to reproduce from the earliest stages of menstruation in their teens and continue reproducing up to their young deaths. Their childbearing life went sort of like this: got pregnant, had the baby, breast-fed for six months to two years, got another period, got pregnant, and started all over again. A woman before the modern era (the last three hundred years) menstruated about twelve times in her whole life. Between pregnancies and breast-feeding, which suppresses menstruation, her reproductive organs were busy or asleep most of the time. Although we are still built to have children in our teens, we are often emotionally and financially unprepared for them until much later.

Many infertility centers make an effort to weed out women with poor egg quality; not only do they want to spare the woman a huge, unproductive expense, but they're looking to keep their success rate high. The only option for a woman with persistent poor egg quality is to find an egg donor.

How Can I Predict My Odds?

When it comes to infertility issues, the number that interests infertility specialists and would-be mothers the most is the follicle-stimulating hormone (FSH) count. This hormone stimulates follicles to grow, mature, ovulate, and get fertilized. An ideal FSH number is in the single digits. A number above this range means that the follicles need extra stimulation to grow and therefore may be less receptive to fertilization. Because FSH levels fluctuate from cycle to cycle and probably vary from person to person, patients should retest several times before getting definitive advice. The FSH test is a good indicator of egg quality, but it is not absolute.

At a level of 15 or over, patients are usually referred to an infertility specialist. The cutoff number varies among infertility programs, but most specialists establish an FSH level above which they consider pregnancy nearly impossible. Some specialists also impose a ceiling on maternal age. If a women has exceeded either the ideal FSH limit or age established by the specialist, the next likely step is for her to consider an egg donor. If you find yourself in this situation, it might pay to find a major medical center with an experienced specialist. However, if a few experts have already told you to seek an egg donor, be wary of the doctor who claims to be able to get you pregnant with your own eggs. If, for example, your FSH persistently stays over 20, it would be unfair to subject you to advanced reproductive technology without first encouraging you to purchase an egg.

The Male Factor

When it comes to the man's role in pregnancy, the key concerns are sperm quantity and sperm quality.

CAN I FREEZE MY EGGS?

A few private companies (e.g., www.extendfertility.com) now offer egg-freezing services. This technology, when perfected, promises to silence the biological clock. However, it's a little early to rely on the new technology. At a 17 percent pregnancy rate, it may leave you disappointed—not to mention poor. Each harvest costs upward of $10,000, and then there are monthly storage fees of hundreds of dollars. Do not despair—the cost of this technology is likely to decrease, while its success rate will continue to increase.

Sperm Quantity

Like the follicle within the ovary, the testicles contain cells that manufacture sperm (in a process called *spermatogenesis*) as well as cells that produce the male hormone testosterone. Both of these thrive at a temperature one degree cooler than the rest of the body, so heat is treacherous to the cells that produce sperm and testosterone. This is why testicles are external, hanging low in heat and retracting in cold.

When a couple is trying to conceive, the man must think of heat as the enemy—such things as hot tubs, saunas, and tighty-whiteys can negatively affect sperm production. Urologists have claimed

THERE IS NO PRECONCEPTION CHAPTER FOR MEN

In Chapter 1 we instructed women who might be pregnant to take certain precautions and take specific vitamins to ensure a healthy pregnancy. Scrap that for guys. Because at any given time sperm are only a few weeks old, men don't have to worry about what they're eating, what drugs they're taking, or whether it's okay to have an X-ray. There are studies that suggest certain medications, nutritional supplements, and the man's age may make a small difference in sperm count, but for the most part men do not have to be concerned with modifying their behavior.

that a high fever can knock out sperm production for up to six months, so if your partner just battled a bad flu or fever, don't be surprised by a bit of a delay in conception. Sitting for long periods may also affect sperm count, especially sitting on material that doesn't breathe, such as a typical truck driver's seat. Conversely, sleeping bottomless may provide a temperature better suited to sperm production. Making adjustments to keep your partner's testicles away from heat may not have a tremendous impact on your ability to conceive, but every little bit can help.

Infections or inflammations in any part of the male apparatus, such as the epididymis, urethra, or prostate, affect the sperm. These problems are readily treated, but first they need to be diagnosed. Certain systemic infections, such as mumps, also attack the testicles. A man who contracts mumps after puberty faces a significant risk that the virus will attack the cells in his testicles and affect his future reproductive capability. (Children today are routinely vaccinated against the mumps.) Further, there is speculation that certain illicit drugs, such as marijuana and LSD, affect sperm count, but definitive data on these risks is not available.

Finally, doctors are not interested just in how many sperm are present in an ejaculation, but also in the total volume of ejaculate. There's an ideal range in the middle; too much or too little can affect the outcome. Men who have a very high volume (two tablespoons or

THEN THERE'S THE OBVIOUS

An erection is what gets the sperm to the top of the vagina, so it should probably come as no surprise to you that erectile dysfunction is an issue if you want to get pregnant. I've had at least three couples as patients who were anxious to have children, but the husband was on medication (for example antidepressants or high blood pressure medication) that affected his erections. Would-be fathers in this situation may be able to work with their doctors to adjust their medication, or they may need to seek help with insemination from an infertility specialist.

more) of ejaculate may have low sperm *concentration*. Although total sperm count may be good and the sperm themselves may be high quality, a low concentration seems to negatively affect conception. For patients who find themselves facing a problem of low sperm concentration, I typically recommend that they get their husbands to pull out after the first spurt, in what is called a *split ejaculate,* because the first thrust of a male orgasm (called an *aliquot*) promises the highest density of sperm.

Sperm Quality

With this kind of high-output production facility—that is, one hundred million sperm per ejaculate—the quality can never be as high as you might like. We evaluate sperm in terms of *motility* (are they moving?) and *morphology* (do they look normal?). When a man's sperm output is analyzed, a really good morphology result would consist of 60 percent normal sperm, 40 percent "seconds." These sperm rejects can lack heads, have double tails, or be nonviable for some unspecified reason. A good result in a sperm motility analysis would be if 60 percent were simply *moving;* it would be even better if they were mostly moving forward. Ultimately, any movement is better than no movement, as the latter typically indicates dead sperm, which, of course, are useless. Typically, dead sperm account for up to 40 percent or so of total ejaculate.

When it comes to fine-tuning conception, the quality of the seminal fluid, the medium the sperm swim in, is important as well. This fluid is mostly water with salt and electrolytes, and it's important that it have just the right pH and viscosity. Infection, which can be detected by the presence of bacteria or white blood cells in the seminal fluid, can also affect sperm quality and interfere with conception. Fortunately, medication can almost always treat these problems.

Structural Issues

In addition to the conception problems already discussed, such as low sperm count and erectile problems, sometimes structural hazards reduce the odds of conceiving.

REVERSIBLE CHOICES

The husband of one of my patients had been, at age 21, keen on zero population growth. So in a spurt of political and social conviction he had a vasectomy (to tie the vas deferens to prevent sperm from getting through). At 30, he started to have a change of heart: Surely *his* one or two kids wouldn't exactly cause overpopulation. Luckily for the couple, a vasectomy can usually be reversed—a procedure performed by a urologist. One note of caution: Although vasectomies can be undone, long-term vasectomies can have a permanent adverse effect on sperm production.

His

A good crop of sperm in the testicles doesn't guarantee one hundred million healthy swimmers in the vagina. Before the sperm even reaches the vagina, it must make a long journey through the epidydimis and vas deferens, over the prostate, and through the urethra. Blockages along the way can interfere with the sperm's arrival at its destination. For example, infections such as gonorrhea can cause a blockage or scarring along the sperm delivery tract, anywhere from the testicle to the urethra. So even if sperm production is good and erection is not a problem, there could be no sperm in the ejaculate if the sperm is getting stuck behind an obstruction. A urologist can surgically correct the obstruction, or an infertility specialist can aspirate (yes, with a needle) sperm from the testicles.

Another fairly common male structural abnormality is something called a *varicocele*—that is, a varicose vein in the scrotum, resting right next to the testicle. Because sperm production is optimal at a relatively cool temperature, a big, blood-filled vein that heats up the testicle can negatively affect sperm quality and quantity. A urologist can readily address this problem with minor surgery.

Hers

Structural problems are more likely to crop up in the woman's body, where the sperm's journey is much longer than in the man. On that three-day trip, any obstruction that might keep the sperm from the egg makes conception difficult. The most common kind of blockage is due to tubal scarring from a prior pelvic infection, usually caused by a sexually transmitted infection, such as gonorrhea or chlamydia. Tuberculosis has also been known to cause jams along the female reproductive tract, but only in cases that are so severe that the bacteria have spread to the fallopian tubes. Fortunately, gonorrhea and chlamydia are highly treatable, especially in the early stages, and tubal tuberculosis is very rare in North America.

There are congenital structural issues that can make it more difficult to conceive. The female reproductive system develops symmetrically from the *Müllerian bud,* which means at a certain stage the female fetus has two of everything she should have two of (ovaries and tubes), and two of everything she should *not* have two of (vagina, cervix, and uterus). As the body develops, the vaginas, cervixes, and uteruses fuse into one, while the tubes and ovaries stay separate. This process can produce perfectly harmless abnormalities, such as a heart-shaped uterus. More serious anomalies might include two uteruses, two cervixes, or two vaginas, or any combination thereof. These are *Müllerian fusion anomalies,* and if you had a significant one, a doctor would have already told you about it. These problems are rarely serious enough to treat, but they can present problems for conception and sometimes in pregnancy if the abnormality affects the uterus. A woman with two vaginas, for example, tends to favor one side for sexual intercourse; the difficulty in conceiving arises when ovulation and intercourse are not occurring on the same side. Thus, if the woman had sex on the right but ovulated on the left that month, she's definitely not going to get pregnant. This structural abnormality cuts down a woman's odds of conceiving by 50 percent. Usually, the problem of two vaginas can be corrected through surgery. Sometimes Müllerian fusion anomalies are slight enough that even the gynecologist doesn't notice.

Weight and Fertility

Your weight is one rough indicator of health. Your hypothalamus, which is the most primitive part of the brain, knows about

START WITH THE SIMPLE

For every high-tech infertility cure, there's a low-tech one. A couple came in complaining of infertility, so I asked, among other things, what kind of lubrication they were using. The man confidently reported that he used "a lot of Vaseline." Of course, petroleum jelly kills sperm, so I suggested a water-based lubricant. They came back pregnant two months later.

how much you should weigh. To your brain, there's probably a big range (plus or minus sixty pounds) of acceptable weights. If you go higher or lower than that, you risk compromising your fertility in proportion to how heavy or light you are. Women and girls suffering from anorexia don't menstruate because the hypothalamus understands starvation to mean there's a famine; therefore, it attempts to fend off starvation by turning off nonessential organ systems until food becomes available. Fertility is a minor concern compared to all the other issues anorectic women face. The mor-

BARIATRIC SURGERY

For a woman obese enough to have surgery to correct the condition, contraception might be a low priority. But it shouldn't be. Women who have an operation that leads to rapid weight loss are likely to face two results: (1) They may get more dates, and (2) their ovaries wake up from their long slumber and start producing eggs. The problem is that the ideal time to be pregnant is not right after major abdominal surgery, when they are often still sick, are taking loads of vitamins, are just learning to control their bowel function, and are often dehydrated. If you are morbidly obese and for any reason lose a lot of weight, you are likely to become fertile before you're physically ready to have a baby. Preempt this by using contraception consistently.

bidly obese have just as many problems with their fertility because the higher the amount of excess weight, the lower the chances of ovulating.

Other Problems

Sometimes hormonal problems can have a negative effect on fertility. For example, if the hormone *prolactin,* the pituitary hormone that stimulates lactation and suppresses ovulation, is out of whack, it can stall conception. Sometimes a benign tumor of the pituitary (*pituitary adenoma*) can stimulate the gland to make prolactin at the wrong times, thereby ceasing ovulation and occasionally causing breast secretions.

Cervical mucus is another minor-sounding matter that can hold up the whole show. Thin, salty mucus helps sperm get to the uterus. Some women have inadequate mucus production, usually because of a minor cervical surgery, such as a loop electrical excisional procedure (LEEP) following an abnormal Pap smear. This is a situation in which doctors might recommend taking Robitussin to thin out the cervical mucus, much as they might recommend it to thin out chest mucus if you had a bad cold. Infertility resulting from a persistent problem with inadequate mucus production can be remedied by having the sperm medically injected right into the uterine cavity through intrauterine insemination (IUI).

Cervical infections can also affect the sperm. The most common type of cervical bacteria are Mycoplasma, which have been associated with infertility for decades. Gynecologists diagnose this condition with a simple cervical culture and treat it with antibiotics. Even more rare, some women are allergic to sperm, and their cervical mucus kills all sperm on contact. These women have the option of bypassing the mucus through in vitro fertilization (IVF) or IUI. They could also try using condoms for six or more months to diminish cervical antibodies to sperm and then try to get pregnant quickly, before their immune response can recover. However, this method is far from foolproof.

These issues are the tip of the iceberg when it comes to potential glitches in the complicated process of conception. If you are

IT'S ESSENTIAL TO RELAX

Fifty percent of couples who think they are having a fertility problem conceive after their first visit to an infertility specialist, *before* any treatment. This is probably a result of the great relief of surrendering control over their ability to conceive and being able to say to themselves, "Okay, the doctor is going to worry about it; we'll just go home and have sex."

having difficulty conceiving because of these or other problems, you will get the best, most up-to-date information from an infertility specialist.

Treating Infertility

Before you seek treatment for infertility, understand that your odds of success depend greatly on why you're infertile in the first place. If you are simply looking to work around a tubal ligation that you had after your last child, IVF should be very effective for you. If you're 40, you've been trying for years, you've never gotten pregnant, and no doctor has been able to tell you why not, you're looking at an expensive long shot.

DON'T JUMP THE GUN

A patient was distraught over her "infertility" after not being able to conceive for one whole menstrual cycle. By the time she saw me, she had diagnosed herself with a hormone imbalance. I was the first in a long line of specialists, acupuncturists, massage therapists, and so forth, whom she had scheduled to help her with this problem. Only she never got to see any of them because she was pregnant. Her anguish was unnecessary.

Some gynecologists conduct basic infertility testing for their concerned patients, while others prefer to refer to a specialist right away. These tests involve semen analysis, cervical culture, blood testing, and an X-ray of the uterus and tubes (called a *hysterosalpingogram*), which should confirm that the uterus is one cavity and the tubes are normal in course and caliber. The cervical culture ensures that the mucus is healthy and conducive to conception. The blood test will reveal a hormonal imbalance.

A standard battery of tests may also include a postcoital test, in which your doctor looks for sperm in the cervical mucus within six hours of vaginal intercourse. If there are a lot of healthy sperm happily swimming in that mucus, it's likely that the man involved has a fairly decent sperm count. If they're all dead, it could be the mucus. If no sperm are present, then he has a problem only a urologist can help with.

In the field of infertility treatment, *advanced reproductive technology* (ART) is an umbrella term for all infertility treatments, except IUI and the drug Clomid, which are considered the least complicated treatment routes and are often attempted before more expensive, intricate measures. Most infertility treatments are thought of in cycles, as in "I've had three IVF cycles." ART is an explosive, complex, evolving, little-monitored specialty. A woman undergoing ART treatments will be subjected to enough tests, shots, sonograms, doctor's visits, consultations, and so forth, to write a book about the subject. The following summary of infertility treatments simply presents a snapshot of the various options—how they basically work, indicators of success, and potential pitfalls. The whole landscape of infertility treatment could change overnight with one significant discovery.

Clomid

A hormone imbalance can cause inefficient ovulation. For example, the follicle appears on the surface of the ovary, then ruptures, but after that it fails to produce enough progesterone. This is treated with fertility drugs that cause the body to produce more of the right hormones. The drug *chlomiphene citrate* (brand name Clomid) is a selective estrogen receptor modulator; it reduces estrogen, which fools the pituitary into making more FSH, which stimulates the follicle to be healthier throughout the process in order to make more progesterone. It's like a vitamin for the ovaries, and gynecologists commonly dispense this pill as a first-line assault on infertility. It's taken early in the cycle (within the first ten days) for five to seven days.

Clomid carries a significant side effect. Because it stimulates the pituitary to produce as much FSH as possible, it increases the chances of producing more than one ripe follicle, meaning it raises the odds of having twins. Although twins make for great photos, it's important to remember that they also double your risk of adverse health consequences, such as high blood pressure, diabetes, orthopedic issues, and premature delivery. Note that although Clomid doubles your chance of becoming pregnant with twins, it does not significantly increase the likelihood of triplets or quadruplets, because it does not introduce any more FSH into your body than your own pituitary can produce.

Intrauterine Insemination (IUI)

When the man produces healthy sperm, and his sperm count is reasonably high (roughly one hundred thousand or more) but still less than optimal, IUI may be the solution. Under the care of a specialist, the sperm can be collected, washed, and concentrated and/or diluted for insemination to optimize the chances of conception. These prepped sperm are inseminated much closer to the egg. In this procedure, a soft pipette (like an eyedropper) delivers the sperm directly into the top of the cervical canal, bypassing the mucus, which may also account for the sperm's inability to reach the egg. This procedure is the optimal choice in the absence of a male partner—for lesbians or women married to prison inmates, for example. IUI is less expensive and less invasive than IVF, and it stands to help a significant number of previously infertile couples; those with cervical mucus problems or a suboptimal sperm count are most likely to be successful with this method.

DOCTORS DO NOT KNOW EVERYTHING

Sometimes a doctor labels an infertility issue as *idiopathic*. This means that the specialists have looked high and low, run all the tests, and just can't find a reason for the problem. Since IVF helps with almost every fertility issue, it can be a good option for patients who have been diagnosed with idiopathic infertility. IVF might bypass something the doctor doesn't even know is there, such as a counterproductive hormone or an anomaly that can't be found.

In Vitro Fertilization (IVF)

In vitro (literally "in glass"—that is, in an artificial environment) fertilization controls many fickle elements of natural conception. Scientifically precise hands put sperm right next to an egg in a test tube, where the hope is that fertilization will occur. An embryologist examines this fertilized egg to make sure everything is just right. After three to five days the doctor moves that fertilized egg into a woman's lush and ready uterus, often enhanced by hormone shots. Even under the best circumstances and after all the variables (for example, the egg definitely meets the sperm, the embryo definitely gets to the uterus) are carefully managed, IVF works only some of the time and costs about $5,000 per attempt.

Whatever your particular problem—be it your tubes or his sperm—the easy thing to do is go for IVF. Originally, the procedure was designed to bypass plumbing obstructions, and it beautifully accomplishes this with scant health risk. Although the potential for a complication always exists with dramatic hormone manipulation and invasive procedures, those risks tend to be lower for IVF than for other surgical options. Doctors therefore prefer to use IVF for a host of conception issues that used to be treated with more complicated, less effective procedures. For example, urologists treat a low sperm count with corrective surgery or hormones that can be more traumatic and less fruitful than IVF. Reopening tied tubes (called *tuboplasty*) involves microscopic surgery, whereas IVF simply bypasses the problem entirely.

Although a patient's choice of treatment will be dictated by her specific fertility problem, one appeal of IVF is that the patient controls exactly how many embryos are put back in the uterus. The downside is that conception is clearly a less romantic experience.

FSH Injections

If Clomid fails, it signifies that the patient's body may not be able to produce enough FSH to kick off a pregnancy. So doctors bypass the natural production facility and turn to straight FSH injections in order to coax usable follicles to mature. Specific treatment varies from center to center and can include daily blood tests, HCG (human chorionic gonadotropin) injections, and frequent sonograms, as well as self-administered shots. This costs thousands of dollars and is not covered by all insurance plans.

The specialist monitors the woman's ovaries by sonogram, and around the time of ovulation, the doctor counts the ripe follicles. When too many eggs are present, the specialist may skip a cycle of insemination to avoid fertilizing too many eggs. This is not an exact science, and there are no rules about how many follicles are too many.

If the FSH shots cause you to produce several follicles, there is no controlling how many of them become fertilized, because unlike IVF you ultimately take care of conception at home during normal

IVF ADD-ONS

There are two common methods infertility specialists employ to improve the odds for their IVF patients, depending on their particular fertility issues. One is *intracytoplasmic sperm injection* (ICSI), in which the doctor drills a hole in the shell of the egg and injects the sperm directly inside. This is a great choice for women whose partners have a low sperm count or poor sperm motility. The second add-on that can give you an edge in IVF is a procedure called *hatching*. In this procedure, the specialist roughens one side of the growing blastula, priming it to stick to the uterine lining. If your problem seems to be with implantation, hatching could help.

SIX BABIES!

For a while it seemed as if stories about sextuplets were a fixture of the evening news. Although such stories are interesting—not to mention entertaining—they represent failures in medicine, because the simultaneous gestation of anything more than triplets exponentially increases the risk of premature labor, which is a high-stakes game for mother and child; the higher the number of babies, the more premature the delivery. In a pregnancy producing more than four babies, each of those babies is overwhelmingly likely to have a visual, auditory, or intellectual impairment. Infertility is a relatively unmonitored field, so choose your specialist carefully.

sexual intercourse. When and if a woman ends up with more than two embryos, her doctor may encourage her to trim that number in a procedure euphemistically called *reduction,* in which doctors selectively terminate one or more fetuses. This guarantees the healthiest outcome for all—so much so that some infertility doctors insist that their patients sign a pledge to reduce if they end up carrying more than four fetuses. Patients can be reluctant to undergo this procedure for any number of reasons, including that the process can irritate the uterus and increase the risk of a miscarriage.

When it comes to FSH shots, there are health risks and no guarantees. Rarely, this treatment can cause the ovaries to swell dramatically, leading to problems requiring hospitalization. Further, many women go through multiple cycles without success. The number of attempts sometimes depends on how many insurance will cover. Some women, however, will reach the limit only when they are out of money or someone they trust says, "Enough!"

Combination Treatments

If you have more than one clearly understood issue negatively affecting conception, then your specialist may recommend more than one treatment. For example, if you have a low sperm count and an ovulatory dysfunction, then Clomid and IUI would be a good

GOOD CARE IS HARD TO FIND

When I was a resident in Jamaica in 1973, a woman hoping to cure her infertility was coming in each month for her Clomid pills. When I reviewed her medical history, I discovered that her pituitary had been destroyed by a blood clot. I said to the chairman of the department, "Clomid is not going to work. She has no pituitary." He said, "Yes, I know. But it's all we can afford."

combination for you. The Clomid helps you ovulate, and the IUI ensures the sperm get to the uterus.

The Last Word on Conception

Women have a window of opportunity when it comes to having children. A cartoon I once saw featured a woman in tears saying, "My God, I forgot to have kids!" If you find yourself approaching the cut-off age for conception, formulate a plan. Decide whether you must have a partner or would consider solo parenting. If the latter is an option for you, consider whether a sperm donor is right for you. If it's the experience of pregnancy you're after, an egg donor might extend your window of opportunity by nearly a decade. And, of course, there's always adoption if your top priority is to become a parent rather than to have the experience of pregnancy.

DIFFERENT WAYS TO SKIN A CAT

A forty-five-year-old patient realized that it was now or never for her and motherhood. She lamented that she hadn't had a date in ten years. Because she could no longer wait for Mr. Right to come along, she went to an infertility specialist, got an egg donor, got a sperm donor, and had the fertilized egg implanted in her uterus. Now she's thrilled to be a mother.

CHAPTER 3

First Trimester: Normal

The First Days of Pregnancy

When it comes to calculating your pregnancy, forget the regular calendar. Obstetricians use a *lunar* calendar to chart pregnancy, which can be confusing. Let's say you are one week late for your period. That would mean you ovulated about three weeks ago, and the fetus implanted itself in your uterus about one week after that. The obstetrician is going to say, "Congratulations! You're five weeks pregnant." Obstetricians always refer to pregnancies in terms of their menstrual age, based on a twenty-eight-day cycle. *Embryonic* age reflects how old the actual embryo is, but only researchers (not clinicians) use this terminology. At your doctor's office, the first trimester is the twelve weeks that began with the first day of your

FIRST BE SURE. BE REALLY SURE.

I had a forty-year-old newlywed patient who had never practiced contraception in her life. Her husband took her practically straight from the altar to an infertility doctor, but when she got there, the doctor said, "I'm happy to meet you, but you're already pregnant." We breezed through the first trimester. When the last test came back perfect, she turned to me and said, "You mean I really have to go through with this?" It turned out that her husband was the sole driving force behind the pregnancy; she had not wanted the baby. She had the pregnancy terminated and told him she had had a miscarriage. Two years later, she changed her mind and to date she has not conceived again.

last menstrual period. It could also be calculated as ten weeks from ovulation. Or nine weeks from implantation. Or nine and a half weeks from fertilization. Confused yet?

Recall that fertilization is the moment when the sperm hits the egg, which happens in the outer third of the fallopian tube, anywhere from twelve to thirty-six hours after the egg leaves the ovary. This free-floating cell (called a *zygote*) starts down the fallopian tube toward the uterus, swimming and replicating simultaneously. The initial one-cell zygote becomes 2 cells, then it becomes 4, then 8, and so on, up to between 50 and 250 cells (called a *blastula*) by the time it gets to the uterus about two days later. During this entire time, the woman's body continues as if nothing has yet happened.

The good news is that you really won't notice much of a difference in your body before implantation. True, many women would like to believe that they feel some magnificent change from the moment of fertilization. However, there is no change in the woman's body until implantation; there's no way to tell she's got a bun in the oven. To the newly pregnant woman, the first sign of pregnancy may be some slight bleeding, caused by the disruption of the capillaries at the point of implantation (known as *implantation bleeding*) as the early pregnancy burrows into the lining of the uterus.

Within the uterine wall, the blastula continues to divide, and we have pregnancy liftoff. At this point, the tiny fetus hooks up to the maternal blood supply. This is when what the woman eats or drinks, what drugs she's on, and what vitamins she takes become important.

DO THE MATH

If you have a twenty-eight-day cycle, and you know when the first day of your last menstrual period was, you can figure out your own due date. Simply subtract three from the month and add seven to the day. For example, if the first day of your last period was October 4, your due date is July 11. If you don't know when your last period was, your doctor will rely more on indirect ways of figuring out your due date with tools like sonograms and serial blood tests, which are often quite accurate.

KNOW WHEN TO ACT AS IF YOU'RE PREGNANT

If you have been trying at all to get pregnant, be extra diligent in that last week before you're due to get your period. Don't be the patient who, after a positive pregnancy test, says, "Oh, there was this wine tasting and I ended up drinking way too much . . ." Many geneticists suggest that exposure to environmental hazards (such as radiation or alcohol) in that first week may have an all-or-nothing effect—that is, the early blastula is so immature and unspecialized that environmental hazards will cause either a miscarriage or no harm at all.

The earliest point at which it is possible to detect a pregnancy is about seven to ten days after ovulation. And even if you could know, it wouldn't matter, because before the egg implants itself, it's out there on its own; it's only with implantation that the pregnant woman needs to exercise extra care. Still, a missed period is one of the most common reasons to think "pregnancy," and by then you've already had a little tyke attached to your bloodstream for a week. So if you're trying to get pregnant, act as if you could be pregnant in the week before your period.

Early Hormonal Changes

Once it's settled in the uterine wall, the blastula starts to make many hormones, the unique one being *human chorionic gonadotrophin* (HCG). Only human placentas make this hormone; therefore, it is found only in pregnant women.

The earliest possible way to detect pregnancy is to test for the presence of HCG, either in the blood or in the urine. Testing the blood yields a 100 percent accurate result and can even identify approximately how pregnant you are (give or take eight or nine days). Unless you have a laboratory at home, you'll need a physician to perform a blood test. A urine test is less accurate (over 95 percent) and can yield only a pass/fail result. The accuracy of urine tests depends somewhat on sample concentration. In other words, if you drink five liters of water and then pee on the home pregnancy test stick, the result may come back negative even if you are pregnant. This is why most home pregnancy test makers recommend that women test their first urine of the day, which tends to be concentrated. Also bear in mind that a negative result may turn positive in a few days as your HCG levels rise.

A blood test can pick up the earliest trace of HCG in the mother's bloodstream about thirty-six to forty-eight hours after implantation. This is about one week after conception, or twenty-one days from the first day of the patient's last period. So time your pregnancy tests accordingly.

Advanced reproductive technology has taught us most of what we know about HCG because scientists have had to develop more precise methods for monitoring extremely early pregnancies. It's just not possible to see on a sonogram whether or not an IVF-implanted embryo takes root in the uterus. However, we can monitor the patient's HCG levels; if they double every forty-eight to seventy-two hours, then we know that the pregnancy is progressing normally. When it comes to HCG levels, numbers vary from patient to patient. The doctor relies on the patient's starting HCG level as the foundation from which a known rate of increase translates into a healthfully progressing pregnancy. For example, a woman who has an HCG level of 20 on day twenty-one of her pregnancy should have a level over 40 by day twenty-three or twenty-four.

Early Symptoms

Once a pregnant woman's body starts producing HCG, she may also begin to experience symptoms. These depend on all sorts of unpredictable variables; perfectly healthy women experience a wide range of side effects, from none at all to the entire list. The symptoms you experience are not an indicator of the relative health of your pregnancy. For example, if you've never felt more alert than you do now, you're just as likely to have a normal pregnancy as the woman taking naps under her desk. The symptoms of early pregnancy may remind you of how you feel before you get your period, when your body also

VAGINAL BLEEDING IS NO GUARANTEE

Don't assume you're not pregnant just because you have vaginal bleeding. As mentioned earlier, some women bleed at implantation. On rare occasions, women have some monthly bleeding through most of the first trimester. Whatever your situation, if vaginal bleeding is different, lighter, or longer than your usual period or if you just don't feel like you usually do when you have your period, the first, simplest option is to do a home pregnancy test.

makes more progesterone, though it's also possible to go through the early stages of a pregnancy without any noticeable symptoms. For most women, of course, this is not the case. Most of the unpleasant symptoms of pregnancy are the likely result of progesterone, which is known to cause water retention, smooth muscle relaxation, and sedation. Sounds a lot like PMS, right? Some of the most common symptoms include fatigue and nausea.

Fatigue

Fatigue is the most common signifier of the first trimester of pregnancy, probably due to both the progesterone and the added biological work of pregnancy. Dizziness and fainting are also common. These might be nature's gentle way of forcing you to slow down so your strength can be directed where it's needed most: the pregnancy and the developing baby. A lot of newly pregnant women want to sleep as much as twelve hours a day and are constantly tired and longing for a nap. If you find yourself always looking forward to bedtime, you can take comfort in knowing that you are having a very common, normal, healthy experience.

Nausea

Probably the most notorious of all the side effects of early pregnancy is the extremely unsavory nausea and vomiting duo. Of course, some women experience only nausea, without the vomiting, while others experience both. Although these digestive difficulties associated with pregnancy are commonly lumped together under the label *morning sickness,* this really is a misleading term, because many women experience them at various (or *all*) times of the day. Once more, progesterone is at least partially the culprit, because of its tendency to relax all smooth muscles. One reason nausea and vomiting are most common in the morning is that during the night the lax stomach fills with gastric juices. For some women this gastric buildup is relieved through vomiting, for others it subsides as the day goes on, while still other women spend the entire day feeling woozy.

For women who are nauseated all the time, the phenomenon (it's phenomenal, right?) is one of the many remaining mysteries of pregnancy, so our ability to understand it extends only to the theoretical. Doctors suspect that the ill feeling is the ironic result of a highly stimulated hunger center in the brain. Have you ever felt so hungry you were nauseated? In pregnancy, hormones constantly stimulate you to eat, but they may overdo it.

In many cases, eating relieves chronic nausea. Some pregnant women feel they must constantly chew on crackers and toast to stave off illness. Not only does eating relieve the overcharged appetite center, it also neutralizes the stomach lining. Of course, eating a big meal may have just the opposite of the desired effect,

EATING FOR VOMIT PREVENTION

What you eat can make a big difference in whether or how often you feel nauseated. Traditionally, doctors recommend that their chronically nauseated patients eat very hot or very cold foods; there's nothing grosser than tepid food to a nauseated person. Also, dry and crunchy beats mushy and soggy, so have a bowl of cereal instead of oatmeal, and toast instead of mashed potatoes. Ultimately, the foods that you'll have the most success with are foods that you find appealing. One of my patients ate bacon, lettuce, and tomato sandwiches three times a day for weeks. Eat whatever feels right and doesn't make you vomit.

because the stomach is in poor shape to handle a huge amount of food and may just reject it. Small, frequent meals or constant nibbling (*grazing*) are ideal.

As long as some food stays down, the mother's weight is steady or increasing, and hydration is not a problem, there's not a huge need to worry about perfect nutrition. Eating enough and correctly does not become superimportant until the second trimester (except for all the things you should have avoided consuming before you got pregnant in the first place; see page 7). A stable blood sugar level is the most important thing for a woman with chronic nausea.

Frequent Urination

One of the most common symptoms of pregnancy is frequent urination. Women who have always slept solidly through the night may suddenly find themselves getting up more than once to pee. Doctors conjecture that this is caused by increased pelvic pressure and congestion as a result of the progressing pregnancy, even in the earliest stages.

Constipation

The same hormone that makes it difficult to hold urine also causes constipation, because it relaxes the entire digestive tract. The intestines are a long tube that pushes food along by contracting— the more relaxed that tube is, the more stagnant its contents. The best thing for constipation is to eat roughage—bulky foods like fiber—which expands and presses against the walls of the large intestine. This pressure encourages the tubelike organ to contract, moving things along more effectively. Hydration is also important to keep the stool moist.

Cramps

Menstrual-type cramps are very common in the first trimester. This discomfort can be a red herring, because it can make a pregnant woman feel like she's going to get her period. Cramps in early pregnancy are a result of the uterus contracting in response to growing larger, whereas contractions to expel blood are what cause menstrual cramps. This is perfectly normal and rarely that uncomfortable. Hearing that there's nothing to worry about is usually enough to soothe a first-timer.

Other Symptoms

There are plenty of other side effects of early pregnancy, including headaches, breast pain, nipple sensitivity, backaches, mood changes, and alterations in libido. Some women are euphoric and horny; others are grumpy and disinterested in sex. Although the symptoms of early pregnancy may reflexively make you reach for a remedy, don't take any medication until you speak to your doctor. Even if the symptoms are familiar, don't take a painkiller for your cramps or a course of antibiotics for an imagined bladder infection.

Monitoring an Established Pregnancy

During pregnancy, the hormone of primary importance to a doctor is HCG, followed by progesterone. A low progesterone level increases the risk of miscarriage. From the first day of the men-

SEE YOUR OB ASAP!

Although many obstetricians today consider it acceptable to have a newly pregnant patient wait a month or more before a first exam, remember that this is an important time in your pregnancy! Do what you can to see a doctor as soon as you know you are pregnant. This is especially true if you are over age 37, if you have had problems with past pregnancies, if you have a medical condition that requires evaluation, or simply if you're really nervous. Women who have had ectopic pregnancies (page 57) in the past are the most in need of *immediate* obstetrical supervision to protect their health.

strual period until ovulation, there is no progesterone in the female body. Within a week of ovulation—that is, when the egg leaves the follicle—progesterone levels should be over 10. This number represents how concentrated progesterone is in the bloodstream. During pregnancy, it should be over 20. In the most high-risk situations, an obstetrician will likely want to monitor the early pregnancy by measuring frequent progesterone and HCG levels.

Guidelines for Prenatal Care

Obstetrical care varies, as does each patient's situation. For example, if you live three hours away from the sonogram machine, you may be unable to have as many ultrasounds as the most cautious physician might recommend. Of course, your care depends on *your* proclivities as well as those of your doctor. You may be happy with an experienced nurse clinician or a midwife. The following recommendations represent the most modern obstetrical care and are drawn largely from the guidelines provided by the American College of Obstetrics and Gynecology. I've heard plenty of women say that they find these practices, from the first-trimester tests to the delivery room, intrusive and "unnatural." However, it's my firm belief that this is the standard of care that comes closest to guaranteeing a healthy outcome for mother and baby. I understand that not everyone can or will choose to follow all my suggestions. My hope is that this information helps you make better choices for yourself.

Sonograms and Ultrasounds (. . . Are the Same Thing)

Once the mother is making a substantial amount of HCG (around one thousand units), a sonogram can usually reveal a small gestational sac, depending on the skill of the radiologist and the sensitivity of the machinery. The level of HCG is proportional to the level of placental cells; the more HCG made, the more placenta must be making it. Superspecialists in major medical centers with the most advanced machinery can probably see something on a sonogram with HCG levels as low as 600, and that number is likely to continue falling.

The first and most important fact to establish with the initial sonogram is that the pregnancy is in the uterus. Sometimes the blastula takes root in another place, most often the fallopian tubes, resulting in what is called an *ectopic* pregnancy. This is an untenable situation that threatens the mother's life, and it occurs in approximately 1 percent of pregnancies—though this number varies from region to region and country to country.

The second sonogram (at about seven to nine weeks) measures the crown-to-rump length, the heartbeat, and the size of the sac. This is the single most accurate way to assess your gestational age. The earlier you have this second sonogram, the more precisely we can estimate the fetal age, and the more accurately we can predict a due date. If the second sonogram is early enough, the doctor can probably tell you, within one week, when conception occurred.

The second sonogram can be one of the most exciting and meaningful tests in pregnancy, because when we see a heartbeat and intrauterine gestation, the risk of a miscarriage plummets to less than 10 percent. Whereas implantation indicates liftoff for pregnancy, the beating fetal heart means it's time to let family members know that you're pregnant!

Blood Work

Once the pregnancy is overwhelmingly likely to continue, it's time for prenatal blood testing. There are a lot of tests, which require a lot of blood (anywhere from two to six test tubes). One of these tests is called the *complete blood count* (CBC), which counts red blood cells, white blood cells, and platelets. This is the most common blood test performed just about everywhere. The red blood cells tell us whether or not the mother's blood is effectively delivering oxygen to her body. White blood cells fight infection, so if this number is very high, doctors worry about an ongoing infection. If it's very low, doctors worry about a blood disorder. Platelets cause blood to clot; a low level of platelets makes a paper cut a potentially dangerous situation, and a high level of platelets can lead to too many clots, cutting off blood supply to critical organs.

A second test is called *type and Rh,* which determines the mother's blood type and her Rh factor. It's essential to know the mother's blood type because there are some common cross incompatibilities between the blood type of the mother and that of the baby. These differences do not matter in pregnancy but can become an issue at birth if, for example, the mother is type O and the baby is type A. In this case, the mother's blood could damage the baby's blood at delivery.

The Rh test looks for a common spoke on the red blood cell, called an *Rh factor* (also an *Rh antigen*). Ninety percent of humans have this factor, whereas the remaining 10 percent are considered *Rh negative.* Pregnant women in the latter group require some precautionary measures (see page 68).

Then we screen for antibodies to specific, unusual red blood cells. This is quite rare, because an individual usually develops the antibodies only after exposure to these other types of cells through a blood transfusion or previous pregnancy.

Another commonly administered test checks for specific antibodies to specific organisms, such as toxoplasmosis and herpes. This information helps the doctor manage each patient in the most effective way, given her particular circumstances. For example, when a patient is tested for rubella (German measles) antibodies, a

KEEPING A SAFE DISTANCE

The gestational sac is foreign to your body. It is genetically different from you, which makes it a miracle that you don't reject it the way you might refuse someone else's kidney. Barriers in the lining of the uterus keep the two systems separate. The placenta, the amniotic fluid, and the fetus itself are all made up of DNA that is different from that of the mother, and frequently the fetus and the mother have different blood types. Ironically, it is ideal that mother and baby stay as separate as possible. This division is critically important and is probably imperfect.

doctor expects to find that she is immune because vaccinations are virtually universal in the United States. However, some people slip through the cracks, while others fail to develop an immune response. These women are advised to be extracautious, taking care to avoid places where German measles is still prevalent. Steering clear of sick children is also advisable, as is requesting a rubella vaccine the day after delivery.

All pregnant women, regardless of their medical history, are tested for antibodies to syphilis and HIV. Both of these sexually transmitted infections carry significant and avoidable health risks for the baby. Untreated syphilis in the mother can lead to cardiac anomalies, neonatal infections, and birth defects when it is transmitted to the baby through the placenta. If caught early in the pregnancy, it can be treated with antibiotics. An untreated HIV mother has a 35 to 40 percent chance of transmitting HIV to her child. We can reduce this risk to 7 percent or less with appropriate antiviral therapy.

In the first trimester, a blood sugar level should be taken to uncover any unknown cases of diabetes. Women who are found to have diabetes require special care.

Another important aspect of the blood work is the screening for genetic disorders. American women are usually screened for genetic disorders to determine their *carrier status* for particular problems. This blood test is usually done in the first trimester or, more ideally, before pregnancy. One in twenty American women carry the gene for *cystic fibrosis*. Another problem is *fragile X syndrome*, which is a relatively common genetic cause of retardation in boys in the United States. Ethnicity-linked genetic testing is standard when applicable. *Thalassemia*, an abnormality of the red blood cell hemoglobin, is prevalent in the Mediterranean basin, particularly among southern Italians and Greeks. Ashkenazy Jews are at risk for *Tay-Sachs disease*, among many other genetic disorders. And then there's *sickle-cell anemia*, common among North Africans as well as those of southern Italian and Greek heritage. All these conditions can be detected through a blood test during pregnancy.

Vaginal Culture

The vagina is not a terribly clean place, and bacteria that can cause problems in pregnancy are normally present. About 5 percent of women have a simple imbalance of normal vaginal inhabitants, called *bacterial vaginosis.* This condition has been loosely associated with obstetrical problems such as premature labor. Obstetricians typically treat this with an antibacterial gel. Approximately 10 percent of all women have *Group B Streptococcus* (GBS) present in their vaginas. Although absolutely benign in the adult woman, this bug has significant implications in delivery and must be treated during labor, prior to delivery.

First-Trimester Evaluation of Risk

At the end of the first trimester, the obstetrician assesses the patient's overall risk of chromosomal disease with a sonogram and a blood test. These procedures are routinely performed on all pregnant patients, regardless of age, and they primarily screen for Down syndrome and trisomy 18, the second most common, serious chromosomal defect. Abnormal results are interpreted as an indication of heightened risk but are not conclusive. Only further tests, such as

---

PREPARE THE BREASTS

Breast-feeding, discussed in detail in Chapter 12, is no walk in the park, but there are things you can do in the first trimester to help pave the way. Because most American women keep their nipples well hidden almost all the time, they become extremely sensitive, tender little nubs. This is where the baby's mouth is going to clamp down and suck, so it would behoove you to start toughening them up. Start by spending as much time as possible topless at home; just exposing the nipples to air helps make them more durable. This is also a good excuse to sunbathe topless, if you're so inclined, although you should use sunblock liberally and shade your face.

chorionic villus sampling (CVS) and amniocentesis, can precisely determine chromosomal anomalies.

The sonogram should happen somewhere between twelve and fourteen weeks of gestation. The radiologist evaluates the thickness of tissue on the back of the baby's neck, called *transnuchal lucency*. A measurement thicker than 1.5 millimeters indicates an increased risk of Down syndrome or trisomy 18. Down syndrome also leads to a diminished or absent nasal bone, which can be detected with the sonogram. However, these results only indicate *risk*. Neither of these findings is absolute; they are only markers. There are many brilliant babies with thick skin on the back of their necks, and there are babies with Down syndrome or trisomy 18 who had abnormal nasal bones.

The blood test is to evaluate two specific hormones that tend to vary slightly from normal levels when the mother is carrying a Down baby. The first is *pregnancy-associated plasma protein* (PAPP), and the other is HCG. Every woman makes these hormones in pregnancy, but fetal chromosomal anomalies tend to shift their levels about 10 percent, either up or down. Again, the findings of this blood test are not absolute; there's such a significant overlap between normal and abnormal that these tests mean little on their own.

The only real purpose of these tests is to advise the patient whether she should seek an amniocentesis (page 92) to determine for certain whether her baby has a chromosomal anomaly. Women under age 40 who are debating getting an amnio, which may carry a very small risk and is an invasive procedure, might skip it after finding out that their specific risks are very low. Some women choose to have an amnio regardless of the results of the twelve-week blood test and ultrasound. Of course, when the results of these tests has put them in a low-risk category, they can approach the amnio with minimal anxiety.

Congratulations!

At the end of the first trimester you have a well-established, recognizable, tiny baby. He or she has arms, legs, a face, and a heartbeat,

FIRST-TRIMESTER NORMAL CALENDAR

Menstrual Calendar Terminology

Day

5	Your period is over and you're trying to get pregnant. You take vitamins, eat healthy, take it easy, and have lots of sex.
11	Great sex.
15	Ovulation.
17	Fertilization.
20	Implantation: Time to abstain from smoking, alcohol, drugs, X-rays, kitty litter, etc. You may feel some symptoms.
28	You miss your period. Do a home pregnancy test. It's positive! Schedule an appointment with an obstetrician within a couple of days.
30	Your obstetrician performs an HCG level and progesterone test.

Week 5	35	HCG levels should be around 1,000, so you get the first sonogram and see the gestational sac.
Week 8	56	Return to your doctor for a second sonogram to see a little fetus with a tiny heartbeat encased in a growing sac and uterus. At the same time, have your prenatal blood work done.
Week 12	84	Your doctor performs a sonogram and associated blood test to confirm the gestational age and evaluate the risk of chromosomal disorders. The first trimester is over.

among other attributes, and measures about seven to twelve centimeters.You have gained between three and five pounds, and your uterus is the size of a small cantaloupe. You may have experienced cramps, backaches, headaches, breast pain, nipple tenderness, sensitivity to smell, nausea, excessive fatigue, fainting or dizziness, horrible mood swings, and all of that will have been "normal." You can probably expect some if not all of these symptoms to improve as you head forward.

You should have had all your basic blood tests. You should have had at least one sonogram, and depending on your or your doctor's anxiety level as well as other factors, you may have had as many as four.

Your chances for miscarriage plummet to way below 1 percent at the end of the first trimester. You're well on your way in an extraordinary journey of growth and development. What started out as a single cell just twelve weeks ago is now a visible baby.

CHAPTER 4

First Trimester: Abnormal

*R*elative to the rest of pregnancy, the first trimester is fraught with risks for the fetus, but light on threats to the mother's health. The vast majority of miscarriages occur in this trimester, but if you're lucky enough to get this far, you've proven that you and your partner can get pregnant together, which is something to take comfort in. Believe it or not, conception is the hard part.

Ectopic Pregnancies

The first, most significant problem in early pregnancy is when the embryo implants itself outside the uterus, which is the only organ that can sustain a pregnancy. This is called an *ectopic* (that is, misplaced) pregnancy. This occurs in approximately 1 percent of pregnancies. Because the vast majority of ectopic pregnancies happen in the fallopian tube, the phrases *ectopic pregnancy* and *tubal pregnancy* are practically synonymous. There are extremely rare instances in which the pregnancy attaches to an organ in the abdomen other than the tubes and uterus. Even more rarely, fast sperm have been known to fertilize an egg before it even leaves the ovary.

Ectopic pregnancies most often start when a structural irregularity in the fallopian tube snags a newly fertilized egg, the blastula, while it is on its way to the uterus. This blastula stays in the tube, grows, and ultimately attempts to implant itself wherever it is when the time is right. If it does not succeed in implanting itself, it will wither unnoticed and be a tiny part of the next menstrual period.

If it does implant itself, the tiny embryo seeks whatever food is available through the local blood supply. Unfortunately, the fallopian tube cannot expand like the uterus; therefore, as the embryo grows, it may cause damage to the tube and slight intra-abdominal bleeding. This blood inflames the lining of the abdominal cavity, leading to discomfort that can range from slight to significant to severe. This is called a *leaking* ectopic pregnancy.

If left to grow, most ectopic pregnancies proceed to a critical mass that causes the tube to explode. These are called *ruptured* ectopic pregnancies, and they almost always lead to a tremendous amount of pain, rapid blood loss, shock, and, sometimes, loss of consciousness. Because there is a plethora of arteries and veins near the tubes, a ruptured tube can cause a woman to quickly bleed to death. Ruptured ectopic pregnancies are still a relatively significant cause of fatalities in women under 30.

Fortunately, these grow rarer each year. Today, women tend to discover their pregnancies earlier through more accurate urine and blood tests. Obstetricians then use sonography to readily determine where a pregnancy is growing, thereby preventing a ruptured ectopic pregnancy and minimizing the health risks for mother.

Generally, there is about a two-week window in which to safely catch an ectopic pregnancy, starting at implantation (roughly day

ECTOPIC PREGNANCIES DON'T MAKE BABIES

It's important to understand that ectopic pregnancies cannot be saved, and they present little choice to the mother and doctor. Do not equate treating an ectopic pregnancy with having an abortion—it's solely about saving the life of the mother. There is no way to remove a viable embryo from the tube. If we could get it out, we couldn't sustain it. And if we did sustain it, we could not heal the irreparable damage caused by poor blood supply.

KNOW THE WARNING SIGNS

One of the biggest challenges in treating ectopic pregnancies is that women are unlikely to equate severe abdominal pain with a pregnancy gone awry, especially if they don't think they're pregnant. If you think you could be pregnant or you know you're pregnant, or you're within five weeks of your last menstrual period, serious abdominal pain (as in pain that is far worse than menstrual cramps) can mean an ectopic pregnancy. If you suddenly experience severe pain below your belly button, go right to an emergency room or call your doctor immediately.

twenty-one) to seven to ten days after the missed period (day thirty-five). The sooner it is discovered, the better. Although there is an increased incidence of vaginal bleeding with ectopics, most often they are close to asymptomatic in the early, unruptured state. The first telltale symptom may be abdominal discomfort caused by intra-abdominal bleeding.

If the obstetrician catches the ectopic pregnancy before the tube ruptures, it can frequently be treated with an oral medication called *methotrexate,* a drug originally developed as chemotherapy. Because this drug destroys all rapidly dividing cells, such as cancer, it also destroys the ectopic tissue. Treatment with methotrexate causes the blastula to simply shrivel up and cease to exist, saving the tube from any damage, and preventing the need for surgery. The earlier the medication is tried, the more likely it is to be effective; most ectopics that have gone longer than five weeks do not respond to methotrexate. Ruptured ectopics cannot be treated with medication, but require emergency surgery to stanch the internal bleeding.

Doctors fix larger or ruptured ectopics with surgery that aims to save as much of the tube as possible while also saving the patient's life. In some cases, laparoscopic surgery through the belly button can remove just the ectopic tissue and any part of the tube that has been damaged. The patient is in and out of the hospital within a day.

If the abdomen is full of blood or laparoscopic surgery is contraindicated (for example, there's scar tissue from a previous surgery in the way), then the situation requires a traditional abdominal incision to stop the bleeding. Even in this case, the tube may still be salvageable, but this depends on a number of variables, such as the location of the ectopic in the tube, the mass of the tissue, and the condition of the patient. If the tube is removed, it will negatively impact fertility, but only by about 10 to 20 percent, as long as the remaining tube is healthy. In practice, this often means it just takes a little longer to conceive because ovulation has to occur on the side of the remaining tube.

There is no way to completely avoid the risk of an ectopic pregnancy. Women are more likely to have a misplaced pregnancy if their fallopian tubes have ever been infected. Untreated or improperly treated sexually transmitted infections (STIs), such as gonorrhea and chlamydia, are the most common cause of tubal infections, which can leave behind scars to snag the fertilized egg as it swims by. Women who have had a previous ectopic pregnancy are also at higher risk of an ectopic pregnancy—they have a ten times increased risk of future ectopics. Before trying to get pregnant again, these women need to have a plan in place with their doctors so that if the blastula implants itself in the tube again, it can be detected and treated at the earliest possible time.

Bleeding and Miscarriage

Vaginal bleeding in the first trimester is always abnormal, but abnormal doesn't mean *pathological* (that is, related to disease). In about 50 percent of cases, vaginal bleeding turns out to be nothing—it stops sooner rather than later, and the pregnancy goes on as normal. Obstetricians call vaginal bleeding a *threatened abortion*, even though the phrase is somewhat misleading because it's impossible to confirm that the patient was, in fact, potentially about to have a miscarriage. For example, if the patient is less far along in her pregnancy than she thought, the blood could be from implantation, a normal occurrence.

If you experience any bleeding in the first trimester, it should immediately be evaluated by your obstetrician. If your cervix is closed and a sonogram reveals a normal intrauterine pregnancy, and there are no signs of infection, then it's not a catastrophe. In this case, the bleeding might be due to a ruptured vessel in the cervix or any number of other nonthreatening factors. Low progesterone can cause spotting or bleeding and, ultimately, a miscarriage, so your obstetrician is likely to check your progesterone levels if you are bleeding in the first trimester. If your levels are low, progesterone pills or progesterone suppositories are an easy and effective solution.

Another recommendation obstetricians often make to patients experiencing vaginal bleeding early in their pregnancy is to get lots of bed rest, although scientific studies have not supported this as an effective means to combat a threatened abortion. Nevertheless, the purpose of bed rest is to diminish the effect of gravity on the cervix and maximize blood flow and oxygen supply to the uterus. If you're staining in the first trimester, it can't hurt to take it easy; avoid the gym and don't move any furniture.

There's no way of knowing exactly what the risk of miscarriage is for each pregnant woman. Roughly 50 percent of all pregnancies end in miscarriage and the vast majority of them are discovered by the obstetrician, often through a sonogram or urine or blood test, before there are any symptoms. This statistic includes pregnancies that end shortly after implantation, when a woman may not have even known she was pregnant. These situations obviously require no medical intervention.

Miscarriages that happen further along are often predictable. For example, the patient is bleeding vaginally, her HCG (human

KNOW THE LINGO

Miscarriage is not a medical term. Doctors refer to all the ways that a pre-viable pregnancy can end, both chosen and involuntary, as types of abortion. The specific label depends on how and when the miscarriage happened and often dictates how it will be medically handled.

chorionic gonadotrophin) levels off or falls, and the fetal sac is not growing—this woman is progressing to an early miscarriage. This does not mean that she will wake up in the middle of the night in a pool of blood, but the way her doctor manages her care depends on how far along she is in her pregnancy. Sometimes, a miscarriage must be completed with the help of medication and/or surgery to protect the woman's health and the health of her uterus. Other times, the safest course of action is to let nature take its course.

Everything in a pregnancy might start off perfectly, with HCG levels rising at an appropriate rate. Then a few days later, hormone levels drop and the patient gets a normal period. Because that pregnancy was only ever detected through hormones and never seen on a sonogram, its end is called a *chemical abortion*.

If, at the first sonogram, there is a sac but the embryo fails to materialize, that is called a *blighted ovum*. If a sonogram finds a fetus, but cannot detect a heartbeat at the appropriate time, it is a *missed abortion;* the nonviable embryo is still in the uterus. If the cervix dilates in very early pregnancy, it's called an *inevitable abortion*. If this is accompanied by cramps and expulsion of tissue, it's an *incomplete abortion,* meaning that the woman's body may benefit from *prostaglandins,* which stimulate uterine contractions, to help fully empty its contents. When a pregnant patient has a sac and a positive pregnancy test on her first visit, experiences bleeding, and then comes in with a negative pregnancy test and nothing in the uterus, it's a *complete abortion*.

In some cases, women who have had a miscarriage require surgical intervention to prevent uterine infection and prepare the organ for another pregnancy. The procedure that empties the uterus is called a *dilatation and curettage* (D&C) or *suction curettage*. Though these are two different procedures, the terms are used interchangeably. It's possible to perform a D&C in an office setting, but it is usually done in a hospital or outpatient facility because the procedure is uncomfortable. Most patients prefer to have some sedation or anesthesia, which may be delivered through gas or intravenously.

The doctor starts the procedure by grasping the cervix with a *tenaculum,* dilating it when necessary with gradient sticks, and inserting a *curette* (a slim spoon) into the uterus. The spoon is used to scrape the superficial fleshy tissue off the lining and out through the cervix, preparing the uterus for the next menstrual cycle. Depending on how much tissue there is in the uterus, the doctor may also try suction, whereby a catheter vacuums the uterine cavity. Suction tends to minimize blood loss, time in surgery, and trauma to the uterus. D&Cs often culminate with a final, gentle sweep of the curette to ensure that the uterus is completely empty.

While D&Cs are very common and extraordinarily safe, they are not absolutely risk-free. Curettage has to be vigorous enough to remove all the tissue but not so strenuous as to scar the uterus. There's a fine line between rough and ineffective, so doctors try to err on the gentle side. Excessive, overly strenuous curettage can cause scarring inside the uterus, which can contribute to infertility, among other problems. A doctor who is too gentle risks leaving some tissue in the uterus, thereby having to perform a second D&C.

Because of these risks, oral prostaglandins are recommended more and more frequently for women experiencing a miscarriage. After all, it makes sense to avoid an invasive procedure when medication can stimulate the body to accomplish the same goal. The downside of using prostaglandins is that the treatment is unpre-

GET THE SOAPBOX

An *infected* threatened abortion can endanger the mother's life and uterus, though it presents a political quandary to some. A PBS documentary detailed the experience of a pregnant woman in New Hampshire who came into a hospital in great physical distress. She had a fever of over 103 degrees Fahrenheit and pus coming out of her uterus. If left untreated, the infected tissue would continue to damage her uterus, if not eventually kill her. But because the sonogram revealed a flicker of a fetal heartbeat, the hospital refused to allow the procedure. Her doctor put her in his car and drove her three hours away to the nearest medical facility, where he saved her life and her fertility by performing an emergency D&C to remove the purulent tissue.

dictable, uncomfortable, and doesn't always work. Sometimes the patient requires a D&C after a failed course of prostaglandins, so many women elect to cut to the chase and have a D&C.

It's hard to believe something as common as a miscarriage can be so devastating. Nevertheless, a miscarriage can often be a significant personal tragedy for the mother-to-be and her family. Depending on the woman, it can stir up lost aspirations, a sense of failure, and basic disappointment. In the early years of obstetrics, women experienced miscarriages in far greater numbers. Even today, about one in four pregnancies ends in the first trimester.

Although it is cold comfort to think of miscarriage as a natural defense, the vast majority of miscarried fetuses have chromosomal anomalies that are incompatible with life, even within the uterus. It's as if nature realizes that there was a misstep—for example, cells replicated with double the chromosomes, the blastula was implanted in the wrong place, or the egg wasn't quite right—and aborts the mission.

Choosing to Terminate the Pregnancy

There are times when, for whatever reason, the woman decides that she cannot or will not be pregnant. Sometimes a wanted pregnancy is terminated due to a confounding medical situation. For example, if a woman who is eight weeks' pregnant happens to be exposed to radiation from a nuclear reactor accident or she contracts German measles, she's guaranteed to have a raft of her own health issues to address as well as myriad fetal abnormalities. The reason for terminating the pregnancy also can be psychiatric—for example, a nervous breakdown in the first trimester might suggest that it's not the right time to become a parent.

There are two options for most women when choosing to terminate: *surgical* and *medical.* Surgical termination can be done up to fourteen weeks. The process is the same as a D&C or suction curettage. Depending on how much tissue is in the uterus, the procedure is likely to incorporate suction first to quickly remove the bulk of the material, followed by curettage to ensure an empty uterus.

The medical option is only recommended up to seven weeks of pregnancy, though these guidelines are constantly reevaluated. The whole process boils down to two pills; the first one is an antiprogesterone (now called Mifiprex, formerly RU-486) that cuts off hormonal support for the pregnancy, thereby terminating it. Forty-eight hours later, a prostaglandin pill (Cytotec) stimulates contractions to empty the uterus.

Each option has its pros and cons. The surgical route is certain; you leave the clinic and know the pregnancy is over. Although 97 percent effective, the medical route may require another try or a surgical follow-up. The advantage of the medical option is that there are no instruments, surgery, or anesthesia involved. Medical terminations are also somewhat safer, with a fatality rate of one in three hundred thousand compared to one in one hundred thousand with the surgical termination. A full-term pregnancy is nearly ten times more dangerous, at an overall fatality rate of one in thirteen thousand.

Excessive Nausea and Vomiting

Nausea in pregnancy is never pleasant, but it becomes a medical issue when the patient is vomiting so much that she's dehydrated and losing weight (called *hyperemesis*). How much weight loss is cause for concern? That's a judgment call. Some doctors let their pregnant patients drop as many as twenty pounds before sending them to the hospital; others, such as myself, get pretty worried when patients lose five pounds or more.

Doctors may also monitor relative nutrition by the amount of *ketones* in the patient's blood or urine. Ketones are acid byproducts of fat metabolism, so when a patient is making a lot of them, we can extrapolate that she's also burning a lot of fat—an early sign of malnutrition. The side effects of heightened ketones include highly acidic urine or extremely bad breath, both of which are common for people on no-carbohydrate diets. These are signs that the body cannot support metabolic function without burning fat. This is not healthy for the mother, whose electrolytes, blood

MEDICAL MYSTERY CORNER

A pregnant patient in my hospital was admitted for excessive vomiting that had been going on for at least eight weeks. When the resident tried to put vitamins in her IV bag, she refused them because the smell bothered her. As the days passed, she drifted further into unconsciousness. Every specialist in the hospital, from infectious diseases to neurology, consulted on her case. They were all flummoxed. One day an intern noted that the patient appeared disoriented. The next morning she slipped into a coma. During an MRI of her brain and chest the technician discovered her heart was no longer beating. It was at about that time that someone thought to investigate her vitamin status and discovered that she had died of a profound vitamin deficiency, something so uncommon in the modern industrialized world that no one had thought to look into it. Not surprisingly, this case is in the lawyers' hands now.

sugar, vitamins, and enzymes are all struggling to stay in balance, or the baby, who isn't getting a whole lot to eat. Additionally, it lowers the pH of the mother's blood, making it more acidic, which is not good for the fetus (this state is called *ketoacidosis*). This doesn't happen after one day of throwing up, but instead occurs after several weeks of nonstop, daily vomiting. Ketones in the blood are a sign of profound illness, and women with this condition are typically admitted to the hospital.

Once admitted, the first priority is making sure the hyperemetic patient is well hydrated through an IV. Vitamin deficiencies can be fatal, so the IV usually includes them as well. Following this treatment, the patient must decide what to do about her nausea. On the one hand, it's good to avoid medications in the first trimester; on the other, extreme vomiting can be intolerable and dangerous.

There are various antiemetics that have been used in pregnancy, some more effectively than others. One class of these drugs is the *phenothiazines* (brand names include Compazine and Phenergan), which safely do the job. These come in IV, suppository, and injectable forms.

Reglen and Zofran are two newer medications that have been used very successfully for nausea out of pregnancy and seem to be very safe in pregnancy. Zofran was developed to combat nausea caused by chemotherapy and is now used for the treatment of significant, life-threatening first-trimester nausea and vomiting. Reglen is usually given intravenously or through injection, whereas Zofran can be dispensed as a tablet that dissolves in the mouth so there's no risk of vomiting it up. Zofran also comes in IV form or, for the more seriously ill, Reglen can be given via a subcutaneous pump that delivers a continuous dose of medication through the first trimester.

For the less seriously ill, vitamin B$_6$ and antispasmodic medication can be helpful. These used to be combined in one medication called Bendectin, which was used for many years by obstetricians to treat nausea. Unfortunately, one patient who used this medication delivered a child with a birth defect and sued the drugmaker. Although all the studies that were conducted on either side of the trial proved the Bendectin was perfectly safe, the cost of litigation ran the company out of business. Luckily, doctors can still prescribe both ingredients separately.

Alternative remedies for nausea abound, although they are of questionable benefit. Some women claim ginger, lemon, gum, or tea

NAUSEA: WHEN THE CAUSE IS EMOTIONAL

Many obstetricians suspect that there is a strong psychiatric component to hyperemesis, but you can't tell that to a puking lady. The last time I mentioned psychiatry to a woman who was vomiting up her guts, she simply went out and got another obstetrician. It seems that women who are particularly anxious, who have a history of emotional problems, and who often have dramatic, emotional responses to stressors may face a greater risk of nausea. This is not to say that they aren't really sick, but that maybe they would get greater long-term relief by addressing their emotional issues. If you are a highly emotional person and are experiencing prolonged nausea in pregnancy, it can't hurt to talk to a mental health professional who can help you get some perspective and a greater sense of control.

are soothing, others rely on an acupressure wristband that puts constant pressure on the nausea meridian to relieve nausea, while still others swear by acupuncture. Although none of these remedies has been proven effective by any real science or evidence, they do no harm. If you find one that works for you, by all means keep using it.

Rh Factor

The *Rh factor* is an antigen, like a spoke, that sticks out of red blood cells. Ninety percent of humans are Rh positive; that is, they have this spoke. The remaining 10 percent do not and are therefore Rh negative. The only time Rh factors matter is when the mother is Rh negative and the father is Rh positive or his status is unknown. Even then, it's a completely treatable problem.

If a pregnant woman finds out she's Rh negative, while the baby's father is Rh positive (or unknown), then the baby has anywhere from a 50 to 100 percent chance of being Rh positive. Because the baby's Rh status cannot be determined, and because 90 percent of all people are Rh positive, it must be assumed that the baby is positive.

An Rh-positive baby in an Rh-negative mother used to be a significant risk, because although there is a barrier between the mother's blood and the baby's, it is not perfect. If a small leak occurred, the baby's Rh-positive blood would trigger an immune response in the mother and the baby's blood cells would be attacked as if they were invaders in the mother's bloodstream. This isn't so threatening in a first pregnancy, but in a second pregnancy, the mother's immune system has a previously constructed, efficient antibody response that can travel back to the baby and destroy its blood cells (called *erythrocytosis fetalis*).

When an Rh-negative mother has an Rh-positive partner today, her obstetrician administers Rh antibodies at the time of potential leakage events to neutralize her immune response. For example, if the patient is undergoing an amniocentesis, which might cause a slight leak between baby's and mother's blood, the doctor gives her an injection of *hyperimmune Rh gammaglobulin* (brand name Rhogam), which is simply a shot full of Rh antibodies. These are like machines that swim through the blood looking to plug up the Rh spoke on the baby's red blood cells. The maternal immune system then remains blind to the Rh-positive blood and does not respond. Rhogam should always be given to an Rh-negative mother after any situation or trauma that could cause a leak between the two blood systems, including an abortion, miscarriage, ectopic pregnancy, and delivery, as well as during the last twelve weeks of pregnancy, when the placenta gets a little leakier.

Unfortunately, once an Rh-negative woman has been sensitized to Rh-positive blood one way or another, her body already has an unavoidable immune response. This means that the next time she is exposed to Rh-positive blood through a pregnancy with an Rh-positive baby, her immune response could be potent enough to kill the fetus. Since medicine can't stop her body from making Rh antibodies, the only way for these women to safely sustain pregnancies is to find Rh-negative sperm donors. Science may solve this problem differently in the future, but as of now, there are no good alternatives.

The Rh factor is the most common antibody for which obstetricians routinely screen. The general antibody screen will catch other, far more rare antigens that live on red blood cells, such as Kell, Dewey, and Duff antibodies, to name but a few. These abnormal antibodies are extremely rare and would only appear in a woman who has had a blood transfusion that was not completely matched to her. These unlikely antibodies are of variable severity and significance. Many of them can be completely ignored.

MOMMY, WHERE DOES RHOGAM COME FROM?

It's esthetically displeasing to learn that Rhogam was developed in prisons. Even today, scientists often pay inmates for their antibodies. Rh-negative volunteers are injected with Rh-positive antigens, which triggers their immune response to make Rh antibodies. Then blood is taken, and all the Rh antibodies are removed, cleaned, and packaged. If you look at the Rhogam label, you'll see that it reads "ultra-filtered human gamoglobulin."

YOU'RE LUCKY TO BE LIVING IN THE TWENTY-FIRST CENTURY

When my roommate in medical school in the late 1960s learned about Rh factors in class, she tested herself. She was Rh negative and, back then, this meant a shaky reproductive future. She cried every single night for weeks on end. Little did she know that just a few years later, being Rh negative would become a totally manageable hurdle rather than a life-altering diagnosis for a pregnant woman.

Abnormal Development of Placental Tissue (Trophoblastic Disease)

Trophoblastic disease is the umbrella term for a group of conditions associated with a dangerous proliferation of placental cells. These disorders are called *partial mole, hydaditiform mole,* and *choriocarcinoma;* the first two behave like cancer, while choriocarcinoma is cancer. There is no way to predict or control which women might develop these problems, though this disease is extremely rare in the United States (around one in fifteen hundred pregnancies). Doctors suspect that trophoblastic disease is associated with poor nutrition, especially vitamin A or fat deficiencies. This would explain why it's much more common in places like Southeast Asia, where these disorders occur in about 1 percent of pregnancies.

The mildest variety of trophoblastic disease is *partial mole,* which produces a highly abnormal placenta and a tiny fetus. Partial mole begins when two sperm fertilize an egg, producing DNA with 50 percent more chromosomes (*triploidy*) than usual.

Hydaditiform mole is more significant. In this case, there is no apparent fetus, just highly abnormal tissue that consists entirely of the father's DNA. Hydaditiform mole commences when one sperm fertilizes an apparently empty egg, probably made vacant by malnutrition, as mentioned.

Mole and partial mole are characterized by abnormally high HCG levels, which may exacerbate the symptoms of first-trimester pregnancy. Vaginal bleeding can also occur, and/or there can be grapelike growths that extend out of the cervix. A biopsy of these growths or the intrauterine tissue confirms the diagnosis.

In the event of any mole diagnosis, all the tissue in the uterus has to be removed by D&C or dilatation and suction (page 62). The obstetrician can rest assured that a patient is mole-free when her HCG levels return to zero. HCG levels are the only way to be sure that the patient is completely healthy, so obstetricians urge these women to avoid pregnancy for about a year, during which time they have their blood regularly tested for HCG to ensure that a possible recurrence is quickly diagnosed and treated.

Choriocarcinoma is a significant malignancy, which is more aggressive and dangerous than mole. This is when the placental cells become malignant, grow out of control, and spread throughout the body. It's so rapid and virulent, doctors are not sure what happens in the earliest stages of this disease. The cure rate is high— even the most advanced choriocarcinoma can be cured over 95 percent of the time with the right form of chemotherapy.

Anyone diagnosed with trophoblastic disease should consult with a gynecological oncologist, preferably at a regional medical center. Do not try to have this disease treated at a small local hospital by an inexperienced obstetrician.

IT'S NOT ALL BAD NEWS

When I was a resident, we admitted a woman who was in a coma with what looked like terminal cancer. It's possible that she had previously been diagnosed and treated for mole, but lacked follow-up care. A simple blood test for HCG would have revealed the presence of placental cells, which in her case were malignant due to choriocarcinoma. Even though she was in an extremely advanced stage when she arrived, after chemotherapy she walked out the door weeks later, cured. No other stage IV cancer has as high a cure rate as choriocarcinoma, but it must be diagnosed correctly and treated quickly.

Testing for Abnormalities: Chorionic Villus Sampling (CVS)

There is a specialized genetic test of the first trimester called *chorionic villus sampling*, or CVS, that some women elect to have instead of an amniocentesis. Somewhere between nine and twelve weeks, the doctor snips off a tiny piece of the placenta by inserting a needle into the uterus through the vagina or abdominal wall under sonographic guidance. This tissue can provide a definitive diagnosis of any chromosomal abnormalities, as well as reveal the baby's gender.

This test is quicker and is done about a month earlier than an amnio, which is a second-trimester test (see page 92). The results come back in three to five days, as opposed to the seven- to ten-day wait for amnio results. The bad news is that CVS carries about a 2 to 3 percent risk above spontaneous miscarriage rates in the same period, and it requires a very skilled hand. Also, an amnio detects more abnormalities than CVS, which requires an additional blood test and sonogram at seventeen weeks to rule out structural problems.

In some cases, CVS is an obvious choice. For instance, CVS seems to be more accurate at assessing cystic fibrosis and is often chosen when both parents are carriers of a particular disease. If a couple has already had a Down syndrome baby, they may want to be tested as early as possible in a subsequent pregnancy. Parents in this situation also appreciate that the test is done earlier in the pregnancy, when they may feel more comfortable terminating.

Couples who know they have some sort of unusual gene or bizarre genetic family history need to meet with a genetic counselor, who can explain all the risks and benefits of aggressive chromosomal testing for each individual woman and her unique circumstances.

The bad news is that the first trimester of pregnancy has the highest complication rate. Many factors can terminate gestation early on, and, unfortunately, doctors don't always understand why. Obstetricians hypothesize that these pregnancies were flawed to begin with. The good news is that most of these negative events simply postpone parenthood. Women whose pregnancies end in the first trimester almost always go on to have healthy babies.

CHAPTER 5

Second Trimester: Normal

The mid-trimester, from the end of the twelfth week to the end of the twenty-fourth week of gestation, is a bit of a lull between the two busier trimesters. Bad things hardly ever happen in the second trimester. Most symptoms improve, and many women report feeling "more like themselves." Although most pregnant women become obviously so during the second trimester, they are still able to get up and around with relative ease. It's a good time to take a vacation, if you are so inclined. It's also a good time to just relax and enjoy gestating.

Eat, Bubelah!

The second-trimester mandate is good nutrition. Food helps build the baby's brain, heart, lungs, and every other body part; without good nourishment, the baby cannot grow. Additionally, there's a growing body of evidence that suggests your baby's nutrition in utero can affect its future risks of diabetes, high blood pressure, and heart disease.

Good nutrition can be tough for women who are usually too busy, picky, or lazy to eat healthfully. It's tough for many women to make the transition to better eating habits during pregnancy, whether it's having breakfast or getting enough greens. Plan ahead, especially if healthy eating does not come naturally to you. Begin incorporating these guidelines early on so that they're a cinch by the second trimester, when it really counts.

Women who tend to eat one big meal a day will have to learn a new rhythm. First of all, the one-meal plan is hard on the mother's stomach. It's also not great for the baby, who needs food pretty much all the time. Skipping meals guarantees a low blood sugar level and poor nutrition for the little tyke. Abstaining from food for more than thirteen hours can trigger a sequence of hormonal events that ultimately stimulates the production of acids in the blood, which increases the risk of preterm labor. Remember to eat regular meals and to graze.

Daily Second-Trimester Diet Requirements

Nutrition is not an exact science, but we do know a few basic facts. It seems that variety is essential. For example, eating foods that are vibrant and varied in color is a simple guideline worth keeping in mind. There always seems to be a new study out that shows how a precise component of food (see section on PUFAs) is extra important in pregnancy, but there could be hundreds left to identify. In short, the goal is to cover all your bases by consuming the broadest array of foods possible.

There are as many pregnancy diets as there are dietitians, so when you choose a nutritional plan, make sure it was designed by someone who knows what they're talking about. The following regimen was designed by the March of Dimes, and it's the one I recommend to my patients. It's simple, safe, and comprehensive.

HAZARDS: STILL WORTH AVOIDING

As the baby grows, external hazards become a bit less concerning. When the fetus consists of fewer cells, one or two going awry can have a tremendous impact. Once arms are formed, for example, they are not going to fall off. Needless to say, it's still worth avoiding unnecessary risks; for example, Chernobyl is not someplace you want to visit while pregnant and it's best to wait before having any plastic surgery.

A Quart of Milk or Its Equivalent

Milk is not just calcium; it's got great value in terms of protein, carbohydrates, and fat. You can mix up the sources, as long as you end
up with the equivalent of one quart (four cups) of milk total. Cot-
tage cheese and yogurt are healthy and roughly equivalent to milk
in their nutritional value. Skim milk is fine. One ounce of hard
cheese is the equivalent of one cup of milk. Ice cream counts, but it
isn't a great idea as a sole source of dairy. People who are lactose
intolerant can substitute soy milk fortified with calcium. Live-
culture yogurt is often safe for lactose-intolerant people because it
contains the enzyme that they lack.

Eight Ounces of Protein (Animal Preferred)

Fish, chicken, and meat are the best and easiest ways to fulfill the
animal protein requirement, and eight ounces every day is ideal. A
helpful nutritionist's tip is that eight ounces is approximately the
size of two decks of cards. Protein consists of many different amino
acids, some of which must be consumed each day because the body
cannot make them. These are called *essential amino acids*. Others
can be converted from carbohydrates, and still others can be made
from other materials in the body. Only animal food has all the essential amino acids. Remember to avoid certain fish (see page 15) and
cook all meat thoroughly.

If you are an ovo-lacto vegetarian, you can eat eggs and cheese
to fulfill your protein requirement, but remember that if you eat a
block of cheese for protein, you still need to fulfill your dairy
requirement. If you are a vegan, you need to work a little harder to
derive all the essential amino acids from vegetable sources. However, there are food combinations that contain a full complement of
protein: rice and beans, *pasta fagioli* (beans and pasta), and vegetarian chili on rice are just a few examples.

Four Grains

For most people, this is the easiest requirement to fulfill, since it
includes pasta, bread, cereal, oatmeal, rice, bulgur, croutons, and so
forth. One slice of bread equals one grain serving, so a sandwich, for
example, counts as two grains. Whole wheat is healthier than white,

but pregnant women benefit from all flour in the United States because it is fortified with folic acid.

Two Leafy Greens

Even with the abundance of fresh and frozen vegetables available in the average grocery store today, there are plenty of women who claim that they don't eat anything green. There are so many options: arugula, mesclun, field greens, kale, broccoli, okra, collard greens, escarole, spinach, swiss chard, and more all count toward this requirement. Figure one handful equals one serving. Sorry, but pistachio ice cream counts as a dairy, not a green.

One Vitamin C

This should be an easy dietary requirement to fill: a glass of orange or cranberry juice is all you need. Obviously citrus fruits count, as do most berries. Vitamins C and B (which are included in most prenatal vitamins) are considered *stress vitamins* because you tend to use them more during times of stress, and you need to eat them every day since you cannot store them (like amino acids).

One Yellow Fruit or Vegetable

These include apples, bananas, potatoes, pears, squash, corn, carrots, and tomatoes. If it's a fruit or vegetable and does not fall into one of the other categories, it's probably a yellow. This is perhaps the least understood of all the dietary requirements in pregnancy, but including it ensures the broadest possible food variety.

Water

Drink at least eight eight-ounce glasses (sixty-four ounces total) each day. Being pregnant makes you sweat and breathe more heavily than normal, draining additional water from your body. The gained weight and blood volume also tax hydration. Even nonpregnant people tend to simply feel better when they are adequately hydrated. Many women who have headaches in pregnancy find that drinking lots of water is a more effective treatment than medication.

PUFAs (Polyunsaturated Essential Fatty Acids)
The latest prenatal nutritional studies show that two omega-3 essential fatty acids, called *polyunsaturated essential fatty acids* (PUFAs), are particularly important in developing the baby's central nervous system. *Docosahexaenoic acid,* otherwise known as DHA, is uncommon in most modern diets. DHA is found in fish, wild game, unprocessed grains, and some prenatal vitamins. *Arachidonic acid,* or AA, is more commonly found in modern diets and prenatal vitamins. AA is present in cereals, whole-grain breads, most vegetable oils, eggs, and poultry.

It's not uncommon for pregnant women to become obsessed with what they're eating. Maybe they entered pregnancy with a strong distaste for milk and have never been able to get over it. Maybe their family never served fish. These are small issues that can be fixed with the help of a nutritionist. The nutritional guidelines provided here will help you achieve an optimal outcome. But if you miss a serving of greens one day or are short on vitamin C another day, it's not worth worrying about, as long as on the whole you follow a healthy, nutritious, and balanced eating regimen.

Common Second-Trimester Symptoms

Despite the second trimester being the calmest, safest, and most comfortable, it's still a time of dramatic change within the mother's body. The symptoms discussed here reflect these changes, but again, not every woman experiences every symptom. If you've never felt better, you are extremely lucky. Most women experience at least a few of these symptoms, and it may help to know that these bodily changes are perfectly normal. Only in pregnancy will you hear a doctor tell you that it's fine to have an elevated heart rate, compromised vision, and relentless constipation. Enjoy it!

ODD SIDE EFFECTS

To improve the blood supply to the uterus, the body has to build new arteries and veins to get blood in greater quantity to more places in the body. This is called *congestion,* and it strikes most noticeably in your mucous membranes (mouth, nose, and vagina) and pelvis. As a result, your gums may bleed when you brush your teeth, a condition dentists call *gum disease of pregnancy.* You may be more prone to nosebleeds. Your vagina might be a little swollen and blue. Other bodily fluids, such as saliva, can also increase.

Palpitations

As the pregnancy progresses, the heart beats not only faster but with greater *stroke volume.* In other words, the heart also beats harder. With pregnancy, total blood volume increases by about three liters. Most of this is water (hydration!) and fresh red blood cells. As a result, the heart has to work extra hard to pump all the extra blood to more places.

Some women notice the feeling of their hearts beating in their chests all the time. Some feel it when they lie down and their ear pressed against the pillow reports each gush of the blood through an artery. Some women don't really notice it at all. Whether you turn

WE'RE ANIMALS, AFTER ALL

Your primitive brain doesn't know about treadmills; it knows about imminent threats to your life. Thus, if you're running, your body figures your best chance at survival is to be able to run like hell or fight the danger. This reflex is called *fight or flight,* and it is automatically, unavoidably triggered by increased pulse and respiration. It's a reflex designed to preserve the maternal unit (you) by giving you a maximum chance at survival and a future shot at reproduction. Fight or flight is not designed with the baby in mind.

out to be the former or the latter, rest assured that increased stroke volume is totally normal in pregnancy.

If you still need reassurance, count your pulse. Put your index finger on your wrist or neck and count the beats for one minute. If the number is under 110, chances are you're fine. Pay attention to the rhythm of your pulse; is it regular or erratic? If your heart is beating like a metronome, chances are you're totally fine. In fact, even if your heart rate is an irregular 120 beats per minute (BPM), it's still probably normal, but it is time to ask your doctor.

Shortness of Breath

Most pregnant women experience some increase in respiratory rate. Whereas a nonpregnant woman may breathe twelve times each minute at rest, that number could increase to fourteen in the second trimester. It's more work to breathe for two; the blood needs to travel through a placenta to drop off some oxygen for the baby and then get all the way back to the lungs to pick up more. The central nervous system stimulates the heart and lungs to work faster to do all this extra hauling.

That stimulation can make the pregnant woman feel short of breath. It's a sign from your nervous system to breathe faster, and if you notice it out of the blue it can feel like an anxiety attack. But remember that if you can still talk, you're still breathing. Nevertheless, if the symptoms worry you, talk to your doctor.

Your Exercise Routine While You're Pregnant
The shortness of breath you experience during pregnancy may affect your exercise routine. It is unlikely that it will keep you from exercising altogether; however, you may have to change your idea of what you consider exercise. Ideal workouts for this time of your life include walking, low-impact aerobics, and swimming. A good rule of thumb is to do whatever you normally do, but cut back the intensity and increase the time. For example, walk the mile instead of running it. It may seem counterintuitive to exercise enthusiasts, but the goal in pregnancy is to maintain, not improve on, cardiovascular fitness.

Cardiovascular fitness is a big part of many healthy women's exercise regimens. This sort of training aims to improve the heart muscle by working it like any other muscle. This is accomplished by stimulating the heart to beat faster through exertion, up to rates of 180 and beyond.

You may be reducing blood supply to the baby when you are out of breath and/or your heart is beating more than 50 beats per minute above your resting pulse. Because a high heart rate stimulates the fight-or-flight reflex in which the body focuses on self-preservation, the adrenal gland directs blood flow to the lungs and muscles and cuts off nonessential organs with a hormone called *epinephrine* (or *adrenaline* from the adrenal gland). The uterus is one of the first places to get cut out of the blood route.

It's important to remember that your resting heart rate is higher in pregnancy and climbs more precipitously with exercise. Let's say your normal heart rate is 70 at rest and goes up to 120 when you get on a treadmill. In the second trimester, it could be 90 at rest and go up to 150 with the same exertion.

Suffice it to say that the pregnant woman should aim to maintain her heart muscle, not improve it. A simple rule of thumb in exercise is that you can do anything you can talk through. If you're

YET ANOTHER REASON TO GET TO THE DOCTOR EARLY

Because your blood pressure will fall in the second trimester and then rise in the third, it can be hard to tell later on if and when it's getting too high. The only way to know what's normal is to establish a baseline blood pressure in the first trimester or, optimally, even before you are pregnant. Let's say you first get to the doctor in your second trimester and your blood pressure is normal, but it starts to go higher and higher. Your doctor can't be sure whether you have chronic hypertension that perhaps predates your pregnancy or if you are developing one of the hypertensive disorders in pregnancy (see page 145); it's important to know the difference because the treatment and risks are handled differently.

so out of breath while you're jogging that you can't talk, you're running too fast.

Vascular Issues

Pregnancy presents unique obstacles to the circulation of blood in the woman's body. First, there's the increase in blood volume (discussed on page 78), but also the weight of the pregnant uterus compresses all the vessels from the legs as they enter the abdominal cavity, preventing the easy flow of blood and leading to swollen veins. Heavier women, those who already have varicose veins, and women whose mothers have varicose veins are all at greater risk and should take preventive measures.

Varicose Veins 101

The heart circulates all the blood in your body by pushing it out into arteries. This pressure moves it along until eventually it flows into a vein to head back to the heart. Veins contain valves that prevent the blood from sloshing around in your feet all day. Each *pump* of the heart moves the blood along past a valve and into the next chamber. Then the valve closes behind it. The next *pump* moves it up to the next chamber, and so on. A varicose vein appears when a valve fails and twice the volume of blood presses down on the valve below, which can cause that one to fail, too. The vein swells with the added volume. Varicose veins happen throughout the leg, but you only see the ones close to the skin that look like thick, blue ropes.

A great way to prevent varicose veins is through exercise. A muscle contraction, especially around a vein, can help the blood move up the leg to the heart. If you make a muscle in your calf, you're squeezing blood in the right direction. Legs that are in good shape from walking, leg lifts, biking, and similar movements, are less likely to sustain varicose veins than ones with no muscle tone.

Support stockings can help prevent varicose veins closer to the skin. The stockings hug the vein, helping the blood to move along. To guarantee the greatest benefit it's best to put the support stockings on before getting out of bed. After lying prone for eight hours or more, the veins are mostly collapsed. Once standing, even momentarily, the veins in the legs fill up with blood, making it harder for the support stockings to do their job.

When you have to be on your feet all day, give the veins in your lower body a break by assuming an antigravity position. Accomplish this by creating a straight path from toe to heart. This means that sitting is bad, because the vein hits a right angle at the knee and at the hip. A better option is to lie straight. It's best of all to lie unbent but at a slight angle, with the legs raised above the heart. The blood will fall back to your abdomen, giving all the veins in your legs a rest.

One of the best ways to effortlessly achieve a vein-friendly position is to put a book under the foot of the bed, so your whole sleeping surface is at a slight, one-degree angle. The goal is to create a straight shot from feet to torso, so pillows under the head are fine even if the waistline becomes the lowest point in the mattress. The slightest slope makes a difference. You can put pillows under your feet as well, in which case you should also put a pillow under your hips so that there's no kink in blood flow at the groin.

Increased blood volume and the blockage of free-flowing blood from the legs to the heart also contribute to swollen ankles, which happen when water oozes out of the veins because the pressure is so high. Salt, which increases blood volume, contributes to this problem. During pregnancy, the feet tend to stay puffy twice as long after a salty meal, waiting for the body to mobilize that extra fluid out of the ankles. Unfortunately, this process of deflating the ankles often happens at night when the pressure of the uterus is alleviated because you're lying down. This may mean several nighttime trips to the bathroom as all that water is finally channeled to the bladder, but at least your ankles should look—and feel—normal in the morning. If swollen ankles are a persistent problem, lower your salt intake and drink more water.

Peeing and Pooping

Constipation increases in the second trimester, once more because of progesterone. This hormone can double intestinal transit time from mouth to toilet bowl and diminish gastric emptying time. Usually, food you ate right now would show up in the toilet bowl by tomorrow. But when you're pregnant, it might be the day after tomorrow. The digestive tract just isn't moving the way it used to. Exercise helps by stimulating the intestines, but most pregnant women encounter some constipation.

When excrement lingers in the system, it tends to dry out. The intestine extracts all the moisture, making for hard, difficult bowel movements. Many pregnant women must strain to evacuate, which increases the risk of varicosities or hemorrhoids around the vagina and rectum. You can avoid this situation by doing what you can to create bulky, moist stools.

Your best bet is to increase the size and fluid content of what's in your digestive system. The intestines are a tube that responds to pressure; when the inner walls of the tube are stretched, they contract in response and move things along. All kinds of fiber including fruit, vegetables, whole grains, nuts, oats, bran, and even fiber supplements such as Metamucil, are a great idea in pregnancy because these materials bulk up the contents of the intestines to encourage motility. Water is the obvious choice to raise the moisture level, but sometimes it's not enough. When increasing your water and fiber intake doesn't do the trick, a stool softener such as Colace is a perfectly safe alternative, as these are not laxatives and do not irritate the colon. They simply help to hold moisture in the stool so what you pass is bulky and moist; ideally, it won't hurt and you won't have to strain.

Prenatal vitamins can also contribute to digestive problems because they are high in iron, which causes constipation. If you are really struggling, talk to your doctor about your constipation. If you're not anemic, you might be able to go without the iron to get some relief for a little while. You could replace this mineral with lots of meat and leafy greens.

Although pregnant women may struggle with bowel movements, they usually have incredible urinary frequency. As the baby grows, so does the number of trips to the bathroom. The uterus presses right on the bladder; every time the baby kicks it's probably in that vicinity.

Kicking isn't the only thing that stresses the urinary tract in pregnancy. The two kidneys are high on the flank, close to the ribs.

A tube (called a *ureter*) runs along the flank and down behind the uterus, connecting each kidney to the bladder. The growing uterus inevitably compresses the ureters. Furthermore, progesterone relaxes these tubes, so urine is free to collect in the kidney. For these reasons, all pregnant women eventually develop a *physiologic hydronephrosis*. This is when the urine does not flow freely to the bladder, leading to swelling in the kidney, which, in an X-ray, would look like terminal kidney disease. But in pregnancy it's perfectly normal and completely painless. The only health concern associated with this symptom of pregnancy is how it contributes to urinary tract infections—swollen kidneys indicate a greater amount of urine throughout the system. This urine is relatively stagnant and, therefore, it is more fertile breeding ground for bacteria.

Urinary tract infections are one of the most common medical problems in pregnancy, if not *the* most common, so it's worth the time to try and avoid as many of them as possible. Your only weapon is water. As you hydrate yourself, the kidney filters the water and pushes the urine down the ureter. Hydration prevents the urinary stream from stagnating. Remember to constantly drink and pee, drink and pee, drink and pee.

BACKACHES

A study was done decades ago that found unwed mothers had fewer backaches than pregnant married women. The researchers concluded that married women's posture was different and more harmful than that of their single counterparts because married women were more likely to have wanted to get pregnant and were subsequently thrilled and wanted everyone to know about their pregnancy. Thus, they tended to stick out their bellies, putting a lot of pressure on their lower backs. Unwed pregnant women, who were less eager to share their news, tended to stand with their stomachs in, backs straight. This created less pressure on their backs. The lesson to be taken from this is to keep your knees bent, hold your stomach in, tilt your pelvis, hold your head up, and keep your shoulders relaxed. This is easier on your whole neuromuscular system, and you will feel better. Everyone will know you're pregnant soon enough.

Skin Changes

In general, skin just becomes unpredictable in pregnancy, but more than anything in terms of its color. The area around the nipple (called the *areola*) grows darker. A dark line called the *linea nigra* appears up the belly, like a racing stripe, from the pubic bone straight up toward the chest. Sometimes, hyperpigmentation (also called *chloasma*) can happen across the bridge of the nose and cheeks, between the eyebrows, and/or on the upper lip, like a mustache. This is romantically dubbed a *mask of pregnancy*. It's not very common, although it also happens to certain women on the pill.

Most hyperpigmentation fades after delivery, but do not expect a complete return to your old self. Your breasts will look different; the areolas are likely to remain a little darker and browner. Pregnancy masks fade, but not always completely. The linea nigra most often disappears. Dermatologists are always coming up with new ways to help this problem; if you have persistent hyperpigmentation, find a dermatologist to help after the baby is born.

Pregnancy also makes sunbathing a risky endeavor. You may burn when you've never burned before. You may get the best tan you've ever had in your whole life. If you develop a chloasma, the sun can make it much worse. For these reasons, pregnancy is probably not the best time to tan your face. (In fact, there is no good time to tan your face, because sun damage and skin cancer are associated with prolonged exposure to ultraviolet rays.) When you're out in the hot daylight sun, wear a hat, big sunglasses, and a lot of sunblock. Even then, take it slow and don't make your first foray onto the beach an all-day event. If you do choose to sunbathe, at least expose your nipples to the sun so they get the benefit of toughening up before breast-feeding.

Pregnant women sometimes sprout skin tags. These are just accumulations of skin cells (*epithilium*) and pose no health risks. They can be removed, but most women don't bother until after the baby is born.

Stretch marks (called *stria*) are probably the least attractive and most permanent mark of pregnancy. A rapid change in figure can lead to these bright pink linear marks. They can happen any-

MY PUBLIC SERVICE CAMPAIGN

In adolescence, the skin is so immature that even girls who rapidly sprout breasts get stretch marks. You can imagine that pregnant teenagers end up with pretty significant *stria* across their bellies. (Perhaps we could lower teen pregnancy rates just by including pictures of real teenagers' bellies, post-childbearing, in teen sex ed texts.) As far as this one small, superficial facet of pregnancy goes, the older you are, the better.

where the skin rapidly stretches as the body underneath it expands, but most often they appear on the belly, buttocks, thighs, breasts, or upper arms. While stretch marks never go away completely, they fade to a silvery skin tone within a few years.

There are some ways to predict the odds of sustaining stretch marks. If you're pregnant and under twenty-five, the chances of getting stretch marks go up. Another bad sign is if your mother got terrible stretch marks when she was pregnant. If you're having twins, you are practically guaranteed to develop bad stretch marks. There are all sorts of creams and emollients available to minimize stria; cocoa butter and vitamin E oil are perennial favorites among pregnant women. Although these creams are unlikely to prevent stretch marks entirely, they might help to make them a little lighter or fewer. Dermatologists are always coming up with new, more effective treatments for this problem.

Increased Susceptibility to Illness

It's a medical miracle that the body doesn't reject the baby like a bad organ transplant, but one way it accomplishes this is by lessening the mother's immunity. Thus, even if a pregnant woman looks like the picture of vitality, she is actually more likely to get sick because her immune system is handicapped. Because the nasal membranes often swell with increased mucus production and blood flow, a little cold can block up the nose and take an inordinately long time to clear.

The American College of Obstetrics and Gynecology (ACOG) and the American Medical Association (AMA) recommend flu shots for pregnant women in the flu season, which is the fall. This protects the mother from getting seriously ill, and it stimulates her immune system to make antibodies that are then passed through the placenta to the baby, so the child is born resistant to the flu.

Increased Body Temperature

As you may recall from the normal menstrual cycle, progesterone kicks in only in the second half of the cycle. In pregnancy, the body simply continues making more and more of it. Because progesterone is *hyperthermic* (that is, it raises the body temperature), the pregnant woman is at least one degree warmer than usual, which means that she feels hotter and sweats more than usual. The sweat may even smell different. This increase in body temperature explains why pregnant women are always opening windows and fanning themselves.

Vaginal Changes

Vaginal discharge typically increases during pregnancy. Further, not only does the discharge smell more than usual, it may also smell a little different. The labia are chock-full of sweat glands—more per square centimeter than the armpits—so you can expect a lot of sweating as your body temperature rises with pregnancy. Further, the vagina is flush with additional blood flow, making it warmer. Huge amounts of hormones stimulate the production of creamy, copious secretions. All of this makes the external genitalia an extra smelly, moist place.

Like everywhere else in the body, the vagina tends to swell with increased blood flow. It can become swollen to the point of being bluish with the added pressure of the enlarged uterus. This swelling can challenge the mechanics of intercourse; some women find it uncomfortable, while others enjoy this new sensation. You may have to make some adjustments. Entry should be slower, and extra lubrication might come in handy. However, sex can play an important, healthy role in pregnancy, so don't let a little congestion get in the way of some intimate time with your partner.

Other Physical Changes

Obviously, the whole body, including the skeleton, has to grow to accommodate a pregnancy. One way nature accomplishes this is with a hormone called *relaxin* that literally melts cartilage—the rubbery stuff that connects bones. This allows the pelvis and rib cage to expand, sometimes dramatically. Your chest has to grow to allow for improved pulmonary capacity, and your pelvis needs to be as big as possible to allow the baby through. The chest and pelvis grow about half an inch in pregnancy and will not shrink after delivery.

Pregnant women are a little more prone to injury. First of all, the pregnancy grows so quickly that you are almost always off balance because your center of gravity is constantly changing. The body is stressed in unique ways in pregnancy; all the muscles in the back of the legs tighten, while the ones in the front stretch. The ligaments relax and stop supporting the body as strongly. Because of this, be extra cautious on your feet—keep your knees bent and look where you're going, especially on irregular terrain. The ACOG advises pregnant women to avoid downhill skiing in particular. I personally do not think skiing poses a significant health risk to the pregnant woman who also happens to be an experienced skier.

Even if you're just walking around, the added strain on your changing body also very frequently leads to leg cramps, usually at the end of a long day. The best way to avoid this is to stretch at night before getting into bed.

CHILDBEARING CAN ENHANCE YOUR FIGURE

It's subtle, but you'll probably look different after having a baby. I like to think of the postpregnancy figure as more lush, voluptuous, and sexy. You end up curvier. Most women bid adieu to straight, boyish hips.

ALAS! THAT THICK, LUSH HAIR WON'T LAST

After the baby is born, you will pretty much lose all the hair you gained in pregnancy: *number of days pregnant × 20 = number of lost hairs postdelivery.* Once the pregnancy hormones stop, it can feel like your hair is coming out in clumps. The stress of delivery and postpartum sleep deprivation don't help. I've had patients think they were going bald, but I've never seen it get that bad.

Healthier Hair and Nails

Pregnant women often have the best hair and fingernails of their lives. Normally, we lose approximately twenty hairs each day. The hormones in pregnancy often prevent that hair from falling out; it grows thick and lush. Fingernails are less brittle and grow long. Pregnant women often assume that it's really the prenatal vitamins that are behind this welcome change, but women who have continued with the vitamins after pregnancy find that it's just not the same.

Because hair and nails are dead cells, you can really do just about anything to them during pregnancy as long as you're healthy. This includes hair dye, which is completely safe (and was probably never dangerous anyway). The active ingredient in most hair dyes is hydrogen peroxide, which you'd put on your finger if you had a cut so it is also okay to put in your hair. If, for some reason, you have open sores on your scalp, you should not get your hair colored. When it comes to nail treatments, avoid any that require the mani-

TREAT WITH CARE

Even though your hair may be thick and lustrous, it is impossible to know how it will react to chemicals. The dye you normally use might not produce the same color as you're used to. Or a chemical straightener might not work. Also avoid anything elaborate or exotic—if your hair turns out to be more sensitive than usual, you might lose it.

curist to wear a mask to protect herself, just to be on the safe side. I would also recommend avoiding any particularly new, drastic hair treatments, again, just because we do not know for sure if it is safe or not.

Vision Changes

The shape of the eyeball can change with pregnancy, compromising vision. Your contact lenses may no longer be comfortable. If you don't seem to be seeing as clearly, try glasses for the duration of the pregnancy. You could also speak to your ophthalmologist. Just remember that if you get a new prescription during pregnancy, there's a good chance you'll revert to the old one once the baby's born.

Dental Work

There's an old myth that you lose a tooth with every pregnancy, but don't let this tale lull you into quietly accepting dental problems and possible tooth loss when you are pregnant. Even though your gums are more likely to bleed, don't skip your regular cleanings and exams. It should go without saying that if you have a real dental emergency—like an excruciating toothache that won't go away—you should always take care of it no matter what stage of pregnancy you're in.

All routine dental work is certainly acceptable, especially in the mid-trimester. Even dental X-rays are okay during pregnancy. These are tiny X-ray machines, and the dentist will blanket you with a lead apron. Local anesthetics, such as Novocain, are also perfectly safe.

The one real hazard in getting dental work in the second trimester is the common dental practice of adding *adrenaline* to Novocain. Adrenaline constricts the vessels nearby, preventing the anesthetic from leaking away too quickly; that is, it holds the drug in that place a little longer. This vasoconstriction can raise blood pressure, which is dangerous for the baby. If you're prone to hypertension, adrenaline can trigger an unhealthy sequence of events. *If you are pregnant, you should not have adrenaline (or epinephrine, which is the same thing).* You can have any plain local anesthetic such as Novocain, but no adrenaline.

Some Good News

Your hearing will almost definitely remain unchanged throughout your pregnancy!

Fetal Movement

Babies start moving at around eight weeks of gestation, and every woman feels movement by the end of the second trimester. However, it takes a certain amount of experience to feel the earliest fetal movement, which tends to be inconsistent and light. The earliest activity usually occurs when the baby is only about one pound and still has a lot of space in the uterus, so it can turn over without jabbing you. A woman pregnant with her first baby may not feel anything until after the twentieth week. Because she's never felt it before, the first-timer might mistake baby kicks for gas or an upset stomach. Women who have been pregnant before recognize fetal movement as early as sixteen weeks.

When the baby kicks, the mother feels it on the surface of her body, even though it ripples out from the uterus. The kick has to travel through the abdomen to the skin for the mother to sense it. This means that thin moms tend to feel the baby moving earlier in pregnancy.

Common Second-Trimester Testing

It can feel like the tests pile up in the second trimester, but this is the most crucial time in determining how the baby is developing. By the end of this period, you and your doctor will know every detectable thing about your child. The vast majority of all structural and chromosomal anomalies are tested for during these three months, so you can enter the third trimester confident about the health of your baby.

Second-Trimester Evaluation of Risk

The second-trimester evaluation of risk happens at around seventeen weeks. This is a quadruple screening, done with a blood sample. The tests seek to measure *alfa feto protein* (AFP), *inhibin*, *pregnancy-associated plasma protein* (PAPP), and HCG. When these four substances are present in certain quantities, it signifies a higher risk of genetic or structural defects. They are evaluated in much the same way as the hormones in the first-trimester risk evaluation; there's a huge overlap of abnormal with normal. It's the aggregate of these tests that gives you a good picture of what's going on with the baby.

The measure of AFP is used to determine the presence of a number of abnormalities, including neural tube defects and Down syndrome. AFP is highly concentrated in the fetus. If there's a hole in the baby that doesn't belong there, AFP will leak into the amniotic fluid and across the placenta. Most of these holes are called *open neural tube defects,* and there's little else that explains a very high AFP level in the mother's blood.

AFP also tends to be a little low in babies with Down syndrome; however, this finding is less meaningful than a high AFP level. There's a very small difference between low and normal, so the other three tests either reinforce or contradict that finding. Genetics labs crunch these four different numbers to estimate the risk of chromosomal abnormalities, of which Down syndrome accounts for 90 percent.

Amniocentesis

Amniocentesis (called *amnio* for short) is also done at fifteen to seventeen weeks. In this procedure, the doctor extracts amniotic fluid, which is fetal in origin, from the uterine cavity. This is done under sonographic guidance, usually with an obstetrician and a sonographer working in concert. Some obstetricians can do both if they're practiced and very good with their hands. The sonogram

A NUMBERS GAME

A lot of obstetrics is numbers. One of my patients had an abnormal quadruple test that suggested her risk of a chromosomal abnormality was one in fifty. The patient asked, "What's the false positive rate for this test?" I said, "Well forty-nine out of fifty times it's wrong." She was not satisfied with that answer because she was expecting something more absolute. But the quadruple test does not in any way say "This baby is sick." Instead, it says "We think there's a higher risk that this baby has a problem." The test is not definitive. It provides odds. There's no such thing as a false positive with screening tests because they do not yield positive/negative results.

allows the technician to watch the needle enter the uterine cavity and thereby completely avoid the baby and umbilical cord. It also allows the mom to see that the baby looks fine afterward.

Many pregnant women dread the large needle involved in an amnio, but this test is really no more or less painful than a blood test. There's a plexus of nerves under your skin; if the needle hits one of them, it hurts. If the needle misses them all, it doesn't. An amniocentesis needle is actually thinner than the ones doctors use for blood tests. It is longer, but the whole thing is rarely used, depending on the thickness of the patient's abdominal wall.

A genetic lab technician cultures (in other words, grows the cells within) the amniotic fluid extracted via amnio and then adds an enzyme to stop the process just as the chromosomes are dividing and at their plumpest. This is the only time when scientists are able to count the chromosomes because they all line up to divide; when cells are not actively dividing, chromosomes wander around the cell incognito. The lab tech typically blows up ten to fifteen nuclei, cuts out the chromosomes, and pastes them on a big board called a *karyotype.*

The geneticist then examines the karyotype for abnormalities such as discrepancies in shape, shading, and number. Twenty-two pairs of chromosomes plus one X and one Y or two XXs is normal. The geneticist looks for unusual shapes or extra pieces and analyzes the dark and light places, which is called *banding.* Through ongoing research, scientists are constantly finding new correlations between the shade of the chromosome and health implications. For example, banding on a particular chromosome could indicate an increased risk of diabetes.

There are normal and abnormal results, although some abnormal findings are insignificant from a health standpoint. Normal is when there are forty-six chromosomes, two of which determine the sex, and these chromosomes are all regular in appearance. The most common abnormality is when there are more or less than forty-six chromosomes. Abnormal results also include a diagnosis of any specific, rare chromosomal problem, in which case the results are either positive or negative (for example, if both the parents are carriers of cystic fibrosis, the geneticists would look for chromosomal mutations associated with this disease). Sometimes, the chromosomes are correct in number, but appear slightly abnormal and unique to the geneticist; this doesn't always have an apparent health effect.

Amniocentesis does not statistically increase your risk of having a miscarriage, but there are some concerns associated with the procedure. When the needle pierces the uterine sac, it leaves a hole in the membrane. That hole puckers and seals when you withdraw the needle, like a thumbtack pulled from a tire. Very rarely, the hole fails to close and water might leak from the gestational sac into the uterus, through the cervix, out the vagina, and down the leg. If you have a watery, heavy discharge the day after your amnio, call your doctor. These leaks frequently seal, but they may require extra care.

"INTERESTING" RESULTS?

I got an amnio report that said my patient's baby had a "funny-looking" Y chromosome. It was abnormal in a way that had never been documented before. When we tested the father's blood, we found the same goofy-looking Y chromosome, and he was perfectly healthy, both physically and mentally. Because of this, we concluded that the baby would be fine, too. There are people who have a piece of chromosome floating around in their cells, but they usually don't know about it until they become parents. The rule of thumb on these highly unusual aberrations is that if either parent has it, we assume that it's just an extraordinary but harmless variation on normal.

Another potential problem following an amniocentesis is uterine contractions. Because the uterus is a muscle, it may tense in response to the pain of the needle—an automatic reaction to a noxious stimulus. The uterus, like the heart, is a rhythmic muscle, meaning that once stimulated, it tends to continue contracting at regular intervals. Once the uterus contracts, it could theoretically contract again ten minutes later, then ten minutes after that, and so on. It's best to rest as much as possible the day of the amnio to avoid stimulating uterine activity. Some obstetricians even recommend a glass of wine just after the test to help keep the uterus relaxed and prevent a continuing contraction pattern from becoming unstoppable; in this case, alcohol can offer more benefits than risks.

The final threat incurred with an amnio is infection. Everyone's skin has tons of bacteria on it, and if there's something unusually pathological on the belly, the needle can track it inside the abdomen. A fever within a week of an amnio could mean a serious infection as a result of a contaminant from your skin. Even though the obstetrician will take all sorts of precautions (Betadine, gloves, sterile equipment), be sure to take the extra step of washing your belly really well on the morning of the amnio.

Ultrasound

The final test in the second trimester is the *twenty-week ultrasound.* This is also called the *anomaly, birth defect,* or *level two sonogram.* Here, the obstetrician takes a very extensive look at the baby, first looking at the overall measurements, which are called *biometrics.* These include the length of the thighbone (femur) and the circumference of the abdomen, as well as the circumference and diameter of the head. From these measurements, the obstetrician can deduce whether or not the baby is *appropriate for gestational age,* or AGA. She'll also measure the volume of amniotic fluid, which should be of a certain quantity. It's important to locate the placenta in the uterine cavity, though an abnormal presentation of the placenta is more of a problem in the third trimester.

This key ultrasound is done at twenty weeks because at that point the uterus isn't yet crowded, which makes details easier to discern. All the internal organs are mature and ready for evaluation.

This sonogram reveals virtually everything the obstetrician would want to examine: the internal anatomy of the brain, the chambers of the heart, the aorta, pulmonary artery, diaphragm, lungs, face, stomach, kidneys, intestines, arms, legs, fingers, toes, and so forth.

Structural anomalies (see page 100) outnumber chromosomal anomalies in the United States, so this is one of the most important obstetrical tests. If it goes well, you know for sure that your baby is structurally and anatomically normal. Usually this sonogram happens right around the time you start to feel fetal movement, so it's nice to feel and see the baby. It makes it easy for a mom to start thinking of the alien in her belly as a real person.

Congratulations!

The end of the second trimester the baby now weighs about a pound and a half and has grown from about twelve centimeters (or three inches) to at least a foot long. All the parts are matured and visible. You have ideally gained another ten to fifteen pounds, for a total of twenty (thirteen at minimum). The top of the uterus is about one to two inches above the belly button—a long way from where it used to be, buried in your pelvis. You can still see your feet, so you don't put on mismatched shoes, and you still look cute and sexy as well as a little pregnant.

SECOND-TRIMESTER NORMAL CALENDAR	
Week	
13	Second trimester begins.
17	Second-trimester evaluation of risk and/or amnio.
20	Ultrasound/sonogram.
20	Fetal movement.
24	On to the third trimester!

CHAPTER 6

Second Trimester: Abnormal

*T*he second trimester *is* the time when bad things hardly ever happen, but when something does go wrong, it can go very wrong. Usually this begins with poor results on a critical test, such as uncovering a genetic anomaly with an amniocentesis.

Genetic Abnormalities

Human chromosomes are meant to come in precise numbers. Every normal human cell contains forty-six chromosomes, of which twenty-two pairs are *autosomal,* meaning that they have nothing to do with the sex of the baby. Unfortunately, any deviation from this basic makeup (or even an abnormality *within* a chromosome) leads to an intellectual deficit; even a child with a mild chromosomal anomaly would need to be very lucky to achieve average intelligence. On the other end of the spectrum, significant chromosomal aberrations often lead to miscarriage. Each genetic problem has its own set of defining characteristics that range in severity depending on the magnitude of the abnormality.

The most common chromosomal abnormality in humans is an extra chromosome at the twenty-first slot. This is called *trisomy 21,* although it is more commonly known as *Down syndrome.* Along with mental deficit, Down syndrome babies have distinct physical characteristics, such as low-set ears, large tongues, bulging eyes, and poor nasal bone development. Down syndrome babies are also at higher risk for cardiac anomalies.

Many experts suggest that children with Down syndrome have exceptional social skills; they tend to be nonaggressive, friendly, and loving. Unfortunately, all Down kids are mentally handicapped to some extent. Nevertheless, there are many individuals with Down syndrome who are able to overcome these challenges and achieve a degree of self-sufficiency in adulthood, usually in independent living facilities. Still, approximately 90 percent of women who receive a Down syndrome diagnosis via amnio elect to terminate the baby.

The risk of Down syndrome increases with maternal age. For a woman under 30, the chances are far less than one in a thousand pregnancies. Once she reaches 35, that number is one in 270. At 40, it's up to one in 80, and at 45, one in 40. And if she's one of the rare women who can still get pregnant at 50, her risk is one in ten. As women age, so do their eggs, and their ability to replicate properly becomes less reliable, raising the chances of an extra chromosome somewhere. This is not to say that young women don't give birth to Down syndrome babies. In fact, there are more Down babies born to women under 35 than over 35, but this is because women under 35 have many more babies than women over 35. This is why the ACOG recommends genetic screening (see page 53) at the end of the first trimester for all pregnant women.

The second-most-common autosomal anomaly is *trisomy 18,* which is an extra chromosome on the eighteenth pair. This is also known as Edwards syndrome and occurs in approximately one in ten thousand pregnancies. Unlike Down syndrome, which may present a truly difficult decision for two eager parents, trisomy 18 is incompatible with a meaningful life; the vast majority of these babies (roughly 95 percent of them) die before birth or shortly thereafter. These children rarely progress past a vegetative state, and they often require a respirator because their brains are not capable of maintaining respiratory function. The extra chromosome comes with an additional host of potential physical problems that can include the malformation of all bodily systems. Most women who receive this diagnosis elect to terminate the baby, and even some religious authorities have supported the decision to end a pregnancy that can never result in an independent life.

Aside from trisomy 21 and trisomy 18, which account for over 90 percent of chromosomal defects, there are enough aberrations to fill a whole library. Of the remaining 10 percent, the majority affect the sex chromosomes—the Xs and Ys. *Klinefelter's syndrome* is the most common sex-linked disorder, affecting 0.2 to 0.3 percent of male babies. Babies with Klinefelter's syndrome have an extra X chromosome (47,XXY). This condition is most often diagnosed at puberty when the secondary sex characteristics (such as facial hair, muscle development, a deepening voice) fail to materialize. Additionally, these boys are mildly retarded and sterile. Like Klinefelter's syndrome, triple X syndrome (47,XXX)—also called *superfemale*—a condition that affects approximately one in one thousand female babies, is often detected later in life, if at all. This condition is also associated with mild retardation.

Turner's syndrome is another sex-linked anomaly, and it occurs in approximately 0.03 percent (three in ten thousand) of pregnancies. In these pregnancies, one sex chromosome is missing (45,X0), often leading to miscarriage. Babies that survive grow up to be short, sterile girls who often have a webbed neck (their skin extends almost directly from chin to shoulder). They tend to be mildly retarded and are at high risk for cardiac anomalies.

BEFORE YOU SAY NO TO AN AMNIO . . .

Some women elect to skip an amniocentesis for religious, ethical, or personal reasons; because they will not consider terminating a pregnancy, they conclude that the test is unnecessary. However, there are other reasons why an amnio may be beneficial for your baby. For example, should the test uncover a significant problem, your doctor can make sure that the right medical personnel are available at the time of delivery. Also, knowing about a long-term issue in advance gives you the chance to seek out a support group for parents of children with the same anomaly and to find the medical center best equipped to manage your child's health issues.

A baby with an extra Y chromosome (47,XYY) is *supermale.* This happens in approximately one in one thousand live male births. An old study suggested that a relatively high percentage of violent criminals had this disorder; for all we know, supermales also dominate Wall Street and professional sports, but no one has done those studies. Although these boys can be challenging to raise— they tend to be hyperactive, aggressive, and mean to their siblings—they are not considered intellectually compromised. There are even pediatricians who specialize in the care of 47,XYY boys, because early appropriate intervention can make all the difference with supermale boys.

Receiving an Abnormal Amnio Result

Receiving abnormal amnio results can leave a pregnant woman terrified and dazed, but there are specialists who can help decipher all the numbers and charts. A geneticist can provide specific details about the health problems, likely behaviors, and intellectual disabilities associated with each child's particular condition, crunching the numbers and telling you how likely it is that the baby will experience these problems and to what extent. The geneticist can also outline the special requirements and challenges involved in raising a child with a specific chromosomal abnormality. In the wake of an abnormal amnio result, seek out as much information as possible from the best available sources (a geneticist, not the Internet) to help you make the best choice for yourself and your family.

Structural Defects

At twenty weeks, the fetus is anatomically developed. There's enough amniotic fluid around the baby to make almost every detail easy to see at your *twenty-week* or *anomaly sonogram.* This is the doctor's first reasonable chance to detect any structural abnormalities; these are defined as any physical aberration that is not caused by a chromosomal problem. While doctors hypothesize about the cause of some specific defects, most of these problems are attributed to an isolated, unidentifiable glitch at some point earlier in the pregnancy.

For a healthy couple, there's a 5 percent chance that there will be some sort of structural defect in the fetus. Of these, at least half have no clinical significance, and most of these, such as a dimple or birthmark, would probably not be detected on a sonogram.These things rarely bother parents, though they are medically character-ized as anomalies. They obviously do not require any intervention. The following discussion focuses on the most common structural problems that are detectable at the twenty-week sonogram.

Many structural defects require minimal medical treatment. For example, a baby may have a nub of skin on his or her hand that looks like a small sixth finger. At birth, the pediatrician ties the base of this sixth finger with silk thread to cut off its blood supply. Before long, the sixth digit simply falls off. Even if that extra finger has some bone in it, a hand surgeon can perform a slightly more com-plex surgery. Other birth defects, such as an *umbilical hernia* or a weakness in the abdominal wall where the intestines may protrude, often correct themselves within a year.

More significant, life-threatening structural defects require more aggressive care. In some rare circumstances, such as a blocked uri-nary tract, it is possible to treat a significant structural defect in utero. This allows the baby to continue growing until it is mature enough to deliver. Sometimes the obstetrician enlists the help of a specialist who monitors the baby to see if she's progressing in spite of the problem. If required, the obstetrician can deliver the baby early in order to perform immediate, lifesaving surgery. In other cases, the pregnancy is continued to term, often because the anom-aly will only be threatening to the infant's health or well-being after birth. For instance, an intestinal obstruction in utero won't cause health problems because the baby isn't yet using her own digestive tract.

Some defects, such as a *cleft palate,* can be fixed completely; others, such as an *open spina bifida* (see page 105), for example, can be surgically addressed but may still significantly compromise the child's quality of life. And then there are those anomalies, like *Potter's syndrome,* in which the kidneys are missing, that are sim-

IT'S NOT JUST YOU

There appear to be worldwide trends in structural anomalies. In the Po Valley in Italy, the leading defect is congenital hip dislocation. In Japan, they tend to see more cleft lips and palates. In Great Britain, particularly Ireland, the most common structural anomaly is a swollen head (called *hydrocephalus*). Cardiac defects are the most common abnormality in the United States. The reason for these differences is not entirely clear, but they can be partially attributed to environmental factors, such as diet, water, and air quality. The vast majority of birth defects are multifactorial; they are the result of a complex interaction of genetic and environmental factors that we do not yet completely understand. Thus, immigrants enjoy a decreased likelihood of the birth defect most common in their country of origin, but their risk will not be as low as it is for natives.

ply incompatible with life. It's worth noting that doctors schedule the anomaly sonogram before the end of the twenty-fourth week; if there's a significant problem with the baby, especially one that makes life outside the uterus impossible, the patient can still elect to terminate.

The Heart

The most common heart defects (approximately 1 percent of all births) are also the least serious, with the majority correcting themselves within one year of life. Unfortunately, these sorts of defects are hardly ever detectable before birth because the baby's heart changes at the moment of the first breath. So what looked normal on a twenty-week sonogram may become problematic after delivery if the heart does not convert to adult circulation. Premature babies are more likely to suffer this sort of defect, since their hearts are not ready for the dramatic change that normally takes place at birth.

At twenty weeks, the sonogram tends to reveal more significant, even life-threatening, cardiac anomalies. For instance, a healthy baby's heart should have four chambers, four valves, and four major vessels that should all appear normal and connect in the right places. Any departure from this basic makeup is extremely rare but potentially catastrophic. While pediatric cardiology is constantly expanding our abilities to help babies with cardiac abnormalities, it tends to be easier to correct anomalies of the vessels than problems with the heart itself. For example, *transposition of the great vessels* is when the artery that distributes blood through the body is attached to the wrong side of the heart. This anomaly is usually successfully treated with surgery at birth, depending on the location of the aberration.

When the sonographer is unhappy with the fetal cardiac anatomy for any reason, it's time to see a pediatric cardiologist. These specialists perform sonograms specifically directed at the baby's heart through the mother's belly (called a *fetal echocardiogram*), and they can accurately assess the health implications. The sooner you know precisely what's wrong, the sooner you can investigate the best medical care for your situation. Don't get anxious if your doctor says something like: "We know this heart will be normal for at least twenty years." This means that the first person to receive this surgery is now only twenty years of age.

If your baby has a defect that requires surgery, bear in mind that the first operation is the most important one. If your baby needs a

FETAL HEARTS VERSUS REGULAR HEARTS

In utero the baby does not breathe, because he or she is underwater. The only oxygen the baby gets is from the mother's blood, which comes through the placenta. This blood travels in the umbilical cord, past the baby's belly button, into the right side of the heart. Outside the womb, that blood is then sent to the lungs, where it picks up oxygen. In the case of a baby in the uterus, however, the blood goes through a hole in the right atrium to the left atrium. From there it goes through the left ventricle to the aorta, which disperses the blood throughout the body. The *ductus arteriosis* catches all the blood that went to the lungs unnecessarily. Once the newborn baby breathes, the hole between the atria close. *Boom.* The ductus arterioris slams shut, and the lungs take over the task of oxygenating the baby.

very complicated and immediate cardiac operation, it may require you to go to a regional center specializing in fetal cardiac care. You might have to interview cardiologists to find someone who is confident doing the procedure your baby needs.

The Brain

Fetal brain anomalies are rare (less than one in a thousand births) and varied, although a good number of them have to do with the fluid that surrounds the brain and spinal cord. These precious items are encased in a lining (called the *dura*) that is filled with *cerebral spinal fluid* (CSF) like a pillow. So there's the brain, then there's fluid, and this is all encased in a covering; this package is called the *neural tube*.

This fluid should be in a constant state of production and absorption, keeping the brain and spinal cord lubricated and cushioned. Sometimes there is an obstruction in the normal circulation of cerebral spinal fluid, which leads to swelling of the head in an anomaly called *hydrocephaly*. When too much fluid collects between the dura and the brain, the pressure can destroy the neurological tissue. When the pressure is great enough and the baby's skull has not yet fused, the whole head can grow bigger and bigger.

Hydrocephaly can almost always be detected from a twenty-week ultrasound. If it's significantly worse by the twenty-fourth week, it's time to call a perinatologist and a pediatric neurosurgeon. It's rare that doctors locate an exact cause of the buildup of CSF, but it's sometimes possible to bypass the obstruction with a tube (called a *shunt*) in utero. When the surgery is successful, these babies turn out fine. When the hydrocephaly is rapidly worsening and intrauterine surgery is not an option, the only choice can be to induce labor so that the baby can have immediate neurosurgery.

Other neurological problems fall under the category of *open neural tube defects,* which involve any abnormal opening in the dura. These occur in about one in a thousand pregnancies, with mothers who take folic acid in their first trimester enjoying dramatically reduced rates of this problem. In general, the closer the defect is to the brain, the worse the prognosis. Thus, the worst open neural tube defect is called *anencephaly,* which is when the top of the brain and skull are missing. Babies with this defect never gain consciousness if they make it to birth, and there is no treatment for this problem. *Meninge mylecele* is an open neural tube defect that occurs at the base of the brain or in the neck and carries an equally grim prognosis.

The only neural tube defect that frequently can be treated with some confidence is an *open spina bifida,* which is when there's a hole in the dura at the base of the spinal cord. This exposes the nerves that control the ability to hold urine and move the bowels, as well as walking, sitting, and feeling, among other functions. An open spina bifida subjects the baby to the risk of permanent spinal cord damage at birth, because the minute the spinal cord is exposed to air at birth it deteriorates. Thus, an obstetrician who knows ahead of time that the baby has an open spina bifida should have neurosurgeons standing by in an operating room to immediately close the defect, preserving as much neurological function to the lower half of the body as is possible. This intervention could mean the difference between a cane and a wheelchair as the child grows.

The rarest structural problems of the brain are when the brain itself is not developing properly. Sometimes parts of the brain or the connections between them are simply not good. As with all structural defects, these problems range from minor, meaning the child will enjoy a relatively normal life, to catastrophic. Only an experienced pediatric neurologist can outline a more precise prognosis, depending on the particular situation.

The Urinary Tract

The urinary tract encompasses two kidneys, two ureters that connect the kidneys to the bladder, the bladder, and the urethra that connects the bladder to the outside world. The most common structural defect in this system is an obstruction of some kind in the flow of urine through all the organs and tubes involved. Like heart defects, urinary tract problems in utero range from the self-correcting to the severe. Moderate obstructions or narrowings can lead to slightly enlarged kidneys that are of mild medical concern.

These kinks and tight fits are often outgrown within a year, although infants born with these conditions should be under the care of a pediatric urologist. Even when a urinary tract problem may eventually require surgical intervention, pediatric urologists prefer giving the baby time to reach an age when surgery is easier. In the meantime, the child might require special care, such as taking antibiotics.

More significant obstructions require intervention. A total blockage anywhere along the urinary tract could lead to backup and kidney damage. If possible, a skilled sonographer can remove the urine directly from the fetus's bladder with a needle, avoiding kidney damage and allowing the pregnancy to continue. As soon as the baby is mature enough to be born, surgery can fix the obstruction. If the fetus has a urinary tract obstruction that is causing permanent kidney damage, and it cannot be addressed in utero, the baby still requires immediate medical intervention at birth, and possibly even an early delivery. In these situations, the obstetrician and urologist must weigh the health risks of prematurity versus kidney damage.

Among urinary tract abnormalities, there are some that are absolutely incompatible with life. The most common (approximately one in three thousand births) is called *Potter's syndrome,* a condition in which the fetus does not develop normal kidneys. The most obvious sign of this problem is a significant deficit of amniotic fluid because this liquid consists increasingly of the baby's own urine as the pregnancy progresses. Thus, a baby without kidneys has no amniotic fluid. Even if you could secure an infant kidney donor (highly unlikely), these children are irreversibly compromised by the lack of amniotic fluid and cannot live. An experienced sonographer can identify this problem 100 percent of the time at twenty weeks.

The Digestive Tract

Defects of the fetal digestive tract range from ones that can be repaired with a simple surgical procedure to those that lead to life-altering or even life-threatening conditions. Problems with the digestive tract occur in approximately one in five thousand births. Among the most common of these defects are those that affect the intestines. The intestines are essentially one big, digesting pipe that runs from the esophagus to the rectum, and this concourse can develop improperly or incompletely. The most common of these issues is an absence of an anal opening, called an *imperforate anus*. Although this condition can cause the fetus's intestines to distend with fluid, it does not become a big problem until the baby is born and begins eating. An imperforate anus can typically be diagnosed with a sonogram; nevertheless, an anus is one of the first things checked for in the neonatal exam. Obstructions or narrowings can also happen between the stomach and the anus, which leads to a distended stomach full of fluid. Again, this rarely poses a problem in utero because the baby in the womb is not depending on his or her own digestive tract for nourishment. Of course, it's best to know about these defects ahead of the baby's birth, so as to have a surgeon at the ready.

Abnormalities in the connection between the mouth and the stomach are called *tracheoesophogeal fistulas* and result in an excess of amniotic fluid (called *polyhydramnios*) and an empty stomach. These blockages do not present a problem in utero, but they do require immediate surgical intervention at birth. The major concern here is that food might get routed to the lungs, an error that can cause the baby to suffocate at its first meal. This diagnosis is almost always made before birth by sonogram, but it is critical that this issue be discovered before the baby is fed.

In a condition called *omphacele,* underdevelopment of the abdominal wall in the fetus leaves the intestines floating free in the amniotic cavity. Since the intestines are bathed in amniotic fluid in utero, this condition poses few problems before delivery. However, these babies must be delivered via caesarian section to protect the fragile, exposed intestines, and then they must be operated on immediately by a pediatric surgeon. With the appropriate care, these children often enjoy normal, healthy lives.

A *diaphragmatic hernia* is when there's a hole in the barrier that separates the abdominal cavity from the chest cavity. Loops of intestines can slide through this defect and fill the chest, preventing the fetal lungs from developing. This defect is corrected at birth by moving the intestines to where they belong and closing the hole between the chest and abdomen. Even if this defect is corrected

> ## C-SECTION PLEASE
>
> There are some birth defect anomalies that all but require a caesarian section. A baby with a goiter (an enlarged thyroid), for example, won't be able to flex his or her head in labor, which is an essential step in a vaginal delivery. If the goiter isn't diagnosed in advance with a sonogram, labor could last for many hours before the reason for the holdup is discovered. Other birth defects that typically require a C-section include those that enlarge the baby or expose sensitive organs, such as an open spina bifida, distended bladder, or hydrocephalus.

immediately following birth, the lungs may never fully recover from the damage already done, which can range from mild to severe. In the worst cases, the lungs fail to expand and function; this condition is called *pulmonary hypoplasia* and is probably fatal. Corrective surgery improves all the time, but it can be difficult at twenty weeks' gestation to predict how successful these measures will be. Obstetricians and pediatric surgeons follow the pregnancy with serial sonograms, in the hope that the baby will be mature enough to deliver before there's been substantial damage to the lungs.

Finally, abnormal-looking intestines can signify a non–digestive tract condition, namely, cystic fibrosis. When the intestines appear shiny and prominent, sonographers call it an an *echogenic* bowel. This finding does not definitively diagnose cystic fibrosis; instead, it is one indicator that the baby might have the condition. When found, the obstetrician will likely make sure at least one of the parents has been tested for cystic fibrosis.

The Face

One of the most common facial anomalies is a *cleft palate,* a condition in which the baby's face doesn't completely fuse together as it forms, creating an empty wedge in the top lip and sometimes in the palate. This is a fixable cosmetic issue; after treatment and surgery, kids born with this defect look perfectly normal.

Doctors can't always identify the cause of a cleft palate, although there are some indicators of risk. There is a strong genetic component and an even clearer connection between this anomaly and certain medications, especially drugs for epilepsy. However, epileptic women can't go off their medication—seizures are extremely traumatic to a pregnancy—thus, they must accept the risk that comes with the medication. Their risk of giving birth to a child with a cleft palate is about 3 percent. If you are epileptic, consult with your neurologist and your obstetrician about establishing the safest possible medical regimen for you and your baby.

The management of cleft lip and palate has changed through the years. In the past, doctors attempted to close the gap in the lip immediately, but surgeons learned that the physical stress of closing the gap in one operation created broader scars. These days, the cleft palate is often treated by a team of specialists, including an endodontist, a cosmetic surgeon, a dentist, a neurologist, and a maxillofacial surgeon. Usually, the process begins with certain exercises and prosthetic devices to help close the separation in the lip or palate. Surgery comes later, typically when the child is six months to a year old. By that time, the tissue has become relaxed and has closed enough to be sewn together without tension, minimizing scar tissue and producing a superb cosmetic result. Children who have

---

BE PREPARED

At a patient's twenty-week sonogram, my radiologist saw what looked like a small tumor on the baby's face, near the eyeball. I arranged to have every kind of relevant specialist available at the delivery—a head and neck surgeon, a neurosurgeon, and an ophthalmologist. Once the baby was born, all these people huddled over her, examining every detail. It turned out that all the fuss was over a clogged tear duct. A resident reached over, squeezed a little, and the problem was gone. Wouldn't you rather have everyone come for a false alarm, rather than everyone hustling at the last minute for the necessary resources?

been treated for a cleft palate often require speech therapy and cosmetic dental work.

The Extremities

Anomalies of the limbs are called *limb bud deformities*. Though they are not life threatening, obstetricians do try and ensure that the baby is complete and normal. A radiologist can usually count the fingers and toes but may not be able to see them all. Sometimes a little piece of a digit can be missing; rarely, an arm or leg fails to develop.

Phocomelia is the most dramatic limb bud deformity, leading to abbreviated, malformed arms and legs. The most famous phocomelia tragedy was the thalidomide scandal of the 1950s. Thalidomide, a sleeping pill, had been proven safe in animals, but among babies whose mothers had taken the drug during pregnancy it produced an outbreak of birth defects that included missing limbs, flippers instead of legs, abnormal arms, and hands coming out of the shoulders.

Strong evidence suggests that phocomelia in an otherwise perfect pregnancy is due to a misplaced piece of tissue in the amniotic sac, called an *amniotic web* or *amniotic band*. This can put pressure on developing tissue and prevent a leg from growing or cut off its blood supply so that it dies. If the radiologist notices a web, the baby should be monitored every three weeks to check on limb development.

Another malformation of the extremities is the *clubfoot*. Because in utero the bones are very soft, the baby's position could lead to a skeletal distortion anywhere, but most commonly in the feet. Clubfeet are turned in, so that the sole is perpendicular to the ground. A milder type of clubfoot can be corrected with massage, a cast, a brace, or exercises; surgery is a last resort.

Complications of Pregnancy

There are two pregnancy-threatening developments particular to the mid-trimester: an incompetent cervix and premature labor or late miscarriage.

An Incompetent Cervix

An *incompetent cervix* is when the cervix—the canal at the bottom of the uterus where the sperm goes in and menstrual blood and babies come out—painlessly dilates once the weight of the uterus hits a critical mass. Typically, a woman with an incompetent cervix would feel the urge to move her bowels at about twenty to twenty-two weeks and find a one-pound fetus in the toilet. Obstetricians monitor the cervix to make sure this doesn't happen. A good sonographer measures cervical length at sixteen to twenty weeks. The shorter the cervix, the weaker it is. It should be three centimeters or longer. If it's less than two, it requires very careful attention.

While an incompetent cervix can happen to anyone, multiple medical procedures in which the cervix is forcibly dilated, such as abortions or D&Cs for abnormal bleeding, increase this risk. A cone biopsy and/or a LEEP to treat premalignant conditions can also lead to a compromised cervix.

The treatment for an incompetent cervix is a *cerclage,* a large stitch to hold it together, much like tying a purse string around it. The timing of a cervical cerclage is very important. On the one hand, there's no point in doing this procedure in the first trimester, when

CERCLAGE CONTROVERSY!

A cerclage can be an effective, simple, safe tool to prevent a miscarriage. However, the procedure is controversial for two reasons. First, doctors prefer evidence-based medicine. We don't have any good studies comparing cerclage to noncerclage patients, because it seems irresponsible to let any woman with an incompetent cervix continue her pregnancy without some help. But this means that we can't quantifiably know how much (or how little) the suture helps. Second, some obstetricians overuse this treatment and put a cerclage in any woman with a multiple gestation or a slightly slim cervix. Unless you have a documented shortening of the cervix, or a history of a previous, painless loss in the mid-trimester, feel free to ask your obstetrician, "Exactly why do you think I need a cerclage?"

miscarriage rates are still relatively high; on the other, the longer you wait, the thinner the cervix might become and the less effective the procedure.

Premature Labor/Late Miscarriage

Premature labor or *late miscarriage* is the second threat to pregnancy in the mid-trimester. While technically these two things are the same, premature labor occurs after twenty-four weeks, when the baby is more likely to be viable. Before twenty-four weeks, should the uterus contract to the point of expelling the fetus, it's considered a late miscarriage. At eighteen weeks and beyond, 0.4 to 0.5 percent of pregnant women will inexplicably start having contractions. A woman more than eighteen weeks' pregnant who starts having rhythmic, menstrual-type cramps that seem to be happening at intervals of ten minutes or less should call her doctor promptly.

Doctors don't always know why these contractions happen, but a frequent, simple reason is dehydration. The bladder is right on top of the uterus. When there's not enough water around, the bladder gets irritated and disturbs its contiguous organ, the uterus. The uterus responds to this nuisance by contracting. Often, IV rehydration at the hospital stops this uterine activity, but once in a while this fails.

TAKE YOUR WATER. SERIOUSLY.

A mid-trimester patient of mine went to the beach on a ninety-degree summer day. Because she thought the bathrooms were inadequate, she decided to avoid drinking water so she wouldn't have to pee. That evening she started having contractions. Over the course of several days in the hospital, we tried to stop her premature uterine activity using every possible treatment, such as IV hydration, sedation, and bed rest. Nothing worked, and she delivered a profoundly immature baby who quickly died. You should aim to exceed eight glasses of water each day, but that is the bare minimum; drink more if you are doing things that could make you dehydrated, like air travel, illness, or sweating profusely.

The most common form of urinary tract infection is in the bladder, which is called *cystitis.* This sort of infection can instigate uterine contractions by virtue of proximity to the uterus. Whenever the bladder is inflamed, it causes the uterus to be irritable. Unfortunately, urinary tract infections are the number one medical problem in pregnancy, and they aren't always accompanied by symptoms. A good obstetrician tests patients' urine at every prenatal visit for bacteria, protein, white cells, and so forth, and investigates and diagnoses all abnormal results. A diagnosis of *asymptomatic bacteria of the urine* means that there are bacteria in the urine but that the condition is not accompanied by burning when you urinate and you don't constantly feel like you have to pee. Twenty percent of these quiet infections can lead to a significant urinary tract infection involving the kidneys. Additionally, urinary tract infections can lead to premature contractions and labor, so it is a general rule that they should be treated in pregnancy.

A third common cause of premature contractions is *intrauterine infection* (also called *chorioamnionitis*). This is sometimes *subclinical,* meaning tests don't reveal the problem; the patient's white count is normal and she does not have a fever. The uterus is supposed to be sterile, meaning free of bacteria. Although intrauterine infection is rare, bacteria can enter the amniotic sac and multiply, leading to an infection not only within the baby, but also within the uterine walls. This can cause the uterus to contract in an effort to expel the diseased tissue and avoid further damage to the womb, such as abscess formation, and infection throughout the abdominal cavity. This can make premature labor very difficult to treat because the obstetrician has to consider the possibility that it is happening for a reason—such as an undetectable intrauterine infection, which can require significant medical attention to protect the mother from a fatal systemic infection. Unfortunately, untrauterine infections almost always lead to the end of the pregnancy and can cost the mother her womb if not her life.

Because premature birth is the number one cause of brain damage and mental retardation, obstetricians have long been searching for a way to stop premature labor. The tragedy here is that the babies have developed normally, but they are simply not ready to live in an extrauterine environment. Prematurity can compromise the oxygen supply to the brain and/or cause damage to other vital organs. At less than twenty weeks old, the baby is not viable. Between twenty and twenty-four weeks, the chances of survival are very remote. Even when these kids do survive, they often have significant physical and intellectual impairments. At less than twenty-four weeks, most obstetricians consider intractable contractions accompanied by cervical change an inevitable miscarriage and allow their patients to deliver. If contractions do not stop with bed rest and IV hydration, and the cervix continues to dilate, the obstetrician's attempts at stopping delivery may risk the woman's uterus if she's suffering from an asymptomatic intrauterine infection, because while preventing the womb from expelling its contents, the doctor is also exposing the mother to continued infection in her abdomen.

Of course, when the patient is at twenty-three weeks or later, doctors have (almost universally unsuccessfully) tried to slow down or stop labor. The medications available to slow contractions have demonstrated limited success in delaying the inevitable. On average, these drugs may buy you an extra week of gestation, which can make the difference between life and death for the baby. Ultimately, the majority of women who go into labor (contractions and cervical change) before twenty-four weeks have a miscarriage. Of these, anywhere from 15 to 40 percent are the result of an undiscovered, life-threatening intrauterine infection.

Terminating the Pregnancy

In the United States, it is legal to terminate a pregnancy up until the end of the twenty-fourth week. This is not a decision women make lightly, but there are strong, rational, healthy reasons to choose to end a pregnancy in the mid-trimester. The amnio and sonogram can reveal issues that range from life altering (for example, an open spina bifida) to life ending (for example, no kidneys). Any of these can be reasons for terminating a pregnancy in the second trimester, which is most commonly accomplished in one of two ways, depending on your medical resources.

A *dilatation and evacuation,* or D&E, is a highly specialized, rare procedure to terminate a pregnancy after fourteen weeks. When handled by an experienced physician, it is the best choice for the woman's health. Unfortunately, there are very few specialists who do enough D&Es to be proficient.

The other method of terminating a second-term pregnancy is to induce labor. To stimulate the uterus to contract, the obstetrician employs medications like prostaglandins and Pitocin, which are also used at term to begin labor. These drugs are intended to cause contractions, cervical dilatation, and a relatively quick outcome. This is the same basic process as delivery, only the earlier in the pregnancy, the more resistant the uterus is to stimulation. At twenty weeks, for example, the uterus can be very hard to force into contractions, and these inductions can go on for days. This is not only emotionally taxing but physically miserable and somewhat dangerous. The advantage to this approach is that it doesn't require surgical technique, and therefore it can be done anywhere in the country, on any labor and delivery unit. For women in a bind, this may be the only choice.

CHAPTER 7

Third Trimester: Normal

The third trimester is the most exciting and dynamic trimester of pregnancy. It's also the longest, from the twenty-fourth week to the end of the fortieth, for a duration of sixteen weeks instead of twelve. In terms of the kind of symptoms you might experience, the last stage of pregnancy is a continuation (and often an intensification) of all the second-trimester symptoms and their treatment, although obstetrical issues come to the forefront during this trimester.

More than ever in the third trimester, your doctor will want to hear from you if anything feels wrong—now she can do something! In fact, obstetricians typically want to see their third-trimester patients more frequently—as much as every week, especially toward the end of the pregnancy. At this point, the doctor must regularly check that the mother's blood pressure, urine analysis, and weight gain are within normal ranges. She also wants to keep tabs on the baby's growth and fetal position, as well as regular check-ins with the mother on the baby's movement.

Throughout the third trimester, the baby is considered viable, although it would be *immature* if born between twenty-four and twenty-eight weeks. Between twenty-eight and thirty-two weeks, obstetricians consider the baby *premature*. From thirty-two to thirty-six weeks, prematurity is less severe and can be minimal. From thirty-seven weeks on, the baby is *mature,* meaning that she is prepared for all the critical aspects of life outside the uterus, such as breathing, digestion, and cardiac and metabolic function.

WHAT POSITION SHOULD I SLEEP IN?

When a very pregnant woman lies flat on her back, the uterus compresses the aorta, which runs along the spine and is the main pipeline of blood to both mother and child. Studies of women with vascular disease have shown that the optimal sleep position in the third trimester is on the left side. However, this does not mean that a healthy woman with perfectly good arteries should get hysterical because she prefers to sleep on her right side. If you like to sleep flat on your back, put a pillow under one side of your torso to shift the weight of the uterus from directly compressing your aorta.

Third-Trimester Symptoms

All the fun of the second trimester continues in the third trimester. The major difference is that your obstetrician will want to see you with increasing frequency, because now if there's a real problem, she is more likely to be able to intervene successfully. The later something goes wrong in the third trimester, the better. For example, at fourteen weeks, vaginal bleeding ahead of a miscarriage is rarely something that a doctor can fix; by twenty-eight weeks, however, the obstetrician can deliver the baby, who will likely go home a healthy infant after a few weeks in the hospital.

The third trimester is characterized by unique symptoms, all perfectly normal. For example, fetal movement, which was nonexistent in the first trimester and potentially mistaken for gas pains in the second, becomes the future mom's constant companion throughout the third. Cramping that might raise alarm in the first trimester could be Braxton Hicks contractions in the third trimester, signaling that your uterus is warming up for labor.

Fetal Movement

In the third trimester, fetal movement (also called *quickening*) should be pretty regular and follow a daily routine. Every baby has its own schedule. Most tend to be active after a meal, but you might find that your baby tends to kick most in the late afternoon or first thing in the morning. Many women perceive fetal movement much more keenly at night when they're in bed. This is because once the lights go out, it's just the dark and the baby; all of life's distractions recede, so it's easier to be aware of the baby's every move.

The vigor of fetal movement generally peaks between weeks twenty-eight and thirty-four, when there is still plenty of room in the uterus for the baby to really wind up and sock you. After thirty-four weeks, the baby has less room to move the whole body. At this point, it's more likely that the baby can move only one limb at a time. The important thing is that movement is as frequent, if not as strenuous, as always.

Be on the lookout for a dramatic, sudden decrease in fetal movement, a prolonged period of inactivity (three hours or more), or quiet at a time of day when the baby is usually active. If you notice any of these things, have a glass of orange juice or a candy bar to raise your (and the baby's!) blood sugar, or try drinking some cold water—rehydration can sometimes perk up the baby.

If you try some food and water, and the baby continues to be inactive, call your doctor. Remember: it's not cause for alarm if the baby is always quiet at a particular time, but doctors are concerned about any prolonged deviation from the normal schedule. When you call your obstetrician, be sure to clearly identify how the current lack of activity differs from what's typical for your baby. Obstetricians rely on full, accurate information about fetal movement from their patients because they have no other way of charting the baby's activity over long periods of time. Your doctor should constantly be asking whether the baby is moving. It's an important indicator of the baby's good health, and the mother's reports are the first line of defense.

Decreased fetal movement rarely indicates anything significant. Babies have quiet days, too. However, if you call to report that the baby isn't moving, your doctor will probably want you to come in for a fetal monitor assessment, because it's difficult for obstetricians to distinguish the rare serious problems over the phone. So don't worry if your doctor wants to evaluate the baby's inactivity in the office or at the hospital; it's just a precaution!

VAGINAL PAINS

As pregnancy progresses, some women get shocks up their vagina as if they had just sat on a cattle prod. This pain is usually gone in a flash. Although it can be scary, it almost never indicates any real problem. It's impossible to know the exact reason for these pangs; they're likely caused by something innocuous and transient, such as the baby nudging a nerve. Of course, any pain between your knees and nipples that lasts more than thirty seconds and repeats every ten minutes or less is a good reason to call your doctor.

Braxton Hicks Contractions

During the third trimester, some women experience Braxton Hicks contractions. These are occasional uterine contractions that actually start in the first trimester, although they generally aren't noticeable that early. Chances are you won't become aware of them before the sixth month of pregnancy.

Braxton Hicks are real contractions like any other uterine contraction; however, they are not part of labor. Instead, these contractions are a way for the uterus to warm up for the big workout that labor promises. The uterus can't lie there for nine months, then go into labor and work effectively; it has to contract to stay in shape and tone itself.

Braxton Hicks contractions are usually not regular, and the discomfort ranges from barely noticeable to severe. Braxton Hicks contractions are also called *false labor,* especially when the contractions

IS IT REALLY LABOR?

If you are having regular uterine contractions accompanied by progressive dilatation and effacement of the cervix, you're in labor. Regular or irregular uterine contractions without dilatation and effacement is *not* labor.

are particularly frequent or strong, leading many women to dash off to the hospital with husband and suitcase in tow. True, the medical team can detect these contractions on a fetal monitor; however, with this false labor, the woman's cervix is still long and closed, indicating that labor has not begun. The further along you are in your pregnancy, the more difficult it is to distinguish between real and false labor. While regular contractions at thirty-four weeks might get you admitted to the hospital right away to ensure you're not going into premature labor, in the last month your obstetrician might be a little more liberal and simply ask you to come into her office or back to the hospital every few hours until your contractions subside or your cervix starts to change, indicating the start of real labor.

Although everyone has contractions in the third trimester, your pain threshold, your anxiety level, and your previous experience affect how you perceive them. In fairness, any contraction is going to surprise a first-timer. Uterine contractions feel like pain, tightening, or pressure somewhere between the knees and the nipples that lasts for thirty to forty-five seconds, then completely goes away for a spell. Braxton Hicks contractions last just a few seconds and are actually much less painful than the booming contractions of labor, but if you've never experienced labor you won't know that. A real labor contraction takes your breath away and makes it impossible to talk, read, or watch television for its duration, whereas women can frequently talk through a Braxton Hicks contraction.

Women who are on their second pregnancy are often better able to distinguish between Braxton Hicks contractions and actual labor. These women might get contractions every three minutes and still recognize that they are far less intense than labor. Or they could have contractions every fifteen minutes and just know that they're going to deliver shortly. When a patient who has had a baby before says that she is in labor, her obstetrician would be a fool not to believe her.

Contractions happen all the time and for many reasons, and how you should react to them depends on your particular situation. If there are no high-risk factors and the cervix is unchanged, there's not much to be concluded from or done about contractions in the third trimester. However, if your cervix was four centimeters dilated at your last doctor's visit, your doctor will certainly be more attentive to any uterine activity. If you are experiencing contractions, consider the following guidelines (although women who live more than four hours away from their hospital might establish a more proactive course of action).

GUIDELINES		
Weeks	*Contractions*	*What should you do?*
24–28	6 per hour for 1 hour	Call your doctor.
28–32	6 per hour for 1 hour	Hydrate and relax.
28–32	6 per hour for 2 hours	Call your doctor.
32–36	More than 6 per hour for 2 hours	Call your doctor.
36–40	6 per hour for 1 hour	Could be labor! Call your doctor. This is your chance to take a shower, get a pedicure, or drive back from your country house. Do not rush to the hospital.

It's understandable that women who have never had a baby want to know exactly how everything is going to feel and what's going to happen; often, explicit directions help. In addition to the guidelines presented here, I tell my patients: If you have a contraction, it could be your uterus responding to something you're doing, something as innocuous as walking. Regardless, the first thing you should do is stop and rest for five minutes. Drink some water. If, at any point, your contractions are less than five minutes apart for one hour, call. If your water breaks at any time, call. If you have decreased fetal movement (see above), call.

Heartburn (aka Acid Reflux)

Heartburn can become unrelenting in the third trimester. As the uterus grows, it pushes all the abdominal contents up against the diaphragm, the dome-shaped muscle that separates the chest from the abdomen. Normally, a hole in the diaphragm allows the esophagus to carry food from the mouth to the stomach. As the uterus compresses the stomach, it can literally push the stomach through the esophagus, up through the hole in between the abdominal and chest cavities. This is called a *hiatal hernia*. Every time the diaphragm (which is a muscle) contracts, it leads to a spurt of stomach acid up the esophagus. Additionally, pregnancy slows digestion, meaning that the stomach takes longer to empty, making it easier for acid to pop up into the esophagus.

Although eliminating heartburn altogether is unlikely, there are ways to minimize it. For example, gravity can be your biggest ally in fighting heartburn. Don't lie down for at least two hours after eating to allow time to digest as much as possible. Because the stomach empties to the right, sleeping on the right side of the body can help. A semirecumbent position can also provide relief, as it allows gravity to help; many pregnant women end up sleeping in a chair because of their heartburn. It's also okay to take a chewable or liquid antacid, such as Tums, Rolaids, Maalox, or Mylanta. If you experience intense heartburn, talk your doctor about a new class of drugs called *proton pump inhibitors* that reduce acid production (brand names include Tagamet, Prilosec, and Zantac), though at this time studies on their use in pregnancy are scanty.

Body Changes

From the twenty-fourth week on, the top of the uterus goes from sitting just above the navel to almost reaching the rib cage. Then it

OLD WIVES' TALE

Midwives used to say bad heartburn in pregnancy meant that the baby had a lot of hair. I expected to deliver a small gorilla.

expands outward. Taller, long-waisted women have more room in their abdomens for the pregnancy, while shorter women tend to watch their bellies grow out. Either extreme—either too short or too tall—can be deceiving. Very short women look like they are carrying ten-pound babies or twins, whereas women taller than five feet, eight inches can appear to be carrying a very small baby.

It may feel like *every* part of your body is growing during pregnancy, but none so much as the belly. The weight gain and distribution contribute to a decreasing sense of balance through the third trimester. It can sometimes feel like you're carrying a cantaloupe between your legs, so sitting down and standing up require extra exertion. And every woman develops a bit of a third-trimester waddle.

The expanded, heavy belly can lead to pain where cartilage connects all the bones of the pelvis. One of these points is right in the middle, below the belly button, called the *pubic symphysis,* which is taxed as the bladder and uterus press down on it. Many women experience *superpubic* (that is, just above the pubic bone) pain from the combination of the stretching cartilage and abdominal wall. Bladder pressure and the growing uterus can add to this discomfort.

There are all sorts of support garments, such as maternity girdles and slings, to help the very pregnant woman feel more comfortable. There's no medical reason to use them, but there's also no reason not to; they are certainly safe, and many women attest to

FOOT SIZE

One old adage is that women gain a shoe size with each pregnancy. True, feet generally get bigger in the last trimester; you may find that your once-comfortable shoes are now too snug to wear. Some women buy bigger shoes "for the pregnancy," only to discover that their feet don't get smaller after the delivery. Most people's feet grow with age anyway, but it seems to happen more rapidly during pregnancy. The other interesting thing about feet in pregnancy is that one study suggested that the smaller your feet, the smaller your pelvis, and the greater the chance of having a caesarian section.

FORGET VICTORIA'S SECRET

If you're a first-time mother, there's a whole new genre of clothing that you have not seen before: clothing with flaps. There are bras with little hooked panels over the nipples so you can breast-feed. There are voluminous nightgowns with a little slit in the side so you can easily whip out a breast. This may not be your idea of sexy lingerie, but you'll definitely appreciate the convenience when it's time to breast-feed. It's a good idea to purchase a nursing bra and bring it to the hospital.

their effectiveness. The goal here is to stand up as straight as possible; even though the weight of your uterus makes you want to arch your back, this posture puts a huge amount of strain on your lower spine.

One body part that grows throughout pregnancy is the breasts, and it's a good idea to keep up with an appropriate bra size. Whenever your breasts seem to stabilize, buy one or two new bras to ensure that you'll have the support you need. This also may be a good time to start investigating nursing bras.

Vaginal Bleeding

In the first trimester, light staining can be ominous; in the third trimester, however, light staining is generally not something to be concerned about (unless your doctor has said that your situation requires special attention). Remember, the vagina is congested, and there's a proliferation of vessels, especially in the cervix, so it's not uncommon to stain after a pelvic exam, or even after sex.

Sex

Sex and pregnancy are related from start to finish. Of course, that's how one gets pregnant in the first place. But sex also plays an important role in preparing the mother's body for birth. The most basic way vaginal intercourse aids delivery is in keeping the vagina stretched and open. Much of sexual activity stimulates the uterus to contract, which is very healthy (as long as you are not at risk for premature labor). Women who are sexually active not only have easier pelvic exams, but they seem to have an easier delivery. I tell patients that every time they have intercourse it will take five minutes off their labor.

Sexual play that involves nipple stimulation, such as sucking or kissing the breast, can have a positive effect on the pregnancy. There's a reflex at the nipple that releases the hormone oxytocin (the natural version of Pitocin, see page 199) from the brain, which causes milk letdown and uterine contractions. Doctors postulate that this response was intended to prevent postpartum hemorrhaging, because as the baby suckles at the mother's breast, she's stimulating helpful contractions. These contractions compress all the blood vessels in the uterus, reducing blood loss.

As the mother approaches the end of pregnancy, nipple stimulation can increasingly cause the uterus to be irritable and contract. The cervix may soften and dilate a little, priming the system for labor. The closer the due date, the more of an impact nipple stimulation can have. Women who are dilating too quickly or too early may have to give up breast play, but this is unusual.

Semen can also affect the pregnancy because it contains *prostaglandins.* This compound, originally discovered in the prostate gland of a sheep, represents a group of new hormones that science is just beginning to understand. We know that prostaglandins

NIPPLES AND TWENTY-FIRST CENTURY MEDICINE

Some obstetricians check the baby's well-being by having a patient stimulate her nipples while she is on a fetal monitor. The doctor wants to see that the baby stays stable through a contraction. Nipple stimulation can also be an at-home way for an overdue mom to try to get labor started.

cause muscle contractions and lead to corollary pain. The prostaglandins in ejaculate are far weaker than the medical ones (see sidebar), but they still have been shown to increase the softening of the cervix. Sometimes, ejaculate leads to a couple of contractions.

Even orgasms help to get the body in shape for delivery. When a nonpregnant woman has an orgasm, she feels some involuntary spasms of her vagina. In fact, the whole reproductive tract tenses, but because the empty uterus is so small, its contraction is unnoticeable. However, women who are eight months pregnant definitely feel the whole uterus contract during an orgasm—anywhere from two to five times. Obstetricians have their own ideas of how many contractions are too many during sex. I advise patients to avoid having more than five contractions before the twenty-eighth week; from twenty-eight to thirty-four weeks, ten contractions are fine, and after that, contract away.

The only women who should desist from sex during pregnancy are those who are specifically advised to abstain. If you're just not sure whether you should be having sex or not, ask your obstetrician.

ANTIPROSTAGLANDINS, PROSTAGLANDINS, AND PREGNANCY

We know that wherever there's pain, there are prostaglandins. Antiprostaglandins (such as Motrin, Advil, Aleve, and aspirin) reduce muscle spasms and pain by specifically preventing the production of prostaglandins. Obstetricians learned from pregnant women with severe rheumatoid arthritis that high doses of aspirin prevent labor. Antiprostaglandins are also well known to cause stomach upset and ulcers. So the treatment for ulcers is…prostaglandins! One oral medication (brand name Cytotec) prescribed for ulcers is often used to induce labor. In such cases, a quarter of a pill is inserted into the vagina; once it is absorbed into the bloodstream, the uterus contracts. Because of their ability to make the uterus contract, prostaglandins are being used more and more commonly in obstetrics, whether it's for getting labor started or for staving off blood loss postpartum.

A WORD ABOUT ROMANCE

After the baby is born, it may be six weeks before you want to have sex again. Avoid being grouchy and having a grouchy partner by getting lots of sex in before the baby. If this is your first baby, this is your last honeymoon for a long time. Try to make this time as romantic as possible: lots of sex, walks on the beach, candlelight dinners, and so on. Reaffirm your relationship, because a third person is about to become the most important thing in your lives. Remember why you're having this baby together. Even if sex is out, there's cuddling, necking, spooning, romance, and all sorts of other wonderful stuff that will soon become a relative rarity.

Reasons to avoid sex include an irritable uterus, a dilated cervix, a history of premature labor, and a poorly located placenta. Women who have any of these conditions should probably hold off from having sex until their doctor says it's okay.

If you're having too many contractions during sex, you can find ways to avoid them. The cause of the contractions may be nipple stimulation, semen, or the orgasm. Try to determine the culprit by giving up one of them to see what happens. For example, if your husband wears a condom or withdraws and you don't get any contractions, then you're probably just especially sensitive to semen and you should avoid it. You may also find that you have to give up nipple play to avoid contractions, and that's fine, too. Of course, if you have to skip your orgasm, then what's the point?

As you get closer to your due date, doctors may recommend sex as a tool to naturally kick-start labor. For example, if the cervix is not dilating, some ejaculate and contractions from an orgasm could help. Italian doctors call this an *Italian induction.*

Routine Tests

Throughout pregnancy, blood pressure, urine, and weight measurements are routinely done at every prenatal visit. In the third trimester, these tests become increasingly important as early warning signs for relatively common but manageable problems in pregnancy, including hypertensive disorders and gestational diabetes. If you had diabetes or problems with your blood pressure before you were pregnant, then you should be under the care of a specialist; these disorders as described here are limited to those that emerge in pregnancy.

Glucose Tolerance Test

Pregnancy is a *diabetogenic* state, meaning that it encourages diabetes, or a resistance to insulin in the body. Insulin is an enzyme responsible for transporting sugar from the bloodstream into the cells, where it can be used for energy. If there isn't enough insulin around, sugar just circulates through the blood without ever being burned up into energy. Therefore, extremely high blood sugar is a sign of diabetes. Without the glucose getting from the blood and into the cells, it's impossible for the mother's body to function, let alone support the growing baby.

Although it hasn't been proven yet, the working hypothesis regarding gestational diabetes is that the placenta produces a compound that destroys insulin. If enough of this compound is present, it can lead to *gestational diabetes,* which usually ends when the placenta is expelled at birth, though not always. For women who are prone to diabetes, it may go away at delivery but return in later years.

Every pregnant woman is screened for gestational diabetes with a *mini glucose tolerance test* (*mini GTT*). Again, this is a screening test; the full glucose tolerance test is the only way to diagnose this problem. The mini GTT is the obstetrician's tool for assessing whether or not the patient is at risk for gestational diabetes.

The mini GTT is usually done around twenty-eight weeks, or toward the beginning of the third trimester. On the day of your screening, avoid carbohydrates in the morning, for a low starting blood sugar. Replace the cornflakes or sugary cereal with bacon and eggs. For the test, you'll be given sugar water to drink, then after an hour, a blood sample will be drawn to assess how efficiently your body processed the sugar. The lower the blood sugar level, the better.

DON'T FLUNK YOUR MINI GTT

Suffice it to say that you should make every effort not to fail your mini GTT so you can avoid the far more troublesome follow-up test. Avoid having lots of sweets the night before, and stick to a low-carb morning. Although it's sometimes difficult to ignore a craving in pregnancy, it's worth the effort. I once had a patient who snacked on a chocolate bar in the waiting room while waiting for her blood test. Needless to say, she flunked the test.

A patient with a blood sugar level under 130 is considered highly unlikely to be at risk for diabetes. No follow-up test is necessary. Anything over 130 mandates a follow-up full glucose tolerance test (see page 145) to confirm or refute the high blood sugar result. The obstetrician's goal is to catch subtle gestational diabetics while at the same time not overprescribing the three-hour test.

Vaginal Culture

As the baby exits the uterus, she faces a vagina full of bacteria, viruses, and funguses. A newborn has no antibodies, so she's vulnerable to all these bugs. She won't always be so fragile—in the first few months of life, she will make her own antibodies and develop

BREAST-FEEDING: BETTER THAN ANTIBIOTICS

Breast-feeding safely transfers to your baby all the antibodies that you've built up in your blood over the years. This is conferring a tremendous immune capability on the newborn. However, this immunity is a short-term benefit. Unlike a vaccine, which makes the body produce its own antibodies, breast-feeding provides immunity only for as long as the mother's milk delivers the antibodies. Hence, it is called *passive immunity*. It takes some time for the baby to build her own immunity.

colonies of healthy bacteria on her skin, intestines, mouth, nose, and so on. But sudden exposure to certain common bugs can be extremely bad for the baby. To prevent this from happening during the delivery, a vaginal culture is done around the thirty-sixth week of pregnancy.

The results of a vaginal culture range from basically harmless (such as yeast) to the relatively threatening (such as herpes). Although it's impossible to make the vagina sterile, obstetricians do strive to make it cleaner. The goal for delivery is *normal vaginal flora,* meaning proportionate amounts of healthy bacteria like acidophilus or lactobacillus, as well as funguses like yeast in small, asymptomatic quantities. If any one organism is dominating the landscape, the obstetrician must determine whether or not it's a serious problem for the baby.

Of fungal infections, yeast (also called *Candida* or *Monilia*) is by far most common and becomes a small, treatable health issue when it runs amok. Because the vagina is congested, lush, and acidic, and the pregnant body in general is hotter, yeast tends to thrive in the pregnant woman. When the baby comes through the vagina, it can catch yeast in its mouth and develop what is called *oral thrush.* Babies with this condition have shiny tongues and can look a little uncomfortable. (We have no way of knowing whether they *are* uncomfortable.) Oral thrush is treated with oral medications. An additional problem that can develop when a baby has oral thrush is that the fungus in the baby's mouth can transfer to the mother during breast-feeding, resulting in a sore, cracked nipple. So if the obstetrician uncovers a yeast infection in the eighth month, she'll probably want to treat it. Of course, there's no reason for you to suffer, so if the itchiness associated with a yeast infection is driving you crazy at any time during your pregnancy, call your doctor.

A more threatening infection that can pass from mother to baby during delivery is genital herpes. If the baby is born when the mother is having an outbreak, the transfer of the virus can be fatal to the baby. If you have visible lesions the day you go into labor, they must be bypassed with a caesarian section. No obstetrician would let the baby go through a vagina with open sores. If exposed, the baby could get systemic herpes; of all newborns exposed to herpes, half are brain damaged and the other half die. Neonatologists and high-risk obstetricians suggest a prophylactic antiviral protocol leading up to the due date to reduce the odds of an outbreak at delivery, depending on the frequency of your outbreaks.

Human papilloma virus (HPV) is an even more common virus that is not threatening to the baby, except in extraordinarily rare cases where the mother's genitalia are covered in warts caused by the virus. In such a case, the baby may sustain warts on the vocal cords that require corrective surgery. This is extremely unusual, but if you have warts on your genitalia, your obstetrician may remove them before labor.

Among bacteria, the big bug is *Group B Streptococcus* (GBS), also known as *beta-hemolytic Streptococcus*. Because 10 percent of women have this bug in their vaginas, it's considered practically normal. Although GBS poses no problem to the pregnant woman or her partner, it can be dangerous for the newborn. About 5 percent of babies who are exposed to GBS in the vagina can become

HERPES: A FEW CAUTIONARY TALES

I had a patient with bad herpes. Her specialists and I discussed a way for her to have a vaginal delivery, which she very much wanted. We all recommended that she either induce labor right after an outbreak and before the next one, or that she start on antivirals. She refused both these suggestions and ironically ended up having a caesarian section because of her wish to avoid medication. Another patient of mine with herpes had never told her husband about it and didn't want to tell him during delivery. She said, "Just make something up to justify the C-section." Another woman came in with her husband for a prenatal visit complaining of a vaginal irritation. As I conducted the examination, her husband turned redder and redder and tried to make a break for it. He had kept his herpes a secret for their entire marriage, until one month before the birth of their first child. Of course, herpes should never be kept secret from someone with whom you are intimate, and it is an especially ridiculous distraction from the magnitude of becoming parents together.

extremely sick or have permanent damage. It can also be fatal, though the vast majority of babies born in a GBS environment are fine. If you are GBS positive, the current standard is to give you IV antibiotics in labor. This diminishes the bacteria in the vagina to guarantee the baby's safe passage.

Sonogram

Some doctors do a third-trimester sonogram, mostly to confirm that the baby is growing normally and to make sure the placenta is in a good place for delivery. If the second-trimester sonogram was at twenty weeks, it's not a bad idea to check in somewhere between thirty-two and thirty-six weeks. If the baby is not growing well or is too large, it can signify a problem. Obstetricians will usually incorporate a comprehensive analysis of the baby and its environment, which is, all together, called a *biophysical profile*.

Nonstress Test

This is a fifteen-minute test to check on the baby's well-being with a fetal monitor (page 169). In this time, obstetricians like to see three heart rate accelerations of at least fifteen beats per minute, lasting at least fifteen seconds. Of course, the baby takes naps, and during that time the fetal heart monitor strip may get a little flat, with fewer accelerations. However, these sleep cycles tend to be no more than twenty minutes' duration. Maybe food or hydration will help to perk the baby up. After that, the obstetrician would move to a biophysical profile.

Prepared Childbirth Class

During the third trimester, many first-time parents take some sort of prepared childbirth class. There are usually plenty to choose from. Virtually every obstetrical hospital offers a course, usually four to seven sessions long. Private childbirth education instructors

A VERY BRIEF HISTORY OF LAMAZE

Lamaze-like techniques were pioneered in Russia during World War II, when all the good pain drugs were sent to the front lines for the soldiers. Because the doctors could not give their patients morphine or Demerol, they encouraged them to follow a particular breathing technique in labor and tried to sell it as being better for the baby. "Lamaze" has become virtually synonymous with any prepared childbirth class.

will come to the home and teach. There are intense weekend-long retreats. You should be able to find a class that not only suits your schedule but fits your labor ideology as well. For example, the course offered at the hospital may not represent the same philosophy as the midwife down the road. While your instinct may be to pick the class that is most convenient, at least consider choosing the

HOW TO PICK A GOOD CHILDBIRTH EDUCATION CLASS

To get the best preparation for childbirth, it's ideal to find an instructor who knows more about childbirth than just Lamaze, such as a trained obstetrical nurse. You'll benefit from comprehensive information about many different aspects of delivery. It's also better to attend weekly courses over a longer time frame rather than over one intensive weekend. Learning gradually seems to make it more likely that you'll remember what you learned when you really need to. Take a tour of the hospital. It can be extremely anxiety provoking to walk though a swinging door in labor scared to death and without knowing what's on the other side. Pregnant women often find peace of mind from seeing the labor room, meeting the nurses, seeing other women postpartum, and checking out the nursery. Being able to visualize the space can make it easier to imagine a future labor experience. Finally, learn infant cardiopulmonary resuscitation (CPR). Make this as much of a priority as childbirth preparation.

course that focuses on those aspects of labor you are most concerned with and interested in.

Lamaze is one of many approaches to labor management based on no medical pain relief. The idea behind Lamaze is that the amount of pain one perceives is dependent on how distracted the person is. Most emergency room visits happen in the middle of the night because the discomfort that you hardly noticed during your busy day suddenly becomes unbearable. A hallmark Lamaze exercise is having the partner squeeze the pregnant woman's leg when she's not distracted and then again when she's practicing her breathing; most women feel less pain when they are focused on their breathing—that is, thinking about something other than the pain.

If you're taking a prepared childbirth class in the hope of avoiding pain medication, the focus will probably be on teaching you how to distract or even hypnotize yourself to get through labor. Good techniques tend to involve increasingly complicated breathing exercises during a contraction. In addition to the breathing exercise, various distraction techniques may be used. For example, sometimes, the coach says random numbers into the mother's ear that she must then repeat with breathing.

Prepared childbirth education classes grew from Lamaze classes, and while they do often incorporate elements of distraction, they usually include many other elements, too. Most of these classes

DOES IT WORK?

In short, rarely. I have had several patients in labor who were lifelong yoga advocates. These women meditated, did deep breathing, focused, and really seemed to be on top of their entire labor experience. This tactic is not as successful for the woman who learns a breathing exercise six weeks before she enters what may well be the most intense pain experience of her entire life. Moreover, long labors wear anyone out. After eight or twelve hours, it's nearly impossible to keep paying attention to one's breathing. This is really more a matter of luck than anything; if you have a quick labor, you might be able to pull off a medication-free delivery. But this shouldn't be something you set your heart on or struggle valiantly toward—because, really, why?

BRING A CAR SEAT, EVENTUALLY

Get a car seat before you go to the hospital. Many states require that you put the newborn in that car seat right out of the hospital. This doesn't mean you need to lug your car seat in with you when you go into labor; you'll have a day or two.

feature a tour of the hospital, an overview of pain relief, and a discussion about the stages of labor and what's going to happen at each. Usually the instructor also explains C-sections and breast-feeding. Sometimes the course extends to infant care and baby baths.

The most important class you should take in anticipation of delivery is a course in how to resuscitate a baby who stops breathing, called *neonatal cardiopulmonary resuscitation* (CPR). Sometimes this is included in prepared childbirth classes. Sometimes it's a separate class at the hospital, and some YMCAs offer it. It is highly unlikely that you will need to perform CPR on your newborn, but if you do, you'll be so thankful you went to the trouble of taking a class.

Choosing a Hospital

Many hospitals have an anesthesiologist on call, meaning that the doctor is home in bed when you show up in labor in the middle of

A SHORT CHECKLIST FOR CHOOSING A HOSPITAL

You should choose a hospital with:

1. A neonatal intensive care unit

2. 24/7 obstetrical anesthesiologists

3. A busy labor and delivery unit (more than three thousand deliveries per year)

AN OBSTETRICIAN'S MEDITATIONS ON LABOR PAIN

First-time prenatal patients say to me all the time, "I have a high tolerance for pain." I want to respond, "Have you had open-heart surgery? Been in a bad car accident? Been in the hospital for more than three days?" Think: What experience do you really have of pain? Most women who are pregnant are young and healthy. Being "really good at the dentist" is not an indication that you are going to tolerate labor just as well.

There are patients who feel that their menstrual cramps are so severe that they're going to do well in labor. This is often true for the early stages, but I've had only one patient who was absolutely right about this. She said to me, "I have terrible menstrual cramps." I told her, "Okay, when your labor pains get worse than your menstrual cramps, we'll talk about pain relief." Either she had a very easy labor or she has terrible menstrual cramps; I'll never know. But she claimed labor was never worse than her cramps.

There are also extraordinarily rare women who experience virtually painless labor. One of my patients had a total of three contractions at delivery. She called at seven in the morning to say her water had broken. I told her she could stay home a little longer, but she said she was "feeling funny," so I told her to head over to the hospital. Three blocks away, she had her first contraction. One block later, she had her second contraction and rectal pressure. At the door to the hospital she delivered the baby in her husband's brand-new Volvo. The car's interior was never the same, and the husband never forgave me.

the night. If you are five or six centimeters dilated with booming contractions and a lot of pain, the obstetrician may not bother the anesthesiologist. After all, you're about halfway through and by the time the anesthesiologist arrives, the whole thing could be over. This is why obstetricians sometimes say, "It's too late to get the epidural."

On the other hand, there are hospitals with anesthesiologists in-house, 24/7, available for obstetrical cases. In many regional centers, this role tends to be filled by a resident—a board-certified anesthesiologist is preferable, but any doctor is better than nothing when you're in the worst pain of your life. When a doctor is just down the hall, it is very rare to find that you are "too late" for an epidural.

Just as many hospitals do not have obstetrical anesthesiologists on staff, relatively few have neonatal intensive care units. In which case, if there's a problem with the baby, they say to the mother, "We're going to helicopter the baby to another hospital." The mother often has the choice to go with the baby or stay where she is; neither option is attractive when you've just given birth.

If you live in a small town, your hospital may not be equipped to provide you with optimal obstetrical services. Unfortunately, only one-third of potential obstetrical problems are known before labor (placenta previa or a breech presentation, for example); a full two-thirds happen in labor or after the baby is born. It is impossible to anticipate which women and babies will require emergent, specialized care. Yet just about everyone prefers to go to a hospital close to home, so relatives and friends can visit, among other reasons. If you're young and healthy, you're looking at a low risk of complications and you may choose to deliver in a small hospital. However, if you *can* get to a regional medical center for your obstetrical care, why not have the best medical tools on hand should you or your baby need them?

MEDICAL CENTERS VERSUS SMALL HOSPITALS

There is a burgeoning movement to close obstetrical facilities in small regional hospitals, which simply cannot provide all the emergency services some deliveries require. These hospitals may do as few as thirty deliveries each year, making them a little rusty. It takes hundreds of deliveries annually to maintain skill and efficiency. If you're shopping around for a hospital, look for a *level III regional medical center*. These places are equipped to do anything to anybody at anytime. They will definitely have a neonatal intensive care unit, around-the-clock anesthesiologist, and the ability to do whatever the baby or you might require.

Other Considerations

In addition to immediate medical concerns for both mother and child, childbearing brings a whole new set of unique decisions and concerns to the expectant parent. What about a pediatrician? Should you harvest the baby's cord blood? If this is your second child, what will your firstborn make of this new addition to the family?

Talk to Your Doctor

In the third trimester, make time to have a conversation with your health care provider about your expectations and options. Is there anything that you simply must have or cannot possibly stand? Are you allergic to anything, especially latex or iodine? Do you want to walk around in labor? Do you want an episiotomy? This is the time to clarify everything you've learned or heard about in your prepared childbirth education class so that there's no misunderstanding at the last minute. What about your doctor's schedule? Is your doctor on a rotating on-call schedule with twenty other obstetricians, and if so, who are they? Do you want to perform any sort of ritual? Do you want to keep the placenta? Be as prepared as possible, even while recognizing that labor can't be a fully planned event.

Cord Blood

In recent years, it has become easier for new parents to save and bank cord blood from their newborn. Blood from the placenta and umbilical cord is loaded with stem cells, primitive human cells that are so early in their development they have the potential to become any sort of tissue in the human body. Individuals can save some of the cord blood at delivery and have it frozen. For an annual fee, a number of private companies will pick up the blood from the hospital, process it, and freeze it.

There are a number of very good reasons to save cord blood. First, cord blood is a perfect match for the baby, and therefore can truly be a lifesaver in certain medical crises. For example, if a child develops leukemia or lymphoma, the saved cord blood negates the need for a bone marrow donor. It also serves as DNA identification in the event a child is kidnapped or lost. Finally, cord blood is at least a partial match for siblings and both parents.

In spite of the advantages, there are potential drawbacks. Key among these is that the procedure and storage can be expensive. Further, it's important to recognize that in the not-too-distant future, scientists may discover that cord blood isn't the best place to collect stem cells or that our method of collection or storage is flawed. Finally, just as with any other business, a company that collects and stores cord blood could go bankrupt and discard your baby's cord blood. For this reason, it might be worth avoiding very new, particularly inexpensive, companies.

Nevertheless, if you can afford to save the cord blood, it's worth considering. If you decide to bank it, be sure and tell your obstetrician before it gets tossed in the biohazard waste bin.

Choosing a Pediatrician

Some parents like to interview pediatricians, making the rounds and selecting their favorite. This is not necessarily the best way to go about finding a doctor for your baby. Even a highly skilled pediatrician who's great with kids can give a bad first impression to adults. Recommendations from friends with children or your obstetrician are an easier way to find a good pediatrician. You can also shop around after your baby is born—start with one doctor and move on to another if the first one is not working for you. Just remember that the pediatric field tends to be a small world; be as diplomatic as possible if you decide to switch doctors.

Take It Easy

Working a full week can become harder and harder as the pregnancy progresses, and it may not be possible for every woman. Since maternity leave and sick days are finite, most expectant moms work until the last possible minute so that whatever paid days off they have they can spend with their newborn. However, taking a day to rest once in a while can make the remainder of your week much easier. Of course, don't overspend your sick days before the delivery, but be good to yourself! Your body is working for two, so if you're exhausted or not feeling well, take a day off.

Weight Gain

A reasonable weight gain in the third trimester is ten to fifteen pounds, not another thirty or forty. Half your pregnancy weight goes to your hips, and that weight is not going to evaporate after delivery. Be sensible now to avoid worrying about how you'll lose the weight later.

If This Is Your Second Child

If you are having your second child, it's a good idea to read up on some of the very natural sibling issues that can arise—believe me, Cain and Abel weren't the last siblings to experience intense rivalry. A first child enjoys the undivided attention of the parents before a new baby shows up to interrupt his or her peaceful, stable world; the firstborn may be less than pleased when the new baby comes around.

There are all sorts of suggestions and ideas about how to help an older child deal with the birth of a new sibling. Sometimes older children struggle with leaving their mothers at the hospital when the new baby gets to stay. You can alleviate some of that distress by calling from the hospital to talk to the kids at home. Another standard recommendation is to avoid taking the new baby home when your older child is out of the house. Consider having another family member wait in anticipation with the sibling to welcome the new baby into the home.

Whatever you do, it's very important to sympathize with how hard a time this might be for the first child. If the child says, "I hate the baby," it's time to sit down and try to explain what's happening. Let the firstborn know that you understand these issues. One of the biggest reasons psychiatrists recommend three-year spacing between children is that by then the older child is verbal and can communicate displeasure, unhappiness, or frustration. It also helps

SIBLING RIVALRY—IT'S FOR REAL

One patient said to me of her firstborn son: "He's so affectionate with the baby that he squeezes her until she cries!" I asked, "Is he that affectionate with you?" She had to admit he wasn't and that her son resented the intrusion of the baby into his world. On another occasion, I waited next to a little boy and his father at a red light on our way out of the park. The child had a brand-new bike, which he was kicking as we all stood there. As the light turned green, he turned to me and said, "They think this is gonna make up for the baby, and it isn't."

when the older sibling is old enough to have friends or a playgroup with whom to share frustrations or provide a diversion. However you decide to handle it, read up—there are many good books that offer helpful strategies for dealing with the complexities of introducing a second child into the family.

CHAPTER 8

Third Trimester: Abnormal

*T*he major difference between medical problems in the third trimester and those of the first or second is that in the last part of pregnancy, should things go very wrong we can usually delivery a viable baby. Significant and unique health risks to the mother, such as gestational diabetes or preeclampsia, present themselves in the third trimester. Since most of the potential genetic and structural problems with the baby have been ruled out by this stage, the baby's environment becomes extremely important. If the amniotic fluid, umbilical cord, or placenta is functioning abnormally, the otherwise healthy baby can be put in jeopardy.

Things That Can Go Wrong with Mom

As a general rule, medical problems that you experience during pregnancy can be an indicator of future health issues. A woman who develops a hypertensive disorder in pregnancy at the age of 30 raises her chances of high blood pressure ten or twenty years down the line by about 50 percent. Same thing with diabetes: If you get it in pregnancy, there's a 50 percent chance that you'll develop diabetes later in life. So while your health issues may clear up after delivery, it's important to stay on top of your diet and cardiac health in order to avoid more problems with diabetes or hypertension.

Gestational Diabetes

Pregnancy is a *diabetogenic* state, meaning that gestation encourages diabetes. About 4 percent of American women develop this disorder during their pregnancy. No one has yet discovered or proven why this happens, but the working hypothesis is that the placenta produces a compound that makes the woman insulin-resistant (that is, the insulin she makes is perfectly normal, but her body resists its effect). Because insulin allows the body to burn sugar as energy, women with gestational diabetes have very high blood sugar and extremely low energy.

It may not sound so terrible, but elevated blood sugar leads to a variety of significant health problems. First, although the mother may not be able to metabolize the sugar in her blood, the baby will most likely have normal insulin function. This means the baby absorbs a huge amount of sugar and packs on mostly fat instead of healthy, nutritious weight gain. Even as the baby grows larger and larger, however, his or her maturity is delayed. At thirty-seven weeks, the gestational diabetes baby will be much larger than average but might function like a normal thirty-five-week baby. Finally and most seriously, as the baby is exposed to relatively high blood sugar in utero, its pancreas responds by making huge amounts of insulin to compensate. Once born, the high levels of insulin in the baby cause a precipitous drop in blood sugar that can be life threatening. Obstetrical professionals, from the nurses to the doctors, can easily prevent this from happening; the key is for them to know of the mother's condition before the delivery.

GESTATIONAL VERSUS NONGESTATIONAL DIABETES

A true gestational diabetic comes into pregnancy with normal blood sugar levels that return to normal after delivery. Women who are diabetic before conception have especially risky pregnancies and require the care of a highly trained perinatologist as well as a diabetes specialist.

The odds of developing gestational diabetes depend on family history and previous experience. For example, if you developed gestational diabetes during your first pregnancy, you run at least a 60 percent risk of developing it during your second pregnancy as well; if your mom had gestational diabetes, you are also more likely to get it. But sometimes it's just the luck of the draw—4 percent of all pregnant women develop this disorder, and many of them have no medical or family history of the illness.

As mentioned in Chapter 7, every pregnant woman must have a mini glucose tolerance test to screen for gestational diabetes. A more thorough three-hour test is done if the GTT indicates the possibility of diabetes. The first test demonstrates a potential weakness in the patient's ability to tolerate sugar (glucose), and the second demonstrates conclusively whether or not the expectant mom is developing diabetes. The first step in a full GTT is to establish a baseline, or fasting, sugar level. This requires the patient to fast on the morning of the test. If you are having your baseline sugar level checked, it is important to abstain from eating beforehand. A normal fasting blood sugar should be very low due to the lack of food and near constant burning of blood sugar by both mother and child. Obstetricians consider an ideal level to be under 95 milligrams of glucose per milliliter of blood.

After the first baseline blood test, the patient is given a sugar beverage, which spikes her sugar levels. Blood samples are then taken after one, two, and three hours so the obstetrician can chart how efficiently the patient's body burns glucose (see table).

For the diabetic patient, maintaining a constant, healthy blood sugar can be a full-time job. Class A1 diabetics should see a nutritionist who will likely advise them to avoid carbohydrates such as sugar, candy, cake, and soda. Pregnant women with class A1 diabetes should graze carefully, selecting an even distribution of protein, fat, and healthier carbs, such as grains and fruits. A woman with more significant diabetes must test her blood sugar with a glucometer many times each day and follow up with insulin injections when appropriate. All diabetics must put in a huge amount of effort just to maintain a normal blood sugar level. These women usually have a team of specialists that can include a perinatologist, a dia-

UNDERSTAND YOUR GLUCOSE TOLERANCE TEST RESULTS					
Fasting	*1 Hour*	*2 Hour*	*3 Hour*	*Diagnosis*	*Treatment*
95 or less	190 or less	165 or less	145 or less	Normal	None
95 or less	Any 2 of the above results are elevated			Class A1 diabetic	Careful monitoring and diet adjustments
96 or more	Regardless			Class A2 diabetic	Insulin injections, perinatologists, diabetologists, nutritionists, careful monitoring, etc.

*Class B diabetics are those who were diagnosed at over twenty years of age, but less than ten years previous to the pregnancy. Class C diabetics have had the disorder for more than twenty years and were under age 20 when they were diagnosed. Class R diabetics have severe vascular issues as a result of their disease, which can result in visual, cardiac, or kidney problems.

betologist, and a nutritionist as well as kidney and eye specialists, depending on the severity of the illness.

Hypertensive Disorders of Pregnancy

In the third trimester, blood pressure can quickly become a problem. Young, healthy women may enter pregnancy with an underlying vascular issue (such as *chronic hypertension*) that becomes apparent only during pregnancy, or they may develop an acute hypertensive disorder particular to pregnancy, called *preeclamp-*

LOW BLOOD SUGAR?

Hypoglycemia, or low blood sugar, is usually caused by diet. Even if you're eating plenty of calories, if they're all at one sitting you're likely to have low blood sugar throughout the rest of the day. A big, sugary snack can also create a rebound effect, whereby your blood sugar spikes and then plummets. Pregnant women with poor eating habits or especially fast metabolisms tend to become hypoglycemic and experience dizziness or fainting spells. Fainting and vertigo are signs that you should be eating more frequently and perhaps avoiding sugary snacks in order to maintain a stable blood sugar level. As long as you continue to gain weight, low blood sugar is not dangerous. But is it really so hard to eat more frequently?

sia (which is nicer than the old term, *toxemia*). Some patients suffer from both disorders. Obstetricians group preeclampsia and chronic hypertension under the umbrella term *hypertensive disorders of pregnancy.*

As with gestational diabetes, science has yet to find a definitive cause for hypertension in pregnancy, but the working hypothesis is

PREECLAMPSIA VERSUS CHRONIC HYPERTENSION

The only quantitative way to distinguish chronic hypertension from preeclampsia is with a kidney biopsy, but this is not ideal at thirty-seven weeks' pregnancy. It's also possible to have an ophthalmologist examine your eyes. If she finds broken capillaries, it's likely you have been suffering from a chronic condition. If the doctor knows that the patient has high blood pressure heading into pregnancy, her health management including medication and fetal monitoring might differ from that of a preeclamptic. However, since it is usually impossible to tell the difference between a chronic and an acute hypertensive problem in pregnancy, obstetricians tend to assume the patient has preeclampsia. The most common treatment for this is to deliver the baby ASAP.

that the placenta excretes a compound that leads to general vaso-constriction (narrowing of the blood vessels). And if you have vaso-constriction to the placenta, the baby gets less blood and fails to gain weight, leading to growth delay (called *intrauterine growth retardation*) and, if the condition is left to progress, death.

Preeclampsia occurs in anywhere from 5 to 8 percent of preg-nancies in the United States. Preeclampsia is identified by four symptoms: elevated blood pressure, protein in the urine, hyperac-tive reflexes, and edema (swelling of the whole body). All of these symptoms are caused by vasoconstriction. High blood pressure in response to the tightened arteries forces water through the blood vessel walls, causing generalized swelling throughout the body (although almost all pregnant women have swollen ankles). The lack of flow through the kidney as a result of constricted blood ves-sels within that organ leads to protein in the urine. All these clenched arteries limit the blood supply to the brain as well, which can trigger a seizure.

So when preeclampsia goes undetected, is not treated appropri-ately, or deteriorates rapidly, the patient could have a generalized convulsion or *grand mal seizure,* which obstetricians call *eclamp-sia.* Hence, all the conditions leading up to the seizure are called

FAINTING IS FIRST AID

A non-preeclamptic patient of mine was feeling light-headed in the recovery room after delivery. She complained that she was dizzy from sitting up in the chair while the nurse changed her sheets. She kept fainting and slumping down in her chair. The nurse would come over and prop her up. After several rounds of this, my patient had a convulsion. The neurologist explained to the nurse that fainting is nature's way of putting your head between your legs; in other words, feeling faint makes a person bring his or her brain down to the same level as the heart, so more blood flows to the brain. If you feel like you are going to faint and you are forced to remain upright, the likely outcome is a seizure caused by lack of blood to the brain. It's always a good idea to lie down if you're feeling dizzy.

*pre*eclampsia. Preeclampsia is the hypertensive disorder unique to pregnancy, although the symptoms of both illnesses are the same, and both carry the major risk of stroke (that is, a ruptured blood vessel in the brain). A key difference between the two, however, is that chronic hypertension alone is unlikely to cause a seizure. After delivery, the preeclamptic patient is cured, while the chronic hypertensive patient continues to have high blood pressure that requires treatment.

Like diabetes, a history of blood pressure problems raises the risk of hypertensive disorders of pregnancy such as preeclampsia. If you've had preeclampsia in a previous pregnancy, there's a 20 percent chance that you'll have it again; a family history of hypertension also raises the odds of preeclampsia. Women with any history of hypertensive disorders should already be under the close care of a nephrologist or a cardiologist.

Obstetricians keep an eye on hypertensive disorders by doing simple, routine tests, including checking a patient's blood pressure during each prenatal visit, testing urine for protein, and checking a patient's weight; a precipitous gain is a sign of water retention and edema.

You should also be on the lookout for symptoms that may be impossible for your doctor to intuit. For example, headaches and visual disturbances can be a sign of preeclampsia, but no one will

HELLP SYNDROME

Hemolysis, elevated liver enzymes, and low platelets, or HELLP, syndrome is an unfortunate variation on preeclampsia. Early symptoms can include severe pain in the pit of the stomach, visual disturbances, and severe headaches. Medical markers for this disorder include high levels of liver enzymes in the blood (probably from vasoconstriction to the liver) and low levels of platelets. In the latter case, platelet levels run low because they accumulate in bad spots, such as damaged arteries and the placenta. These clots (also called *thrombi*) can form in arteries that feed the placenta or in the placenta itself. This is a dangerous condition that requires immediate intervention. If your doctor discovers HELLP syndrome, it doesn't matter how far along your pregnancy is, the baby's only hope is to be delivered right away.

DIC: AN ACRONYM TO AVOID

Three letters represent something that you should avoid at any cost: DIC, which stands for *disseminated intravascular coagulopathy*, a condition that can follow unaddressed HELLP syndrome or be a part of any hypertensive disorder of pregnancy. The primary characteristic of DIC, one of the most serious conditions that can occur in pregnancy, is that all blood platelets are used up by little clots in the vessels, leading to bleeding from just about everywhere—the IV site, gums, nose, vagina, placenta. Basically anywhere there are swollen blood vessels, tiny breaks can lead to endless bleeding. DIC can also be caused by an *abruptio placenta* (see page 156), hemorrhaging, or any trauma, in and out of pregnancy.

know you're having these symptoms unless you say something. Edema can cause your face to look like it's been stung by a swarm of bees because it's so swollen first thing in the morning. You may notice before your obstetrician does that you have gained a lot of weight in a short period of time (for example, more than five pounds in a week). Preeclampsia can restrict blood flow to the kidneys, leading you to urinate less (when you should be going all the time). Many of these developments can be totally normal, but if you experience any of these symptoms, call your doctor. As with so many other problems in pregnancy, the earlier your obstetrician becomes aware of any potential problem, the better for mother and child.

As far as treating preeclampsia, the rule of thumb is to stabilize the patient and deliver the baby as soon as possible. A precise course of action depends on how sick the mother is, as well as how far along she is in the pregnancy. Borderline or mild cases of preeclampsia might be treated with bed rest and medication and followed with frequent monitoring in the hospital. More severe cases might require an emergent delivery, because the baby is simply not getting the necessary nourishment. Of course, it's much easier to induce labor at thirty-eight weeks than, say, at twenty-eight weeks, when the medical team might make a greater effort to treat the preeclampsia without having to deliver the baby.

If you have developed a severe hypertensive disorder in the third trimester of pregnancy, do not dally over considering your course of action—this is not the time to get a second opinion. An obstetrician whom you like and trust will get as many other opinions as necessary to ensure that your health management is comprehensive in any complex situation. Hypertensive disorders of pregnancy change rapidly and require quick intervention in order to maintain optimal health for both the mother and the baby.

Premature Labor

Premature labor is defined as regular, frequent contractions accompanied by cervical change between the twentieth and thirty-seventh weeks of pregnancy. This problem seems to be on the rise, occurring in as many as 10 percent of pregnancies. If you've had a premature labor before, you're four to five times more likely than the average pregnant woman to experience it again. Additionally, bacterial vaginosis, a shortened cervix, and having multiple babies increase the risk of experiencing this relatively common problem, although there isn't always an obvious precursor.

Because contractions in the third trimester are normal, it is a challenge to diagnose premature labor. A relatively new method of diagnosing premature labor involves testing for a particular compound called *fibronectin,* which can be found in the vagina just before labor. A negative result—indicating no fibronectin around the patient's cervix—is 100 percent accurate, while a positive result accurately diagnoses premature labor only 50 percent of the time. Nevertheless, this simple swab test promises to save a huge number of women from unnecessary treatment.

The best way to treat premature labor is to avoid it, because obstetricians frequently fail at stopping it. The newest approach to preventing premature labor involves weekly injections of progesterone from the middle of the second trimester for pregnant women at higher risk. The additional hormones support the pregnancy by stimulating intrauterine health. Proactive progesterone shots lower the risk by 35 percent.

Once premature labor has commenced, the patient is admitted to the hospital, hydrated, put on a fetal monitor, and possibly given antibiotics to rule out urinary tract infections, which can lead to contractions. At this point most obstetricians notify the neonatal intensive care unit, in the likely event that labor proceeds. Medications to stop contractions all aim to relax the uterus and include Terbutaline, Ritidrine, magnesium sulfate, and newer, more experimental drugs. These all carry some cardiac risk for the mother, and they are rarely successful; their benefit is to allow time to move the patient to a medical center, if necessary, and administer steroids. Steroids are injected into the mother and stimulate the baby's lungs to mature, dramatically improving the infant's prognosis. Steroids require forty-eight hours to take effect, so the obstetrician may prescribe them along with the medications already mentioned.

Obviously, outcomes of premature labor vary greatly with gestational age. In regional medical centers, pregnancies over thirty-four weeks are often allowed to simply proceed to delivery because these infants have great chances out of the womb. Earlier than that, the doctor may attempt to stall labor; the more premature the baby, the more effort the doctor will make.

Abnormalities of the Pregnancy Apparatus

As the pregnancy rounds the home stretch, the structure around the baby must continue to nourish, oxygenate, and support the infant. Defects in any of the peripheral elements (placenta, cord, and fluid) can compromise an otherwise healthy baby's environment and well-being.

Growth Delay and Placental Insufficiency

During pregnancy, the placenta is of paramount importance; in spite of this, its role is often poorly understood. The placenta is where maternal blood transfers all the oxygen and nutrients to the baby's blood across a membrane. This process requires a lot of blood constantly flowing in and out of the placenta. Everything the baby needs for growth, nourishment, and metabolic activity—glucose, amino acids, carbohydrates, fats, and so forth—travels across this same membrane. Similarly, all the waste products are transported across this layer to the maternal kidneys and liver to be filtered out of the bloodstream.

If the placenta is not functioning at an optimal level, the result is *intrauterine growth retardation* (IUGR), also called *growth delay*. This term applies to any fetus that lags behind established developmental standards. Growth retardation is not the same thing as mental retardation, although nutrition to the brain can also be compromised by an underperforming placenta. Placental insufficiency causes over 90 percent of growth delay, although problems with the umbilical cord, maternal infection, hypertensive disorders of pregnancy, or poor nutrition can also retard the baby's growth. A malfunctioning placenta also leads to decreased amniotic fluid, a condition called *oligohydramnios* (see page 158). Finally, insufficient placentas tend to be smaller than normal ones.

Placental insufficiency has many causes, although hypertensive disorders are the most common. High blood pressure, for example, could cause all the arteries in the placenta to narrow and reduce the blood supply to the baby; the placenta's ability to transfer oxygen, energy, and nutrition is then compromised, and the baby's growth is slowed. Placental insufficiency is pretty common among older mothers; no matter how young you feel and look, your arteries and uterus are still forty or forty-three or forty-five years old. Placental

MEASURING GROWTH DELAY

What distinguishes a healthy six-pound baby from a growth-delayed six-pound baby? Obstetricians look at their rate of growth and whether or not they've fallen off their trajectory. They also compare a baby's size to that of thousands of other babies at the same gestational age. Similarly, a radiologist measures the baby's skull, abdomen, and thighbone and compares the measurements to those thousands of other babies.

insufficiency unrelated to age or hypertension can be caused by an infection or a genetic problem.

Growth delay may be symmetrical and asymmetrical, both of which can be caused by a range of minor and major issues. Sometimes the baby's growth slows a little and can be managed without medical intervention. Other times the baby can actually get smaller, a situation that calls for extreme measures. Any delay of growth indicates that somehow the flow of blood to the baby is compromised or that there is some other problem with the baby's health.

Asymmetric growth delay happens when the baby's body compensates for less blood by sending the majority of it to the most important place—the brain. Therefore, this disorder is characterized by continuing healthy brain development while the body lags behind. The first sign of a developing health risk can be a relatively slim abdomen; because the belly is mostly soft tissue and fatty deposits, it would be one of the first parts of the baby's body to receive less nourishment.

In asymmetric growth delay, food and rest are your only weapons. The fewer calories the mother uses and the more she consumes, the more nutrition is available for the baby. Her overall caloric intake must be high, and she should definitely give up visits to the gym. This is not to say that mom has to stay in bed, but she should definitely take it easy. The idea is to overload the placenta with food and oxygen, because it has become inefficient in transferring these essential elements to the baby.

If the obstetrician finds and manages asymmetric growth delay from an early stage, the baby has the best chance of getting to maturity. If, however, the baby isn't growing so well, and other indicators start to worsen (such as lessening amniotic fluid), the baby may be better off out of the uterus. Choosing the best course of action calls for the input of a perinatologist, an obstetrician, and a radiologist, as well as, of course, the mother.

In symmetric growth delay, the baby's overall growth lags at every sonogram. First, the baby is a little small, then he or she is one week behind, then two weeks, and so on; however, all the baby's measurements remain proportional. This type of growth delay could be due to an infection or simple placental insufficiency and demands more concern than asymmetric growth delay for two reasons. First, symmetric growth delay can reflect a congenital problem, such as an undiscovered chromosomal anomaly or congenital infection. Worse, this type of growth delay is alarming because it negatively affects the development of the brain. Depending on the severity of the situation, symmetric growth delay can call for an early induction (see page 215).

In addition to assessing the baby's growth, doctors assess placental health by monitoring blood flow from the baby to the placenta. Even though the heart circulates blood through rhythmic pulsing, commonly called beats, the blood should always be flowing forward, even between beats. Each contraction of the baby's heart should be enough to push the blood through until the next beat. An interruption in the flow of blood is significant cause for concern because it suggests a resistance in the placental vessels, where the exchange of oxygen and nutrients occurs. If there is reverse flow, it's time for an emergency caesarian section. Bear in mind that reverse blood flow doesn't happen overnight—growth delay is a relatively early indicator of placental insufficiency and should clue your doctor in before reverse blood flow becomes a problem.

Blood Flow Is Important

Doctors can sonographically examine the blood flow in the uterine artery, the main blood supply to the uterus. If the uterine artery is compromised, it's likely the baby's blood supply is lessened, too. Finally, radiologists can examine the blood flow within the baby's brain to assess that this most important organ is receiving all the nutrients it requires. If either of these examinations turns up a negative result, the course of action depends on gestational age, although there is no treatment for these problems except delivery.

Placenta Previa

The placenta can sometimes stick to the wrong place in the uterus. Although this rarely has significant medical implications, if the placenta implants itself low in the uterus, toward the cervical opening, then it can cause some obvious routing problems during delivery. A

PICTURE THE PLACENTA

One of the many delicious treats of Indian cuisine is naan bread. To make it, dough is flattened into a thick disk and slapped onto the inside wall of a tandoor oven like a fat pita bread. That's what the placenta looks like—a thick round of tissue flattened against the inner wall of the uterus and flattened out like a big pancake over time.

total placenta previa is when the placenta is square over the cervical opening, blocking the baby's path into the world. A *partial placenta previa* is when the placenta is a little to one side or the other, but the edge still covers the cervical canal. And if the placenta abuts the edge of the cervical canal but does not cover or cross it, the condition is called a *low-lying placenta*. As the cervix dilates in labor and exposes the edge of this placenta, significant bleeding results.

The most common side effect of placenta previa is painless vaginal bleeding during the third trimester, and it can be quite heavy. Because placenta previa is usually diagnosed in the second trimester by sonogram, most women with this condition are forewarned of the possibility of vaginal bleeding and instructed to go directly to the hospital if it occurs.

A C-SECTION CAN BE A REAL LIFESAVER

A patient with a low-lying placenta very much wanted a vaginal delivery. A nurse and I were attending to her as she labored. We put absorbent blue pads under her bottom to catch the heavy amounts of liquid pouring out. The nurse said, "I think that's blood," and I said, "Oh, no, that's mostly amniotic fluid." Her labor was progressing nicely and I wanted to try to let her have the vaginal delivery of her dreams. Then the patient said, "I'm getting a little dizzy." We took her blood pressure and discovered she was going into shock. So we did a C-section. (And now I always use white pads.)

If the bleeding persists, the usual course of action is a caesarian section. However, if you're bleeding heavily and the baby's still immature, your obstetrician will most likely admit you at the hospital, where you'll put your legs up and pretend you're having a very heavy period. The goal is to maintain normal blood volume and pressure. Occasionally, a patient may require a blood transfusion. Frequently, the bleeding stops as the healthy patient's natural clotting mechanisms kick in, which can mean a real advantage for the premature baby.

The risk of placenta previa increases with age. A previous caesarian section also increases the risk because the section leaves a scar in the uterine wall. The scarred area lacks the vessels necessary to support the placenta, so the placenta grows broader and thinner in order to reach a better blood supply. As it spreads out, it becomes more likely to cross the cervical opening. However, low-lying placentas or even partial previas diagnosed earlier in pregnancy can "get out of the way" by the end of the third trimester, because the growing uterus can move the placenta away from the cervix.

Abruptio Placenta

Abruptio placenta is a dramatic and terrifying condition (informally called an *abruption*) in which the placenta separates from the uteruine wall. In a *partial abruption,* the placenta remains partially attached to the uterus, sustaining the baby; a *total abruptio placenta* means the baby has been separated from its source of oxygen and could be dead in minutes.

Doctors don't really know what causes an abruption, but high blood pressure is commonly associated with this problem. Trauma, such as from a car accident or falling on your belly, can also cause abruptions. Cocaine use—a bad idea anytime but especially dangerous during pregnancy—can also cause an abruptio placenta. And, of course, an abruption sometimes just happens.

The placenta can separate from the uterine wall along its edge or from its middle. If it separates at the edge, the event is accompanied by vaginal bleeding. If it starts in the middle, the edges of the placenta can hold the blood in place. Regardless of where it starts, once the placenta separates from the wall of the uterus, the mother's health is also at risk. The gap leaks blood and can quickly drain the body of platelets. Disseminated intravascular coagulopathy, or DIC, (see page 149) is the great danger with abruptions.

The most noticeable symptoms of abruptions are pain and vaginal bleeding. Of course, if the placenta is sealed to the uterine wall along the edges there will not be any bleeding, but there will be pain, and it will feel different from the pain of contractions (false or real). Abruptions hurt continuously and significantly. If you experience these symptoms, getting to the hospital quickly is your best shot at saving the pregnancy. If the obstetrical staff determines that you're having an abruption, you must have an emergency C-section. This is certainly the only way to save the baby's life, and it is critical to saving both the mother's life and her uterus.

Conditions of Amniotic Fluid

The third trimester is full of miracles, and amniotic fluid is one of them. In the beginning, it's mostly just a watery secretion from the gestational membrane, but as the pregnancy progresses, the amniotic fluid consists increasingly of the baby's own urine. At twenty weeks, it's about fifty-fifty. At delivery, it's virtually all fetal urine.

A sonogram can roughly measure amniotic fluid. It's reported as an *amniotic fluid index,* or AFI, which measures the amount of fluid around the baby's body. These numbers do not represent a specific unit but, rather, they are a reflection of a complex equation that considers multiple measurements. A result of over 10 is a normal score, between 7 and 10 is borderline, and below 7 is low.

The right amount of amniotic fluid is absolutely critical because it performs so many important functions. The baby develops all its muscles through constant calisthenics in utero, and the fluid makes it possible for the baby to kick and wave his or her arms around. The right amount of fluid also allows the baby to get into the head-down position for delivery.

The amniotic fluid also helps the intestinal and respiratory tract develop because the baby constantly drinks the surrounding liquid. The liquid travels through the intestinal tract, gets filtered through the kidneys, comes out as urine, and the baby drinks it again. This stimulates the esophagus and muscular activity of the stomach, initiates the swallowing reflex, and helps the stomach and esophagus mature.

Babies also breath amniotic fluid, expanding and developing their lungs. It forces all the little ducts and alveoli to expand, and it stimulates the chest to go in and out. Sonographers know that one of the most important signs of a healthy baby is breathing movements, so they include this measurement in their biophysical profile (see page 132). Amniotic fluid becomes a matter for concern in the third trimester, when there is too little of it (*oligohydramnios*) or too much (*polyhydramnios*).

Oligohydramnios

Oligohydramnios can lead to a number of problems. Without enough amniotic fluid, babies are unable to float, swim around, move, or kick, and their little arms and legs stay flexed against the body, resulting in malformed limbs. The intestinal tract suffers because it can't develop muscles through its practice with the amniotic fluid. The lungs fail to grow without amniotic fluid. The dearth of amniotic fluid also means less cushioning around the umbilical cord, which raises the risk of it getting squashed and cutting off blood flow to the baby.

Oligohydramnios can range from a temporary condition to a significant problem and can have a number of causes. For example, if there's an obstruction in the urinary tract (page 105), there will be very little amniotic fluid. Premature rupture of the membranes also leads to low levels of amniotic fluid, as it leaks out of the body. Oligohydramnios can be the result of a hypertensive disorder of pregnancy, failing placental function, dehydration, and many other causes, including some that are simply unknown.

An expectant mom diagnosed with oligohydramnios requires frequent checkups, typically weekly sonograms and nonstress tests (see page 132), to be sure that there are no other problems developing, such as slowed fetal growth or a case of preeclampsia. Women diagnosed with oligohydramnios should also monitor fetal movement very closely on their own. This is another condition that the doctor can only monitor; ultimately, the decision is whether the baby will be better off in or out of the uterus.

Polyhydramnios

Polyhydramnios is a condition of excessive amniotic fluid. This can be common in diabetics. It can also occur if the baby is making too much urine and not swallowing, typically because of an obstruction somewhere in the digestive tract. Polyhydramnios overextends the uterus, lending the appearance of twins or multiples and increasing the mother's discomfort. The extra fluid makes it very difficult for the uterus to contract because the muscle is overly stretched. An overabundance of fluid also makes it less likely that the baby will find the optimal, head-down position for delivery (see "Abnormalities of the Baby"), and a prolapsed cord (see page 161) becomes more likely when the mother's water breaks.

Conditions of the Umbilical Cord

The umbilical cord is a long, braided tube that contains two arteries and one vein. It connects the placenta to the baby at the belly button. The cord can be poorly developed and have only one artery instead of two—this is not catastrophic, but it does require extra care. First, the obstetrician must rule out all defects that are associated with abnormal cords, such as kidney problems. A compromised cord might lead to more fetal heart irregularities in labor and, therefore, a somewhat higher section rate. Also, because babies with a poorly developed cord get a little less food and oxygen, they're at risk for mild growth delay (see preceding discussion).

KICK COUNT

A doctor who suspects a problem with the baby may ask you to do a *kick count,* where you count the baby's kicks for one hour. Don't pick a time when the baby's always quiet. Look at the clock and count each time you feel the baby move. Obstetricians are comfortable with kick counts of at least ten during a customarily active hour. If you have several movements, but not as many as ten, have something to eat and drink, put your legs up, relax, and do it again. If the baby still doesn't move ten times in the hour, call your doctor.

THE FUTURE OF CORD ANALYSIS?

Coiling is the newest, hottest term in umbilical cord analysis. Radiologists have long noticed that good, healthy umbilical cords coil, like a slinky. This theoretically means that if the baby presses it against the wall of the uterus, the cord has the springy ability to protect itself, whereas a flat and uncoiled cord might lose blood flow if squeezed between baby and uterus. Some radiologists already include the measurements of umbilical coils in their reports. Whether this is a significant development in obstetrics or just a fad remains to be seen.

The remaining abnormalities of the umbilical cord tend to present problems at delivery. For example, a short cord can create a stalled labor, because it yanks the baby back up into the uterus after every contraction. A long cord can get twisted, creating kinks that obstruct blood flow. When the cord wraps around the baby's neck, the danger is not that it will strangle him, but rather that the process of labor will squeeze the cord and cut off the blood flow before the baby has been fully delivered. These abnormal presentations rarely create a problem in utero, when there is a lot of space and liquid to keep pressure off the cord.

PROLAPSED CORDS IN LABOR

In my days of training, there were times when the senior resident, upon doing a pelvic exam on a woman in labor, would turn to me and say, "This is very interesting. Why don't you check it?" I'd reach in, discover a prolapsed cord, and have to push the baby's head off it to keep the blood flowing. Because I was the junior doctor, I'd have to stay in that position, with my hand up the patient's vagina, as they wheeled us down to an operating room, anesthetized the patient, prepared for the section, and so forth. Obstetricians still handle prolapsed cords pretty much the same way; however, I now pass on the honor of holding the baby's head away from the cervix to my junior colleagues.

A *prolapsed cord* is an acute emergency that can happen only once the water breaks. If the baby's head is high in the pelvis, the cord can slip between his head and the mother's cervix. With the first contraction, the head squashes the cord against the pelvis, cutting off blood flow. The good news is that sonograms can frequently (but not always) predict an excess of cord around the baby's head or neck, indicating a heightened risk of cord prolapse. If a woman's water breaks and the umbilical cord is coming out of her vagina, she should lie down with legs elevated and call 911.

Abnormalities of the Baby

Two key abnormalities involving the baby in a late-term pregnancy involve the baby's position and stillbirth.

Position

An optimal pregnancy for human beings is one baby, born headfirst. All other numbers and positions increase the risk to the baby at birth.

In a normal pregnancy, the uterus is shaped like an upside-down pyramid. The head is the single biggest part of the baby's anatomy, but the buttocks, thighs, knees, and feet are the bulkiest. So the head, even though it is the biggest body part, should find its way into the lower part of the uterus, as the bulky parts naturally seek out the most room. Not only does the head in the lower position make for smoother vaginal deliveries, but when the mother's water breaks, the baby's big head acts like a cork, keeping everything else inside the uterus and relatively stable.

At thirty-two weeks' gestation, 30 percent of babies still have their buttocks facing the birth canal. This position is called *breech* and is not good for delivery. By forty weeks, however, only 3 percent of babies are still breech.

A baby can remain in a breech position for a number of reasons. Anything that distorts the normal shape of the uterus, such as a placenta previa, increases the risk that the baby will be in an abnormal position. Polyhydramnios, or too much amniotic fluid, for example, provides a vast expanse of fluid to swim around in, making it less likely that the baby will be confined to a head-down, feet-up orientation. Similarly, anything that changes the shape of the baby's head, like hydrocephaly (page 104) or a goiter, could also force the head to the top of the uterus.

If the baby is still not presenting well when the mother goes into labor, the likely choice is to perform a C-section; contractions will preserve the baby's original position as the walls of the uterus compress all around her. If you know ahead of time, you can attempt an external version (see page 203), in which the obstetrician attempts to reorient the baby through the abdominal wall before labor begins.

Stillbirth

Stillbirth is when the baby dies at twenty-four weeks or later, but before delivery. It is one of obstetrics' saddest events, but happens only about 0.1 percent of the time. Usually, stillbirths are discovered when the mother reports no fetal movement for three hours or more or at a routine visit when the monitor fails to show a fetal heartbeat. Stillbirths can be caused by a number of factors, including infection, hypertensive disorders, postdate pregnancies, acute placental insufficiency, and cord accidents—sometimes the baby gets tightly wrapped in the umbilical cord, compromising the blood supply. A

BE SAFE BUT STAY SANE

Anything that can happen to a nonpregnant woman can happen to a woman when she is pregnant (except getting pregnant). You can get in a car accident, you can have a ruptured appendix, or you can catch chicken pox. We all try to diminish these risks every day, especially during pregnancy, but that doesn't mean you should quarantine yourself. That said, I would suggest that the last trimester is not the time for a trek through Patagonia. You might want to avoid going places that require you to have live-virus vaccinations, where the blood supply is questionable (should you need a transfusion), or where health care is shaky. As your due date approaches, it makes sense to stay closer and closer to home, but don't stay *at home*.

A NEWLY IDENTIFIED SYNDROME

Antiphospholipid syndrome is a rare blood condition that causes recurrent fetal deaths and miscarriages, and ultimately can lead to a maternal stroke. In this autoimmune disorder, continuous mini blood clots form throughout the mother's body and placenta. Of course, this disorder has health implications outside of pregnancy, but it is often discovered in the wake of a stillbirth. Once a woman has been diagnosed with this condition, anticoagulation therapy to avoid clots can make a healthy pregnancy possible.

diagnosis is usually made after the fact or not at all; it's not always possible to tell why these tragedies happen.

Once a stillbirth has been diagnosed, the doctor wants to deliver the baby quickly, because dead tissue in the uterus can lead to blood-clotting disorders such as DIC (see page 149). Women sometimes want to take a few days to begin coming to terms with their loss, before medical intervention. In these cases, patients must have their clotting factors checked at least every other day. Most women want to have the baby delivered sooner rather than later. Some say, "I don't want to go home with a dead baby in my uterus," and they go right to the hospital.

The treatment for stillbirth is an induction, which can take anywhere from half a day to several days. Doctors can use large amounts of drugs such as Pitocin and Demerol for this procedure.

A stillbirth can be so emotionally traumatic that many patients choose to not see the baby and instead prefer to just leave the hospital as quickly as possible. However, in my experience, having some closure by seeing the expired child is helpful. Most obstetrical wards are prepared for these situations and have a kit to dress the baby appropriately and allow the parents to hold the child, say goodbye, and maybe even take a picture. Although this might sound morbid, these parents don't see anything grotesque; instead, they see a member of their family who tragically died. Seeing the stillborn baby can be therapeutic, because it makes both the baby and the death real and helps the parents cope with the loss because they are not left to imagine what their baby looked like.

CHAPTER 9

Labor: Normal

As Your Body Prepares for Labor

Labor and delivery are serious undertakings for the body. The uterus has been warming up since the second trimester, and up to four weeks before your due date, the cervix and baby may also begin preparations. Once you're in your ninth month of pregnancy, your obstetrician should see you as frequently as once each week to evaluate these changes. The more progress made before labor, the

GETTING IN THE RIGHT MIND-SET FOR LABOR

Many new prenatal patients come in for their very first obstetrical visit and are already scared to death about labor after hearing their friends' gory tales. I had already delivered hundreds of babies when I got pregnant, so I was sure it wasn't going to get to me. After my labor, in which I lost control and practically assaulted the anesthesiologist, I asked the obstetrical nurses who were also mothers, "Why didn't you tell me?" They said they didn't want to scare me. There's really no way to be totally emotionally prepared for labor, especially since no one can predict what your labor will be like. If you're like me and think you'll breeze through it, you're probably in for a few surprises, too. Of all the labors I've seen, the best have been with patients who have a healthy respect for the process. Don't be terrified, but don't be cocky, either.

NESTING IS NOT FOR EVERYONE

A common old wives' tale is that just before labor, you will get a spurt of energy that drives you to clean out closets and cabinets. Sure, I've seen one or two women experience this nesting urge right before going into labor, but it's far from universal. Don't think to yourself, "I haven't nested yet, so this can't be labor."

shorter the labor. This means that when you call with contractions in the middle of the night, the obstetrician can advise you whether to head to the hospital (if your cervix was effaced or dilated at the last visit, for example) or make some tea and stay at home (if your cervix was unchanged last time the doctor checked).

Cervical Changes

In the last month of pregnancy, the cervix softens and *effaces* (thins), it becomes axial (changes orientation), and then it *dilates* (opens and practically disappears). At each checkup, the obstetrician evaluates the cervix for all these qualities. Normally, it's three centimeters long, but ahead of delivery a run of contractions can thin the cervix 20 to 30 percent, and it can dilate one centimeter or more.

ENVISION THE CERVIX

The best way to think of how the cervix behaves toward the end of pregnancy and in labor is to think of a turtleneck sweater, where the cervix is the turtleneck and the uterus is the rest of the sweater. When you don a turtleneck, there's a moment when the slim neck stretches over the head when the turtleneck part effectively "disappears, leaving a small hole at the top. The cervix behaves the same way, becoming part of the uterus. Then it dilates to allow the baby's head to come out.

The Baby's Presentation

Presentation is the term that refers to the part of the baby that is coming into the pelvis first. If the baby's head is presenting, that's normal. Feet are not so good. A pelvic or abdominal exam usually reveals the baby's presentation, although sometimes a sonogram is required.

The Pelvis

Station measures the position of the baby's presenting bony part in relation to the narrowest part of the mother's pelvis, where bony protuberances called *ischial spines* narrow the way. In a pelvic exam the obstetrician can feel the top of the baby's head through the cervix to evaluate her station. *Zero station* is when the presenting bony part of the baby's head is even with these bones; −1 means the baby's head is one centimeter above the ischial spines; +1 means the baby's skull is one centimeter lower than the spines. If the baby's head is just entering the pelvis, obstetricians call it *dipping,* and if it's higher than that it's *floating.*

   Engagement is when the widest part of the baby's head has negotiated the narrowest part of the mother's pelvis, called the

---

IT MADE SENSE AT THE TIME

From the 1950s to the early 1970s, X-rays of the mother's pelvis at eight months' gestation and/or during unprogressive labor were standard practice. This, along with other physical assessments, was done to predict whether the baby's skull would fit through the pelvis. It turned out that women who were told they needed a C-section would often come into the hospital with the baby's head half out already, and women who were supposed to breeze through labor frequently ended up having C-sections. What obstetricians learned from this is that the only true test of a pelvis is labor, since there are so many important variables that affect the process, such as the force of the contractions and the position of the baby's head.

THE BABY'S STATION

Floating in the uterus

Dipping into the pelvis

−3: three centimeters above the ischial spines

−2: two centimeters above the ischial spines

−1: one centimeter above the ischial spines

0 = *engagement:* at the ischial spines

+1: one centimeter below the ischial spines

+2: two centimeters below the ischial spines

+3: three centimeters below the ischial spines—the baby's head is now visible during contractions and pushing

+4 = delivery

(Some hospitals and doctors use a five-point system.)

pelvic inlet. The term *zero station* is commonly used interchangeably with *engagement* because when the bony part of the baby's head is even with the ischial spines, the widest part of the skull is also at the pelvic inlet the vast majority of the time. If and when the baby gets to zero station, there is very little chance that the skull will be too large to fit through the mother's pelvis. When the baby's head is too large to squeeze through, it's called *cephalopelvic disproportion,* or CPD, and it is the classic reason for a caesarian section.

Status of the Membranes

While many women are sure they'll know when their water breaks, your obstetrician will still check on the status of the *membranes,* or the two layers of the amniotic sac, at each visit. Once the seal on the baby's sterile environment is broken, bacteria can climb up into the uterine cavity and cause an infection. So it's very important to know whether there's any kind of break in the integrity of the amniotic sac.

The conditions in the vagina toward the end of pregnancy can make it difficult to tell whether the membranes are still intact. The vagina is at its most congested and secretions are at their most voluminous. The pressure on the bladder can cause occasional bursts of urine. All of this can mimic the presence of amniotic fluid in the vagina.

The obstetrician tests for amniotic fluid in your discharge with nitrizine paper (a form of litmus paper). Vaginal secretions and urine are acidic; amniotic fluid is very alkaline (or basic). Another way an obstetrician can check for the presence of amniotic fluid is by taking a vaginal smear and looking at it under a microscope, because the high salt content in amniotic fluid makes it crystallize when it dries. Dried amniotic fluid looks like ice crystals on a window in winter. Under a slide, amniotic fluid also reveals fetal cells.

Once the membranes rupture, amniotic fluid continually leaks out of the vagina until the baby is born. So if you think your water has broken and you call your doctor, she may tell you to urinate, put on a pad, and check it after an hour for fluid. If the pad is wet after an hour, call your doctor back and let her know your water has probably broken.

During the last month of pregnancy, before the water breaks, the doctor may try to stimulate uterine activity by *stripping the membranes*. This is a benign, noninvasive, simple way to initiate uterine activity in which the obstetrician sweeps the space between the membranes and the cervix to break up any mucus and allow the amniotic sac to rest with more force on the cervix. The cervix has to

THE STINK TEST

Amniotic fluid has a very characteristic smell, so you may find your doctor sniffing your panties. Remember, amniotic fluid is mostly baby's urine, so it smells like a weak ammonia solution or a very clean bathroom.

THE MUCUS PLUG?

Pregnant women sometimes talk about passing "the mucus plug," but this term is not mentioned in any medical journal or textbook. What it refers to is the extra cervical mucus produced as the cervix effaces and dilates, resulting in what seems like a big glob of mucus, which some midwives dub a "plug." The mucus is not plugging anything, and the term is meaningless to obstetricians; you could pass a "mucus plug" every week toward the end of pregnancy.

be dilated enough to allow the doctor to insert a finger or two into the cervix to accomplish this.

Monitoring Your and Baby's Progress

The fetal monitor is the most common and easy way for the obstetrician to evaluate the baby's well-being in utero, and it is likely to make many appearances toward the end of pregnancy and through labor. Although there are several varieties, a fetal monitor often

WALKING AROUND LABOR AND DELIVERY

While there are excellent labor and delivery wards that offer handheld fetal monitors to allow the mother free mobility, most do not. But if the results of the monitoring are good, you will probably be able to take a break from the fetal monitor every fifteen minutes or so, particularly in the very early stages of labor. Obstetricians try to avoid continuous fetal monitoring until active labor. Pregnant women sometimes get agitated if the hospital staff won't let them walk around. However, a woman in labor who still wants to go for a stroll is probably still in the very early stages of labor; if being mobile is that important to you, hold off on going to the hospital until your doctor says you have to go. I recommend that women having their first child come to the hospital when their contractions are five minutes or less apart.

looks like a loose elastic belt that goes around your belly. The monitor does two things: It picks up the sound of the baby's heartbeat with a Doppler machine (an instrument that measures sound waves) and it measures the frequency and duration (not intensity) of each contraction with a pressure gauge. So a normal fetal monitor readout has two lines—one represents contractions and the other represents the baby's heartbeat.

A normal fetal heart rate is between 120 and 160 beats per minute. This is a lot higher than the normal adult's resting pulse, which is about 70. Babies are metabolically hyperactive and continue to have a rapid pulse as late as their teenage years. However, like an adult, whose heart rate rises with activity, the fetal heart should be responsive to stimulus, such as the baby's own kicking or a uterine contraction. Also, just as with a normal adult heartbeat, there's no regular length of time between the beats of a baby's heart. Different hormonal and neurological forces in a healthy person push and pull the heart, resulting in what's called *beat-to-beat variability.* This variability is apparent on a fetal monitor and is an important indicator of the overall health of the baby. Therefore, the more squiggly the fetal heartbeat readout line from the fetal monitor, the better; however, it's also important to keep in mind that normal events, such as the baby napping, can flatten the line.

A normal fetal heart tracing has a 100 percent predictive value, meaning that there is never a tragic surprise after the monitor has reported the baby's good health. However, a *bad* fetal heart tracing is only 50 percent accurate, which means half the time obstetricians think babies are in trouble, they're actually perfectly fine. Therefore, doctors no longer refer to an abnormal fetal heart tracing as *fetal distress;* instead, they now use the term *nonreassuring fetal heart rate pattern.*

Any *deceleration,* or falloff, from the baseline fetal heart rate is considered abnormal, although no labor is deceleration-free. Abnormal does not mean dangerous or pathological; it just gets the doctor's attention. When deceleration occurs, the delivery room suddenly swarms with a variety of medical personnel; the nurse is there with oxygen, the obstetrician does a pelvic exam to make sure there's no prolapsed cord, the anesthesiologist does a blood pressure check, and so on. Often, this crowd of people is gone within ten minutes, once the baby's heart rate has returned to baseline and everything is stable once more.

There are many different kinds of decelerations, some benign and others significant. About ten minutes after an epidural, for example, there is occasionally a deceleration in the baby's heart rate as the mother's blood pressure drops, the baby's head descends into the pelvis, and both mother and baby relax. *Mild variable decelerations* are another relatively benign event. These are brief dips that look like little V's on the monitor. Doctors hypothesize that these depressions are the result of a brief temporary cord pinching that interrupts blood flow; once the baby moves, blood flow is restored.

Recurrent variable (Type III) decelerations, meaning at least six times an hour for more than one hour, can be cause for concern, depending on how far the mom is from delivering. If the baby is going to be out in twenty minutes, there's far less reason to worry than if there are still hours of labor left, along with the potential for continued decelerations.

When the baby's head descends through the pelvis, there is often a *Type I deceleration*. These decelerations are inversely related to contractions; as the contraction intensifies, the baby's heart rate goes down. The peak of the contraction is the trough of

MEASURED PRAISE

The fetal monitor has been controversial since it was first introduced in the 1960s, before doctors came to rely primarily on evidence-based medicine. Since then, a number of studies of the efficacy of fetal monitors have been done, some refuting their efficacy and others supporting it. For good or ill, fetal monitors are an integral part of obstetrical care in the United States. OB units rely on them, and the majority of obstetricians think they have been extraordinarily beneficial for millions of babies. Proving the utility of fetal monitors is tough because it would require a few thousand pregnant women to go through labor without a monitor, and no one, doctors or patients, is willing to take that chance.

the baby's heart rate, and then it returns to normal as the contraction wanes. Doctors hypothesize that these decelerations are the result of the baby's head being compressed in the pelvis, which slows the heart rate. Therefore, Type I decelerations are a sign that the patient is fully or close to fully dilated.

What obstetricians do not like to see on the fetal monitor are significant, prolonged decelerations. Any persistent deceleration from the baby's baseline heart rate should be further evaluated. One way to do this is with a *scratch test,* in which the obstetrician stimulates the baby by reaching up and scratching his head. This stimulus should cause an acceleration or return to baseline, which is a sign that the baby is still responsive and the deceleration is not too alarming. An alternative way to investigate a prolonged deceleration is with an internal scalp electrode. This corkscrew-shaped wire is screwed into the skin of the baby's head to pick up the electrical conductivity of the baby's heart. Like an electrocardiogram (EKG), this is a direct report on the baby's heartbeat and is a more accurate way of assessing the baby's well-being. The scalp electrode is frequently used instead of the external fetal monitor in cases where the fetal monitor fails to work—for example, when the baby is in a difficult position or the mother is obese—as well as in some high-risk pregnancies.

PREMIUM BABY

In the 1970s and 1980s, obstetricians came up with the phrase *premium baby* to differentiate among the levels of treatment various prenatal patients should receive. For example, if a patient already had seven children, doctors conjectured that one of them turning out a little off, physically or mentally, wouldn't be so bad because that one would just blend in with the other children; perhaps they worried a little less about the level of care this expectant mom received. On the other hand, an older patient—say, age 38—pregnant with her first child might have garnered more attention from the doctors, who felt they were required to deliver to this woman her one premium baby. Not to worry, in twenty-first century obstetrics, *every* baby is a premium baby.

Persistent decelerations that occur when the mother is less than two centimeters dilated—precluding the possibility of checking on the baby via the scratch test or scalp electrode—most often culminate in a C-section. In these cases, there's simply too much time left before full dilation and delivery, and there's no other way to evaluate the baby's health.

Prodromal Labor

The first stage of labor, where contractions are less frequent than every five minutes and the cervix is mostly unchanged, is called *prodromal labor.* This is pretty much confined to first pregnancies, though not every woman experiences prodromal labor even then. This stage can last a few hours or a few days. Although prodromal labor can be uncomfortable, as long as your contractions are more than five minutes apart and your cervix unchanged, this stage of labor doesn't require you to go to the hospital. However, your doctor will probably want you to come into the office to check on the baby with the fetal monitor.

While you're there, the doctor will perform a pelvic exam and say something like "You're still one centimeter, 50 percent effaced. Take a walk and come back in a few hours." Obstetricians prefer to wait for the mother's body to be in active labor before sending her to the hospital.

MY ADVICE ON PRODROMAL LABOR

If everything in your pregnancy has been good and normal, stay at home until you want something for the pain or the contractions are less than five minutes apart. You're probably better off at home, staying as active as possible and keeping yourself distracted. One of my patients decided the best way to do this was by going to the movies. Unfortunately, her groans at steady six-minute intervals didn't go over well with the rest of the audience, and management asked her to leave.

THE ENEMA SOLUTION

Enemas are a classic way to kick labor into a higher gear because they irritate the colon, which in turn produces prostaglandins that can increase contractions in the nearby uterus. The colon-uterus relationship is why some midwives recommend a spoonful of castor oil to stimulate labor, because it causes diarrhea. Of course, castor oil also causes dehydration, so don't try this remedy on your own.

Prodromal labor doesn't happen to everybody; conversely, some women get stuck in this early rut. Depending on how mother and baby are holding up, prodromal labor can last days. Obstetricians prefer to avoid stalling in this stage for too long because it's exhausting for the mother and hard on the baby, who may tolerate only so many contractions before his or her heart rate starts to become irregular, movements decrease, and other signs of stress begin to show. Different babies and mothers can handle varying lengths of these inefficient contractions; some women and babies can go on for up to a week without distress. However, if this stage drags on, your doctor is likely to recommend medication to stimulate more effective contractions.

Speeding Labor Along with an Amniotomy

In labor, the amniotic fluid sac may rupture spontaneously or it may be ruptured by the obstetrician. The membranes can rupture spon-

LOW-STAKES GAME

At my hospital, labor and delivery doctors and nurses commonly bet on how dilated patients are when they first get to the hospital. In general, the most dramatic patients—the ones who are doubled over, huffing and puffing and moaning, are the least dilated. The ones who come in by ambulance are usually not even in labor yet.

MOVE IT ALONG

A patient was six centimeters dilated and contracting every five minutes. Though she was doing well, her membranes had not ruptured, and I suggested she might benefit from an amniotomy. She begged me not to because it was "not natural." She stayed in that holding pattern for sixteen hours, at which point *I* was reduced to begging. I ruptured her membranes, and we delivered her within an hour.

taneously before labor, which is called *premature rupture of membranes*. The majority of women (up to 80 percent) go into labor on their own within twelve hours of breaking their water. As long as the amniotic fluid is clear and you don't have Group B Strep (page 131) your doctor may tell you to stay at home and wait until you do go into labor. Membranes can rupture spontaneously during labor, or not at all, and delivery progresses anyway. However, if labor is not progressing, your doctor might also rupture your membranes in a procedure called an *amniotomy.*

An amniotomy requires that the cervix be at least one centimeter dilated for the obstetrician to reach the membranes, using an instrument called an *amniohook*. Despite its ominous name, this tool, which looks something like a long crochet hook, is designed to avoid accidentally scratching the baby. An amniotomy is no more painful than a pelvic exam, but like a pelvic exam at this late stage, it can be a little uncomfortable.

In general, rupturing the membranes can promote a better labor because the pituitary gland responds to this event by releasing oxy-

BORN UNDER THE CAUL

Babies can be born without membranes rupturing, and they emerge encased in the gooey sac that's been their home for nine months. This is called being born *under the caul*. This is a medically meaningless event, but in certain cultures it is thought of as good or bad luck.

tocin, a hormone that stimulates contractions. It also improves the mechanics of labor, because the diminished volume inside the uterus allows for shortened uterine muscles, which can act more effectively. Finally, rupturing the membranes removes the soft cushion of amniotic fluid between the baby's skull and the cervix; the hard skull is a more effective dilating wedge than the amniotic sac. A paramount reason to rupture membranes is to get a look at the amniotic fluid, which should be a clear, pale yellow.

Normal Labor: A Hypothetical Tale

You are within five days on either side of your due date, and at your last doctor's visit your cervix was 50 percent effaced (meaning about 1.5 centimeters long) and the baby was at −1 station.

You wake up in the middle of the night with painful contractions that last about forty seconds and feel like very strong menstrual cramps. Before you can think about what to do, you fall back to sleep. Then something wakes you up again. Now look at the clock. Start keeping track of the frequency of these contractions. Let's say they're ten minutes apart.

If you have no high-risk factors (such as diabetes or high blood pressure) and your membranes are still intact, it is too early to wake up your doctor and it's way too early to go to the hospital. But you're probably not going to get back to sleep. Get up, have some water, take a shower, recheck your bag, all the while charting your contractions. They may come every six or seven minutes and become so intense that you have to stop what you're doing and wait them out. In the morning, call your doctor's office to describe your contractions. At this stage you are in early labor, and your doctor may advise you to either go to the hospital, come into the office to be checked, or stay at home for a while.

Early Labor

Once your doctor has told you to go to the hospital, the obstetrical staff will admit you with a diagnosis of *early labor*. A nurse, resi-

DON'T FOOL THE DOCTOR

Doctors tend to respond to the tone as well as the content of what you say. If you call up and report in a flat, unemotional voice, "The contractions are every two minutes and they're very painful," your doctor may deduce that you are far too calm to be in real labor. If you call up and you're huffing and puffing, and you suddenly hand the phone to your partner, your doctor is more likely to think it's "go time."

dent, or doctor will take a medical history to double-check that there are no high-risk indicators, general health problems, allergies, and so forth. The nurse will put you on the fetal monitor for twenty minutes to half an hour to make sure the baby is doing okay. She will put in an IV to keep you hydrated, take your blood pressure, and check your urine for markers of preeclampsia or infection. The hospital may want (or be required by law) to do a few blood tests for anemia, white blood cells, and clotting factors, among other things, as well as for HIV and/or syphilis. This may feel redundant or unnecessary, but these tests are harmless and guarantee the hospital is taking the utmost caution with you and your baby.

DO *NOT* CALL AN AMBULANCE

A patient once called to tell me that her water had broken. However, the baby was still moving around and it was clear that she was not in labor. I told her, "Have your husband drive you to the hospital. Or if you want you can call a cab, get a car service, drive, walk, or take the subway, but whatever you do, do *not* call an ambulance." She hung up and promptly called an ambulance. Because paramedics are only obligated to take patients to the closest emergency room, my patient ended up having an unpleasant delivery experience at the wrong hospital and threatened to sue. Ambulances are frequently used by frightened women in labor without a plan. Have a plan!

Then you'll mostly be left alone with your partner, who, ideally, is encouraging you to breathe and relax. Your nurse will be in and out checking on you and the baby, although many hospitals equip their nurses' stations with a display of all the fetal monitors on the ward. Depending on how you're feeling and how your contractions are going, you might be encouraged to get up and walk or to sit on a big ball and bounce up and down, or simply to doze between contractions.

Bloody Show

Bloody show is the colloquial name for bleeding as the cervix dilates, which happens as capillaries on its surface rupture. Patients sometimes get nervous when they hear me say to the nurse "Great bloody show," but it is a good sign that the patient is in the advanced stages of labor. Bleeding in labor is expected.

One thing you should not do during early labor is eat a big meal to "get up your strength." Once you go into labor, your stomach literally stops functioning. Vomiting in labor upsets everyone, and the bigger the meal and spicier the food, the more awful the vomiting is for patient and caregivers alike. If you're feeling hungry, keep your choices small and simple: Try a plain poached egg or a little toast. I tell patients, "Eat something pretty, because we're going to see it again." This is no time for pork chops and gravy. Best of all, forget food and focus on hydration instead. If your stomach is up to it, drink lots of fluids, such as clear broth, water, club soda, or tea.

Active Labor

Active labor has three stages: The first is when the patient is from four to ten centimeters dilated (as in, *fully dilated*). The end of the first stage, from eight centimeters to fully dilated, is called *transition,* and it is the most tumultuous part of labor. The second stage is from full dilation to delivery. The third stage is from the delivery of the baby to the delivery of the placenta. Then you are *postpartum.*

WHEN WILL YOUR DOCTOR ARRIVE?

It's hard to say when your doctor will get to the hospital. Twenty years ago, doctors frequently *labor-sat,* meaning that they were in the hospital as long as you were. Today, doctors often ask nurses to call them at specific times—for example, when the patient is six centimeters or when she wants pain relief. With managed care, doctors tend to come to the hospital later and later. Personally, I feel that if my patient is uncomfortable enough to require an epidural, then it's time for me to be there. Ask your doctor when you can expect to see her. She might say, "When you're eight centimeters" or "There are seven doctors in our group, and one of us will be there for the entire time." It might make you feel more relaxed to know exactly when you can expect to see your obstetrician.

First-Stage Active Labor: Four Centimeters to Fully Dilated

Active labor is somewhat predictable. For a first-time mom, once the cervix is dilated four centimeters we expect it to continue dilating at the rate of one centimeter per hour, till it is fully, or ten centimeters, dilated. Once fully dilated, Mom can face two or even three hours of pushing. So active labor for a first baby is normally about eight hours.

If your first-time labor is shorter than eight hours, it's not called abnormal, it's called *lucky.* If active labor is two hours or less, it's called *precipitous* and is very rare in a first pregnancy. If the cervix fails to dilate and the baby's head is not descending into the pelvis at the appropriate rate, this is called *poor progress.* Obstetricians don't like to see women stall in active labor (where the cervix stops dilating or contractions peter out), and they may recommend some medication if things are not moving along (see Chapter 10). Poor progress is a common indicator for a caesarian section, but only after all the other available modalities have been tried.

Even though things are warming up during active labor, there's still not much to do but wait until you're fully dilated. With fetal monitors, there's someone constantly checking the baby's well-being, even if they're not in the room with you. The nurse should make sure you're comfortable. If you've had an epidural, your doctor will probably recommend a catheter so your bladder doesn't get distended, because you may not notice when you have to pee. Even if this stage drags out, it's still best to not eat, because if you do you will probably vomit.

Transition: Eight Centimeters to Fully Dilated

Transition is when the last bit of cervix disappears and the baby's head comes down farther to prepare for delivery; it's usually the last hour or so of active labor, before pushing. It's also the most painful part of the whole process, especially, of course, for women without pain relief. Even women with epidurals tremble and vomit; sometimes they even require a top-off to get through this stage. During transition, contractions become longer and stronger. You may feel like you have to move your bowels; this sensation is caused by rectal pressure as the baby's head descends and presses the rectum. This sensation intensifies with contractions.

Second Stage: Fully Dilated to Delivery

If all through active labor your baby's heartbeat is good, and you have pain relief, your doctor may not find it essential to know the

OBSTETRICIANS' SECRETS

By the time the cervix is four centimeters dilated, it should also be paper thin. It's relatively easy and safe for the doctor to gently spread the cervix farther during a pelvic exam. This can dilate a cervix from four to six centimeters in a few seconds, trimming two hours off labor. It's called *manual dilatation of the cervix* and should be done only on a woman who is fully effaced and who has had an epidural, because these conditions maximize the effect. Manual dilatation should be used gently and sparingly. Whether obstetricians use this technique or not, don't expect to hear them talk about it. While it's a tool many rely on, it's generally done "off the record."

MULTIPS

Typically, a mom who's had a vaginal delivery previously gets through labor in about half the time it took her the first time around. This is because her cervix dilates more quickly, she pushes more effectively, and her vagina may be a little stretched out from the last child. Obstetricians call these experienced women *multips* (which is short for *multipara*).

exact moment that you are fully dilated. Each contraction still pushes the baby's head down a little farther, saving you from some of the pushing you're about to do. Once you are diagnosed as fully dilated, you are directed to push with every contraction, which in a healthy, normal labor comes every two or three minutes.

Throughout the United States, the standard pushing position is semireclining (at roughly a twenty-degree angle) on your back with your legs up and bent, and your hands under the crooks of your knees, with elbows out. Your partner may hold a leg or a foot, the nurse will have a leg or a foot, and you will be directing all your focus at your vagina.

Pushing *with* each contraction is much more effective than pushing outside a contraction. To push effectively, take one cleansing breath, then throw your head back and fill your lungs. Drop your chin to your chest and push down like you have never pushed before. Do and think whatever you can to push—get mad, get furious!—like you're having the biggest bowel movement of your life. Hold the pressure for a count of eight, then quickly exhale, and do it again. The goal is three long pushes with each contraction.

The force of pushing and the contraction may blow small blood vessels in your face or eye. Each push engorges the perineum (the area between the vagina and the rectum), while the baby's head prevents the blood from draining after the contraction. The whole area can swell up and turn blue. Your obstetrician or nurse may massage your perineum with mineral oil or some other lubricant to stretch the vagina and ease the baby's passage. The aim here is to help the baby ease out in a controlled manner and prevent injury to the maternal tissues.

The pressure on the rectum is intense, and almost every woman gets hemorrhoids in labor. Some say they are the worst part of their postpartum experience, while others do not even notice them. Generally speaking, the later in pregnancy hemorrhoids show up, the quicker they depart. So if they pop up in the last hour of labor, they will probably go away within the week. If you have already had them for five months before labor, they might not go away so quickly. The veins will ultimately drain, but your rectum will probably not look quite the same.

While all this is going on, everyone is looking at your crotch. Sometimes, it's possible to set up a mirror so you can see too, although this can be pretty frustrating because as you push you can see the baby come out an inch or so, only to slide back nine-tenths of an inch as you stop pushing.

If the baby is of normal size and position (see page 199) and you have a nice-size pelvis, you should deliver within two hours of pushing. With a potent, numbing epidural, most obstetricians allow a third hour if the patient requests it. After the third hour, there are diminishing returns. You're tired and not pushing effectively, the vagina is bruised and swollen, the hemorrhoids look like African violets, and the baby's skull needs a break. It's time for a C-section (see page 228).

DON'T FORGET DISCRETION

Once while making postpartum rounds, I heard a patient's husband regaling his sister with tales from the labor: "...and then she threw up, she was scratching herself and whimpering, then screaming." Of course, the sister had a glorious, "natural" delivery by a stream somewhere, and even I felt like she was gloating. I pulled the husband out into the hallway and suggested he reconsider how private these stories were to his wife. What goes on in the delivery room stays in the delivery room.

STRATEGIC PLANNING

Even at hospitals like mine, with obstetrical anesthesiologists available 24/7, there are busy times when there may be a wait for an epidural. Every so often, I have to go to my patient and say, "Look, you're five centimeters and you're doing very well. Our anesthesiologist is going to do a C-section now, which will take about forty-five minutes. During this time, you will not be able to get an epidural if you want one. Do you want it now, or do you want to wait?" Half of them say, "I'll take it." The other half say, "I'll wait." As soon as it's too late, the second half suddenly wants their epidurals. Just remember, if you get caught in an unavoidable wait, you don't want the anesthesiologist rushing with your epidural or anyone else's.

Pain Relief

While no one wants you to be in terrible agony, it makes sense to wait for pain relief until you are in real pain. For most women, this is after their membranes are ruptured, their contractions are three minutes apart, and they have to breathe through every contraction. Women who receive pain relief before they are really in an active labor pattern risk slowing down the whole process.

Epidurals

The standard for pain relief in labor is the *epidural,* so named because anesthetic is injected around the *dura,* or the casing of the spinal cord. The spinal cord is at the core of the nervous system. This delicate tissue is surrounded by protective fluid, which is contained by the dura like a balloon. There is empty space between this vital package and the bones that make up the spine, which is where the medicine in an epidural injection goes—that is, *epi* (around) the dura. Often, quite a lot of numbing anesthetic was required to address the patient's pain, which could make it difficult for her to move from the waist down. This would also compromise the patient's pushing ability, because she was so numb she couldn't feel anything at all.

Most hospitals and doctors have adjusted the procedure to include a *subdural* (that is, into the spinal fluid) narcotic injection to combat common problems with the traditional procedure. The newer cocktail is sometimes called a *walking epidural,* even though most women in active labor are not interested in taking a stroll. The new epidural-subdural cocktail provides for the same pain relief, but with much less anesthetic, allowing for better motor function and ability to feel and push.

If you are in a hospital with a dedicated, round-the-clock obstetrical anesthesiologist, you will be able to get an epidural anytime up to half an hour before delivery, which is typically when you are fully dilated if this is your first child or eight centimeters if you're a multip. That's the deadline, because the epidural takes at least ten minutes to work after the time it takes the anesthesiologist to perform the procedure (roughly twenty minutes). If you get to the hospital with only half an hour to spare, the medical staff will tend to focus on more pressing matters to ensure your well-being, such as putting you on an IV for hydration. You may also be told that it's too late for an epidural if you are at a hospital where the anesthesiologist has to be paged (and may be at home in bed), and you are already six centimeters dilated. In this case, your obstetrician will probably factor in travel time, and if she figures that by the time the anesthesiologist gets there you'll be half an hour from delivery, she may tell you it's too late.

Once you're in the rhythm of a good labor, an epidural can only help things progress. Additionally, patients who experience some (ten minutes to an hour) active labor tend to appreciate their pain relief with diminished fear and anxiety about the epidural. If, for example, you're still worried about the needle, then you can probably wait. No one should be foisting an epidural on you; however, chances are that eventually you'll be asking for it.

The procedure for an epidural—or the newer epidural cocktail that includes a narcotics injection—typically is done with the patient lying down on her side, although some anesthesiologists request that their patients sit on the edge of the bed. Either way, you'll be asked to arch your back like a cat, maximizing the space between the vertebrae. Then the anesthesiologist swabs the area with a cold antiseptic, as is done before a blood test, and injects a little local anesthetic to numb the area. She then injects morphine into the dura and passes a catheter through the bore of the needle into the epidural space for the numbing anesthetic. The anesthesiologist removes the needle and tapes the flexible catheter in place so she can readily give the patient more anesthetic as it wears off. In some hospitals, that catheter can be hooked up to a computerized drip to provide continuous pain relief.

The most common drawback of the newer epidural cocktail is that most women get very itchy from the narcotic for about twenty to thirty minutes. Some women don't, and most don't care. If you are uncomfortably itchy, ask for some Benadryl. Another innocuous event associated with most epidurals is a brief deceleration in the fetal heart rate. This is anticipated, monitored, rarely significant, and happens less and less frequently as we become more proficient with this anesthetic tool.

There are extremely rare health risks associated with an epidural. Less than 0.1 percent of the time, a little nick in a vessel in the epidural space sends the medication right into an artery. This can lead to convulsions, which anesthesiologists are prepared to treat. It's possible to administer an epidural too high, which can numb and/or paralyze areas above the waist until the medication wears off. In the worst of these cases, the patient's chest becomes

BE GENTLE WITH YOUR ANESTHESIOLOGIST

Anesthesiologists are unique among doctors in that they typically deal with immobile patients in a nice, quiet operating room. An epidural can be chaotic. The patient is often trying to hold still but could get a contraction at any moment and want to pause the operation. Anesthesiologists can be especially sensitive to performance anxiety, and they often ask all nonmedical people to leave the room. The added pressure of having people watch you perform this delicate procedure is not good for doctor or patient. Don't be upset if the anesthesiologist asks your husband to leave the room; the nurse will be there at every step along the way.

paralyzed and she may require some help breathing until the epidural wears off. The good news is that she will continue dilating during this time.

The most serious complication is when the epidural causes a hematoma (a small blood clot) inside the epidural space, which can end up pressing on a nerve. Although anesthesiologists have been known to have nightmares about epidural hemotomas, they almost never happen. In thirty-five years, I've *heard* of this happening only one time in a nonobstetrical case.

Nonepidural Pain Relief

If you can't get or don't want an epidural, there are injectable analgesics. The most commonly used in labor is a narcotic called Demerol (the generic name is meperidine). Demerol is *somewhat* effective with the pain; as the nurses say, "It takes the edge off."

Demerol is most often given to women in very long or very uncomfortable prodromal labor. Demerol can be nauseating, so it is often given with antinausea medication and/or a mild sedative to reduce anxiety. On it's own, Demerol can be very sedating and helps women who are uncomfortable catch some sleep. Sometimes when

THEN THERE ARE FREAK COMPLICATIONS

After one delivery, the anesthesiologist reported to me that the catheter was inexplicably stuck in the patient's epidural space. Lucky for me, this particular patient happened to come from a family with a number of medical professionals, so we had a conference in the waiting room. The consensus was to simply pull harder. We gave the patient some Valium and told her to lie on her side. I pulled her head to her knees, to separate the vertebrae as much as possible. The anesthesiologist began pulling on the catheter, trying to get it out without breaking it. Sweat was dripping down his face. All of a sudden, *pop!*—out it came. It turned out there was a knot in the catheter—a one-in-a-million aberration. The patient was just fine, and the anesthesiologist probably had the catheter bronzed.

A BRIEF HISTORY OF OB PAIN RELIEF

In historical efforts to provide pain relief in labor, doctors have occasionally overdone it. In the 1950s and 1960s, Demerol with scopolamine was often used because these drugs were more potent when combined. Scopolamine had the added questionable benefit of making women in labor forget their whole experience, which could be a good thing because scopolamine is also a truth serum and is extremely uninhibiting. Women in labor would run down the halls naked or call out an unknown man's name. Husbands were not allowed in the labor room in order to protect the privacy of these women. Thankfully, epidurals are a vast improvement.

the prodromal patient wakes up afterward, she's contracting more efficiently. Of course, if an epidural is not available or is contraindicated, then Demerol is better than nothing for pain relief in active labor as well.

Demerol, like other narcotics, is a respiratory depressant; when people overdose and die from narcotics, it's because they simply stop breathing. A woman in labor does not have to worry about drifting off and ceasing to breathe, because every three minutes she gets woken up by the pain of a huge contraction. This means that the woman in active labor can tolerate quite a lot of Demerol. However, because Demerol crosses the placenta and therefore gets to the baby, obstetricians try to avoid giving Demerol in the last two hours preceding delivery. Although the Demerol poses no risk to the baby in utero, if the mother has a lot of Demerol in the last two hours before delivering, it's possible that the baby is so sedated that he doesn't breathe right away at birth. If it's impossible to avoid giving the mother Demerol leading up to delivery, a pediatrician stands by to take care of the baby at birth. Sometimes, a little stimulus (rubbing the back or tickling the toes, for example) is all the baby needs to perk up. If that doesn't work, the pediatrician will give the baby a shot of the antidote to Demerol (called Narcan), which is perfectly safe and wakes the baby immediately.

AN OBSTETRICAL NURSE WEIGHS IN ON PAIN RELIEF

Obstetrical nurses see more deliveries than anyone else, and perhaps they, better than anyone, are excellent predictors of how an
individual woman's labor might go. These professionals are far more
likely to work with your nonmedical requests, such as music or aromatherapy, if they think you have a chance at making it through the
delivery using these nonconventional methods instead of painkillers.
As one nurse says, "If you show up at the hospital eight centimeters
dilated, I'll jump through hoops for you. I'll bounce on the ball, play
your CDs, and do whatever you want. But if you come in insisting
you're not going to get pain relief, and you're one centimeter dilated
and crawling around on the floor shrieking in pain already, give me a
break."

For some reason, nowadays it seems like having a "natural" childbirth (that is, one without pain relief) is a heroic and virtuous choice.
I have had patients refuse pain medication, then later ask, "Aren't you
proud of me?" And I've had patients who felt ashamed about "caving
in" and asking for an epidural, even though over 95 percent of the
deliveries at my hospital include epidurals. Of the remaining 5 percent, some were too late for an epidural, some patients delivered in
the cab, and some were intentionally unmedicated.

Do not look at your sister-in-law's easy labor and delivery by
the stream and think, "If she can do it, I can, too." Some women
seem to have a very functional uterus—their contractions are efficient, the cervix changes at a nice, even pace, and the baby gets right
to where it should be. These women are *lucky*. For many women,
these things don't happen in sync, and the pain of labor and delivery can be long and intense. In the end, there are no awards for the
woman who skipped the drugs.

Have no illusions. Labor hurts like hell and pain relief is not a
frivolous bonus. The anesthesiologist Gilbert J. Grant, author of the
book *Enjoy Your Labor* (Russell Hastings Press, 2005), reports that 7
percent of women who go through labor without pain relief sustain
posttraumatic stress disorder—they have nightmares and flashbacks
that make them anxious and jittery. There's also a higher incidence
of postpartum depression in "natural" situations. Along with providing relief from the pain, an epidural or Demerol helps to relax the

vagina, making transit much easier for the baby. Women without pain relief tend to have tight, closed vaginas. Finally, women who have an epidural tend to participate in and enjoy their labor more than just grimly trying to get through it.

I've spoken to doctors who specialize in pain management, who express amazement that the labor and delivery unit is the only part of the hospital where pain is considered to be par for the course. No one asks before gall bladder surgery, "Do you want anesthesia or should we remove your gall bladder *naturally?*" Pain relief is part of the doctor's code, and it so happens that these days we can treat pain in labor within very safe parameters.

If you're thinking that women have done this—given birth—for millennia and that the pain is just a natural part of the process, here are two things to think about: First, throughout the ages women have died giving birth. In New York City in 1900, 1 percent of women who went into labor did not survive. Second, "natural" is not always best. Cancer is natural. Heart defects are natural. Diabetes is natural. Would you treat these ailments? Would you deny your new baby surgery to correct her cleft palate because surgery is not "natural"? Would you avoid infertility treatments because they're not "natural"? Do you wear glasses and take aspirin? Why become so rigid and righteous at the time in your life when you will be most in need of "unnatural" measures?

Of course, doctors, nurses, and hospitals are not perfect, but your odds are much better with medicine than without it. One in thirteen thousand women in the United States dies in pregnancy. In Afghanistan, where obstetricians are in short supply, pregnancy is the leading cause of death for women of childbearing age. Keep an open mind about all aspects of labor, including C-sections and pain relief.

One older form of anesthesia that certain cases may call for or certain small hospitals may still rely on is the *pudendal,* an injection of local anesthetic into the pudendal nerves that go to the perineum (the crotch area). These nerves are on either side of the pelvis and can be accessed through the vagina or the perineum. It can be tricky to administer a pudendal and it offers little pain relief during labor, but it can help with delivery. If this is the only pain relief option offered to you, take it. Sometimes patients who are very far along get a pudendal if it's too late for an epidural.

Episiotomy

An *episiotomy* is an incision made by the deliverer (a midwife or doctor, usually) to widen the vaginal opening. The purpose is to cut down on trauma to maternal tissue, preventing future vaginal health issues like prolapse and incontinence, as well as providing a wider, faster, and safer route for the baby. This practice was adopted as standard obstetrical procedure in the 1920s without much scientific analysis. While some obstetricians still perform episiotomies routinely, and certain cases call for them, the evidence suggests that they are generally unnecessary.

In the last decade, doctors have examined whether or not episiotomies actually do encourage vaginal health and have found that Kegel exercises are a much more effective means of preventing problems like prolapse and incontinence. A Kegel exercise is like strength training for your vagina; simply clench the vaginal muscle and relax it. It may be easiest to remember to do these exercises during urination by trying to stop the flow of urine several times while on the toilet.

Recently, doctors also started to consider that episiotomies may make it easier for vaginal tissue to tear. Just as a piece of material can more easily keep ripping after an initial cut has been made into

NEVER SAY NEVER

Some doctors still do episiotomies routinely, while others flatly refuse to ever consider them. Neither position is optimal. Episiotomies still have their place as the exception, not the rule. For example, a large baby that can get stuck at the halfway point for hours may be delivered more quickly with the aid of a small incision at the vaginal opening.

FECAL INCONTINENCE

In the past, doctors treated the woman's rectum pretty cavalierly during childbirth. Decades later, gynecologists are finding that their older patients who experienced a fourth-degree laceration during childbirth are struggling with fecal and urinary incontinence. Most women find their bowel function somewhat changed after a fourth-degree laceration; usually, they cannot hold their gassy emissions as well as they used to. These days, there's a much greater sense of urgency around protecting the rectum; doctors are less likely to cut a large episiotomy, which could extend into the rectum, and instead recommend a C-section.

it, when an incision is made from the vagina toward the rectum, it's easy for that tear to extend into the rectum, creating a fourth-degree laceration (see page 192).

There are two types of episiotomies: *median* and *mediolateral*. The median is an incision between the vagina and the rectum and is more frequently performed because it is where the perineum most often tears in labor anyway. The median incision also has the advantage of separating muscles where they meet as opposed to cutting into discrete muscle tissue. The mediolateral episiotomy is a diagonal cut from the posterior wall of the vagina toward the inner thigh in one direction or the other. Because this approach cuts through muscles, it hurts more and is harder to suture. The mediolateral provides more space for the excessively large baby or an alternative for the patient with a short perineum, because when there is relatively little distance between the vagina and the rectum, the median cut carries a greater risk of extending into the rectum.

In labor, vaginal tissue frequently tears a little in several places, and the argument in favor of an episiotomy is that the procedure offers a controlled laceration rather than an unpredictable tear. Doctors have ominously said to their patients, "You don't want to tear, do you?" That makes it sound worse than it usually is. A *first-degree* laceration is when there is a break in the superficial tissue of the vagina and/or the mucous membranes. This is pretty common. A *second-degree* laceration means the underlying tissue is also involved, just like in an episiotomy, only the "natural" lacerations are irregular and unpredictable. A *third-degree* laceration extends into the muscles around the rectum and happens very rarely without an episiotomy. Finally, the *fourth-degree* laceration extends from the vagina to the rectum so that there's a gaping hole where the perineum once was. The chances of this are extraordinarily remote without an episiotomy.

The Baby During Labor

Throughout labor, the baby is still attached to the umbilical cord, which is still attached to the placenta, which is still attached to the wall of the uterus. This system is almost always able to sustain a healthy baby through labor; however, if the baby gets into trouble, the fetal monitor immediately alerts the medical team. It should comfort you to know that while labor may be difficult for you, at least you don't need to be anxious about how it's affecting your baby because he will be under constant surveillance. If the medical team thinks that he is in trouble, you will have an emergency C-section.

The stages of labor from the baby's perspective are *engagement, descent, internal rotation, extension, restitution, external rotation,* and *delivery.* Obstetricians chart the baby's position by using the bones on the head as a map. The *occiput* is the back bone of the baby's head. The *parietals* are the two side bones, and then there are two frontal bones (the forehead). In a newborn, these are all free floating like continental plates, with spaces between them called *suture lines. Fontanelles* are the soft spots where suture lines meet.

Engagement is when the widest part of the baby's head is at the narrowest part of the maternal pelvis. At that point, the pelvis is wider than it is tall; in other words, there's more distance from hip to hip than from belly to back. This dictates that the baby adopt a transverse, or sideways, head position.

At the ischial spines, the pelvis is broader from front to back than from side to side, so the baby has to rotate the head to the facedown position. The baby must also flex the head to negotiate the midpelvis. Since the jaw is one of the last bones to ossify, a baby can bury its face in its chest. This presents the back of the head at the vaginal opening, while the contractions continue to push the baby out and down, toward the rectum. Eventually, the baby has to extend the head slowly out of the pelvis until the chin plops over the perineum and the head is out.

During this process, the baby's skull accommodates the tight passage by *molding,* which occurs when one of the freely floating bones in the baby's skull slips under another, diminishing the skull's overall diameter. In many cases, the baby's head has been hitting a pelvic bone for hours during labor. This can traumatize the baby's head, leading to swelling called *caput succedaneum.* The swelling goes down within twenty-four hours, but it can look dramatic at first.

What You (Could) Bring to the Hospital

Obviously, there is no absolutely perfect list of what you will want to have with you at the hospital; if you are a music person, that might be important. If you find a specific item comforting, like a pillow or a stuffed animal, bring it, just don't expect to be taking anything that was in bed with you home again after you've been through the

STAY ON TASK

A patient and her husband were followers of an obscure belief system that required a silent delivery room where the first thing the baby would hear was the name of God. The husband asked that no one speak until he had a chance to whisper in the baby's ear. I complied. However, when the baby was delivered the father went to la-la land for a few minutes. I (quietly, of course) waved and signaled to him to move along and perform his ritual. When he finally got the message he quietly whispered something into the baby's ear.

If you're going to follow a particular ceremony in the delivery room, or even just take a picture, stay focused and get it done.

mess of labor and delivery. I tell my patients to bring what they'd want for a weekend away from home if they were going to spend the whole weekend in their pajamas.

- *Ice/lollipops:* Many Lamaze instructors recommend having ice pops or lollipops during labor. These are to get the bad taste out of your mouth, not for nutrition. Clear ice pops are best because they are the easiest to vomit up later. Don't bring anything that requires active digestion, like chunky fruit bars. Small pieces of hard candy are questionable because the surprise of a contraction could result in choking. Lollipops are not only safer, they're also easier to hand off to a coach or nurse during a contraction.

- *Music:* You can bring a little stereo or speakers for your iPod. I've heard all sorts of sounds that are supposed to be soothing: wind chimes, oceans, classical music. Bring what you think you'd like to listen to.

- *Aromatherapy:* Potpourri or aromatherapy oils heated by electricity are fine. Anything that requires flame is not fine. No incense, no candles. Even Sabbath candles are forbidden, although most hospitals provide electric menorahs so observant Jewish women can turn the bulbs and pray.

- *Camera:* Flashes are discouraged by many hospital administrators, so try to find a camera that functions well with indoor lighting.

- *Comfortable clothes:* The hospital provides a gown for labor, but be sure to pack for the postpartum period, which is two to four days. Bring personal toiletries, lots of pajamas, and some slippers. If you're going to try breast-feeding, bring a nursing nightgown (the kind with slits for your nipples). Hospitals tend to be hot, but also public. Layering is a good idea so you can cover yourself up when you go to the nurse's station to pick up a Percocet.

- *Phonebook:* I've seen patients fill out their birth announcements the day after delivery. Feel free to bring stationery, your address book, a cell phone, and, of course, your cell phone charger. A nice trashy book or some magazines can also prove useful.

- *Food:* Hospital food is notoriously bad, so consider packing some snacks or ask your partner to bring you some takeout. Certainly feel free to eat foods you haven't had in a while, such as raw tuna, rare beef, and unpasteurized dairy products. I saw a gestational diabetic in the recovery room with a milk shake; she had been dreaming of it for months and her husband brought it for her.

- *Gifts:* A mom who's just been through labor may not be thinking about gifts, but after a little rest she is likely to enjoy receiving a pretty package. Partners often give the mother of their child gifts postpartum, especially if they've been in the delivery room and seen what went on in there. There are other, better reasons to have the father of your child there; he should be involved in your health and the health of your baby. But a gift box is always nice.

- *Lip balm:* You may want some goo for your lips; you'll be huffing and puffing for a while and your mouth will be dry. There's no reason to add chapped lips to the list of potential discomforts.

- *Pillows?* Lamaze instructors frequently seem to recommend bringing all sorts of pillows and/or bedding. If you have money to spare, by all means, bring linens. But they're not necessary. I've seen plenty of expensive designer bedding get ruined. The pillows themselves are often lost.

- *Glasses?* Rarely will an obstetrician ask you to take your contact lenses out in labor, but it's possible, so bring your glasses. (I haven't heard of asking a patient to remove false teeth, but it's also conceivable. If you have a prosthetic limb that's difficult to clean, better to take it off beforehand.)

- *Interpreters:* Hospitals often have a staff member who speaks a foreign language, especially if it's widely used in the local community. Hospitals should also have someone on staff who can sign and translate for deaf patients. However, those who are hearing impaired or do not speak English may find it more efficient to bring their own interpreter.

- *Seeing Eye dogs:* A patient in my hospital had a blind husband with a Seeing Eye dog. He refused to leave the dog outside, and when she ultimately needed a caesarian section, he insisted the dog come into the operating room. The nurses were all trying to put a mask, hat, and four little booties on the dog when the hospital supervisor sent word that no animals were allowed in the operating room. Needless to say, pets should stay at home. If you bring a working animal to the hospital, do not expect it to be welcome everywhere.

A Doula?

A *doula* is a nonmedical companion in labor, like an assistant coach. There are few, if any, professional requirements for being a doula. They're not midwives, doctors, or even necessarily nurses. They do all sorts of other things: They can come to your house in early labor and sit with you during those long prodromal hours, rubbing your back, making you tea, and helping you in the shower. A doula should be comforting and maternal, making you feel like you're back in the proverbial village with the other, older women all around you. Doulas can be helpful, supportive, and encouraging.

The advantage of having a doula is probably greater now than ever. Nursing shortages are relatively common, and you may not feel as connected as you should to your obstetrician. Finally, women seem to be taking a great interest in creating as pleasant a delivery experience as possible. All together, these factors suggest that having another pair of experienced hands and eyes around might be a smart idea.

Be warned, however, that having a doula present can complicate the situation. As things heat up, it can be easy for an experienced doula to sideline the inexperienced partner. Some men are especially resistant to being involved in labor, and doulas make it easier for them to stay unengaged by taking over all the little things they

DOULAS AND DOCTORS: A DELICATE DANCE

Obstetricians tend to hate doulas, and I am no exception. First of all, it's just distracting to have another person around who wants to be included in everything that's going on. Particularly aggressive doulas can also interrupt an obstetrician's communication with the patient by giving priority to their own personal issues. A doula's job is to pay attention strictly to you, the patient. A doula is not qualified to engage the doctor in an adversarial conversation about your episiotomy or to instruct you to push one way while the doctor is telling you something else. These situations can be unpleasant. If you must have a doula, talk to your obstetrician ahead of time so both you and the doula know what her role in the delivery should—and should not—be.

could be doing, like holding the mom's hand, encouraging her to breathe, walking with her, and rubbing her back. Some husbands see the doula doing these things and take it as a sign that they can leave, sleep, or sit with the grandparents. Some couples are grateful for the doula's involvement because both of them know the guy's just not going to get the job done. However, if it's important to you that your partner be very involved with your labor, a doula may not be for you.

Even the medical team can feel a little displaced by a doula. Nurses tend to spend less time in the patient's room because the doula takes over some of their nonmedical jobs, such as plumping the pillows. Worse, doulas can make waves with the obstetrician by questioning her management of the situation. If you're considering a doula, talk to your doctor about it first to be sure the three of you will be comfortable together in the delivery room.

CHAPTER 10

Labor: Abnormal

*L*abor is like a rickety bridge: On one side, you're relatively stable in pregnancy; on the other, you've got a newborn baby. You do not want to dillydally on the bridge admiring the view. Keep your eyes on the prize and move expeditiously toward motherhood. Labor is something you must get through to have a baby. There is no magic, no mysticism, and no right way to do it.

In addition to being exquisitely painful much of the time, labor is a brief window of heightened risk. Two-thirds of complications of pregnancy and childbirth occur in the critical time from active labor until the placenta is delivered, called the *intrapartum period.*

Luckily, we live in a time when we can detect many of these problems at a very early stage and, when needed, perform a caesarian section (page 228), which now carries no increased risk over a vaginal delivery. A C-section may not be the way you envision delivering your baby, but a safe alternative to a vaginal delivery can be a wonderful, lifesaving, reproduction-preserving event.

Problems with the Baby

There are two key issues with the baby that obstetricians especially look for during labor: The baby needs to be in the right position for a vaginal delivery and the placenta, cord, and baby need to function optimally throughout the intrapartum period.

Positional Problems

Obstetricians use the terms *lie, presentation,* and *position* to describe the baby's general orientation. *Lie* refers to the direction of the baby's entire body—is it parallel to the mother, and therefore *vertical,* or is it sideways, and therefore *transverse?* It could also be oblique, which means somewhere in between verticle and transverse. All babies with a nonvertical lie are in an abnormal position and are highly unlikely to be delivered vaginally. *Presentation* refers to the major body part that is closest to the cervical opening: the head, buttocks, or shoulder (which would be a transverse lie). If the head is closest, which it should be, this is called a *vertex* presentation. Therefore, normal orientation for a baby in labor is a vertex presentation, vertical lie. *Position* describes the relationship of the baby's presenting part to the maternal pelvis; because the baby rotates several times in labor, the "normal" position changes throughout the intrapartum period.

Assuming the presentation is vertex, the baby still needs to do some reorienting to make it through the maternal pelvis. The baby enters the pelvis with her head sideways, as if she was looking at your hip; then she *rotates* her head downward, so that her nose is pointing toward your spine; next, she *flexes* her head, pressing her face into her chest; and finally, she *descends* into (and ultimately out of) the pelvis. Any one of these steps—*rotation, flexion,* or *descent*—can fail to happen. In addition to making labor more painful, any departure from the ideal birth position is more likely to lead to what's called an *obstructed labor,* meaning that there's a partial, temporary, or real obstruction preventing the baby from passing through the birth canal.

When a baby is in a suboptimal position, it is standard obstetrical practice to ensure the mother is contracting effectively. The medication Pitocin (synthetic oxytocin) is often used to stimulate contractions, though this requires an evaluation of the mother's pelvis (see "Problems with Mom")—if she is too narrow, Pitocin will not help and could actually hurt. If, having evaluated the mother's pelvis and prescribing Pitocin, the baby still has not been delivered vaginally after an adequate trial of labor, which could be anywhere from twenty minutes to eight hours, depending on the particular situation, the obstetrician usually diagnoses an obstructed labor and recommends a caesarian section. The vast majority of C-sections happen because labor is simply not progressing; while doctors can't know why every patient ceases to labor effectively, the baby's position is one known cause of stalling.

Inadequate Internal Rotation

At the narrowest part of the maternal pelvis, *the ischial spines,* the baby's head should turn from sideways, facing a hip, to down, facing the rectum. Some babies turn up instead, toward the mother's navel. This position is called *occiput posterior* (as opposed to the normal position, *occiput anterior*). This is also glibly called *back labor* because the hardest part of the baby's head presses on the mother's sacrum bone, and in addition to the "standard" labor pains, every contraction ignites all the nerves of the back; women who have experienced this have described it as severe low back pain that coincides with the contraction. Some women experience back pain like this in normal labor, too, but it's virtually guaranteed when the baby is in an occiput posterior position.

Along with increased discomfort, back labor carries some unique risks, including longer and harder labor with more fetal heart irregularities. Furthermore, the mother's rectum and the baby's skull may suffer added trauma. After all of that, the chances of making it to a vaginal delivery remain reduced; women in back labor receive a C-section about half the time. If you're in back labor due to an occiput posterior position but still keen on a vaginal delivery, be prepared for more intense contractions and stronger pushing because delivering a baby in an occiput posterior position is like adding a pound to the baby's overall weight. Some doctors try to help the delivery along by attempting to manually rotate the baby's head as the mother pushes.

In addition to turning the wrong way, the baby can fail to turn at all at the ischial spines, staying sideways; this situation is called a *transverse arrest.* Because more forceful contractions can sometimes help to turn the baby, the doctor might give Pitocin to a patient in this situation. Alternatively, an epidural may also do the trick, as it can help relax the soft tissue in the pelvis and reduce any resistance. Here, too, some doctors attempt to manually turn the baby's head. However, if these measures fail, most obstetricians recommend a vaginal bypass—a C-section.

Flexion Flaws

If, after rotating her head to face downward, the baby does not flex her head, pressing her face into her chest, she is in a *deflexed* position, meaning that a wider part of the baby's head leads the way through the pelvis. This sometimes happens if a few loops of cord are around the baby's neck, preventing the chin from lowering, but it can also happen inexplicably. The baby's head may be only partly deflexed. This is called a *military position,* because it looks like the baby is a soldier at attention. A baby can also have a *face presentation,* a deflexed position in which the face leads. Babies delivered in a face presentation look a little battered, but the swelling generally goes down in a day or so.

The most difficult deflexed position for a vaginal delivery is when the baby's head is halfway between a face and a military presentation, with the brow leading the way, because this requires the widest dimension of the baby's head—from the top of the head to the chin—to pass through the birth canal. A baby presenting this way is almost always delivered via a C-section.

Descent Failures

Sometimes the baby's head simply does not enter the mother's pelvis. This can be due to a disproportion between these two bony structures, called *cephalopelvic disproportion* (CPD). However, it's not always possible to know why the baby isn't coming, so obstetricians usually call this situation *failure to descend.* This diagnosis is usually made after two hours or more of pushing, when the baby's head is stuck at zero station or higher (see page 167).

Traditionally, a trial of labor is four hours of pushing at full dilatation. If the baby is still not deliverable, even after trying mid-forceps (see page 228), then this is identified as a failed labor and a C-section is mandated.

However, today it is not necessary to go through a whole trial of labor because it's fairly easy to predict whether a woman will ultimately need to have a C-section by looking at her progress. If the baby's head does not descend or the mother fails to dilate at the rate of one centimeter an hour in active labor with good contractions, she most likely needs a C-section. Because protracted, stalled labors can lead to fever, infection, and fetal distress, obstructed labor can usually be diagnosed within three hours of when things stop progressing. Therefore a C-section is generally done earlier to avoid the health risks associated with a prolonged, nonprogressing labor.

Presentation

A *breech* presentation is when the baby's bottom half enters the pelvis first. A breech vaginal delivery is one of increasing dimensions, meaning that it's all too possible to end up with the baby's body outside the mother while the skull is still stuck in the pelvis. The baby is unable to breathe until the head comes out, and the cord is compressed between the baby's body and the mother's pelvic wall. This can compromise the child's oxygen supply, accounting for the tenfold increase in neurological deficit with breech vaginal deliveries. There is also an increased risk of fetal death. These are needless risks mothers and their obstetricians are not willing to tolerate; therefore, if you go into labor with a breech presentation, you are likely to end up with an abdominal delivery.

A WORD ON CAESARIAN RATES

It's true that the C-section rate continues to climb, and there are many good reasons for this. C-sections have come to all but replace forceps deliveries, which were extremely common three or four decades ago. There were deliveries where I would apply the forceps to the baby's head, put both feet up on the delivery table, and pull with all my might until the veins in my neck stood out. If that didn't work, I'd ask a nurse to pull on me from behind. Babies delivered this way would have bruises on their heads big enough to make them anemic. Most of them failed to breathe right away because of the shock to their brain. And then there was the extensive damage done to the mother. Doctors don't like to do this anymore when there's a safer option for the mother and the baby.

THE GOAL IS THE BEST POSSIBLE OUTCOME

I was at the nurses' station at my hospital and overheard a doctor talking to his patient about her breech presentation. The doctor said simply, "We have to do a section or the baby will die!" Then he walked off. The patient turned to us at the nurses' station and said, "In the country I come from, breeches are born all the time. Is it true they die *all* the time?" We didn't know what to say. The truth is, of course, that many healthy breech babies are delivered vaginally. I've personally delivered dozens of breeches and will still do it under specific circumstances. But do you want to take the chance that your child is going to get on the short bus to go to school? The risks are compounded by the fact that breech vaginal deliveries are not even routinely taught in American obstetrics anymore, so doctors under age 45 are likely to have very limited experience.

If a breech presentation is diagnosed before labor, the obstetrician can attempt to reorient the breech baby, in a procedure called an *external version,* whereby the doctor physically manipulates the baby into a vertex position through the mother's abdomen by pushing it around. This cannot be done with a preterm baby because if something goes wrong, the doctor needs to deliver the baby right away. The mechanics of an external version require adequate amniotic fluid and a relaxed uterus because it's almost impossible to turn the baby through a tensed, contracting uterine muscle.

Some obstetricians do an external version and send their patients home; others prefer to deliver right away because the turning may tax the cord or placenta. In the latter case, the obstetrician follows an external version with an immediate induction, which is successful at getting labor back on track up to 80 percent of the time. These women are not guaranteed a vaginal delivery; their odds revert to those of a normal, vertex presentation labor.

There are exceptions to the ironclad rule about not delivering breech babies vaginally, but the criteria are unusual and stringent. If you've had a previous vaginal breech delivery, for example, then maybe your doctor will take a chance with you. If the baby is especially small, it's not your first child, and you're in booming labor, your doctor may consider delivering you vaginally. However, be sure that you understand and accept the heightened risks; in extraordinary situations, a vaginal breech delivery may be as safe as a C-section, but only your obstetrician and you can decide what route to take.

Shoulder Dystocia

Shoulder dystocia is when the baby's head is delivered but the shoulders are stuck in the maternal pelvis. Generally this happens after a long, arduous labor and two or three hours of pushing, when the baby's head finally squeezes out and characteristically bounces back against the perineum as the shoulders hit the pelvis. This position compresses the cord between the baby and the mother's pelvis, cutting off blood to the baby.

Once the head is out, there is no going back; the baby must be delivered vaginally. And because during the entire time the baby is stuck in a shoulder dystocia position, he's not getting any oxygen, the obstetrician must do whatever she can to get the baby out as quickly as possible. This means that in shoulder dystocia situations, there is an immediate increase in delivery room activity as the obstetrician works to release the stuck shoulders. She might try lifting the mother's knees to her chest, which can widen the pubic diameter. She could try pushing in on the mother's pelvis, applying what is called *superpubic pressure,* in an attempt to get the shoulder down and out. Another approach is to rotate the baby, creating a corkscrew effect, which can help ease out one shoulder. In a pinch, the obstetrician might break the baby's clavicle (or clavicles). Although this sounds brutal, such breaks heal quickly and safely. While you may have seen doctors on television shove babies back into the uterus after the shoulder gets stuck so that they can do a C-section, this procedure has been successful only about a dozen times in this country. It's very rare and is not considered a standard obstetrical option.

The primary goal in addressing a shoulder dystocia situation is to get the baby out without any brain damage from lack of oxygen; however, the force required to accomplish this may lead to nerve damage in one or both of the arms, which is called *Erb's palsy.* This happens in about one out of every thousand shoulder dystocia situations. The majority of these children have normal limb function within the first few years of their lives; a minority have permanent compromised function to the affected arm(s).

There are factors that increase the risk of shoulder dystocia. Certainly, if you had a problem getting the baby's shoulders out at your last delivery, your obstetrician will be quick to suggest an earlier induction (before the baby gets too big) or a C-section. An extralarge baby, especially as a result of gestational diabetes, also increases the odds of shoulder dystocia. Because of this, most obstetricians at least discuss an abdominal bypass (a C-section) with women carrying very large babies before labor. However, 50 percent of the time, shoulder dystocia is unpredictable. Some women have eleven-pounders that slip right out, only to have their next, *smaller* baby get stuck in that same pelvis.

The Fetal Heart

There are two types of fetal heart monitors: external and internal. Both of these produce reports on the baby's heart rate called *tracings.* The external monitor, usually just called the fetal monitor,

DELIVERING MULTIPLES

Most obstetricians recommend a caesarian section anytime there is more than one baby to be delivered. With twins, when the lower one is vertex, there is a shot at a vaginal delivery, but only if the doctor is experienced in this procedure. If the first twin is breech, then a C-section is a must.

At my hospital, I am one of the few doctors who still attempts vaginal delivery of twins, and the procedure continues to become more rare. Back when sonography was a new technology, I delivered triplets vaginally, but only because a radiologist had told me to expect twins. After delivering Twin B I told the medical student to deliver the placenta. He said, "I don't think this is a placenta." I reached up, grabbed the foot, and delivered the third baby. Obstetricians hate surprises like that.

uses sound waves through the maternal abdomen to establish the baby's heart rate. The internal version is called the *internal scalp electrode* (ISE) and is a fine corkscrew needle that is inserted into the baby's scalp to pick up the fetal electrocardiogram (EKG). The ISE is more continuous and sensitive, but it is not more accurate than a good tracing from a regular fetal monitor. However, the ISE requires at least two centimeters' dilatation and is usually reserved for abnormal circumstances, such as a nonreassuring fetal monitor tracing, or when the external monitor is failing for some technical reason, such as the baby's position or the mother's weight. Since most women don't like the idea of a wire corkscrew in their baby's head, obstetricians tend to employ ISEs less frequently.

Fetal monitors err on the side of caution. That is, when the fetal heart rate looks good on the monitor, it means the baby is definitely fine; when the fetal heart rate looks bad on the monitor, 50 percent of the time the baby is still fine. The other 50 percent of the time, a bad result on the fetal heart monitor is indicative of a real problem in utero.

As explained in Chapter 9, any deceleration from the fetal baseline heart rate will catch the attention of your obstetrician, although some types of deceleration are nothing to worry about. *Type I decelerations* (see page 171) mirror the contraction and tend to represent a healthy baby's response to the increased pressure on his head. These are generally benign and, in fact, indicate that the baby is descending into the mother's pelvis. Similarly, *Type III decelerations* (see page 171), also called *variable decelerations* because they vary in length, configuration, and incline, are most often benign. These decelerations are unrelated to contractions; doctors hypothesize that they happen when the umbilical cord is pinched momentarily.

If your baby experiences Type III decelerations, the way your obstetrician handles them may depend on how close you are to delivery. Variable decelerations are well tolerated for an hour or so, but if they set in at the beginning of labor, the obstetrician might try some simple tools to address them. For example, she might move the patient around, from side to side, in an effort to get the baby off the umbilical cord. She might try giving the patient nasal oxygen;

although this has limited, if any, effect, it certainly does no harm. Dehydration can lower the blood volume and lower blood pressure, which can lead to fetal heart irregularities; therefore, the obstetrician may take the mother's blood pressure and provide IV fluids if blood pressure is low. The doctor may check for a prolapsed cord, which would mandate an emergency C-section. Finally, the doctor will look for a dramatic change in the cervix. Rapid dilatation can cause a sudden fetal heart rate deceleration, and very likely a quick delivery soon follows.

In the face of recurrent, profound decelerations, most obstetricians encourage a C-section. Even though doctors know that 50 percent of the time these decelerations are false alarms, there is no other way to guarantee the baby's health.

Type II decelerations are more subtle heart rate changes (of as little as twenty beats per minute), but these can indicate that the baby's oxygen supply is compromised. On the fetal monitor, a Type II deceleration begins at the peak of a contraction and lasts until well after the contraction is over. Recall that the baby does not get blood during a contraction but relies on the blood already in the pla-

MANAGING HEART DECELERATIONS

How to correctly manage fetal heart decelerations depends on many variables. For example, in a patient whose amniotic fluid is clear, who is dilated six centimeters, and who has had two Type II decelerations, I would make sure her blood pressure is normal, give her more IV fluid, turn her from one side to the other, and then do a vaginal exam to see if she's suddenly at eight centimeters with the baby's head crowning. I'd make sure the contractions aren't too close together and would possibly slow down any medication that stimulates labor. I'd also take into account the patient's age and whether or not this is her first baby. At six centimeters, thirty years of age, and a second baby, she could deliver in twenty minutes; if she went much longer than that we'd have to discuss a C-section. At six centimeters, age 40, first baby, we'd give it twenty minutes and then consider a scalp pH and/or an emergency C-section.

centa. If, at the peak of the contraction, the heart rate slows down, it means the placenta is not healthy enough to maintain the blood supply through the contraction. This is a symptom of *placental insufficiency* (see Chapter 8) and may call for further evaluation through a scalp pH.

Scalp pH

In a scalp pH test, a sample of the baby's blood is extracted to measure the acidity/alkalinity (pH). The procedure entails inserting a cone into the vagina and against the baby's head, so that a patch of the baby's head can be clearly seen and cleaned off; this requires at least four centimeters of dilatation and ruptured membranes. After inserting the cone, the doctor nicks the baby's scalp, sucking up two drops of blood for testing. The lower the pH, the more carbon dioxide is building up, and the less oxygen the baby is getting.

A pH of 7.28 is considered pretty good. The American College of Obstetrics and Gynecology considers 7.24 the lowest acceptable scalp pH level and calls for a repeat test in twenty minutes. Doctors and hospitals encourage C-sections for scalp pH levels between 7.20 and 7.24, depending on the physician, the patient, and the facility. Also depending on the medical center, a pH level of 7.19 or 7.20 calls for an *emergency* C-section.

Certain studies have suggested that the scalp pH sample is too inaccurate to be reliable. Criticism includes that it's impossible to

---

MECONIUM WARNINGS

A major factor in assessing nonreassuring fetal heart rate patterns is whether or not the amniotic fluid is clear. Baby poop, called *meconium,* in the amniotic fluid, is a sign of intrauterine discontent. Although sometimes the presence of meconium can be a completely benign event, signaling that the baby has had its first bowel movement a little early, it can also signal trouble. So although on its own the presence of meconium in the amniotic fluid is not a reason to do a section, it is a red flag.

guarantee that there's no amniotic fluid or maternal blood in the sample and that tests done right after a contraction may yield a different result than those done during or beforehand. However, although the scalp pH has come under fire lately, we have very few tools to evaluate the baby during labor, and this test can be one more data point in assessing the baby's well-being.

Problems with Mom

The biggest issue with the mother in labor is mechanics: Is her pelvis big enough to allow the baby's skull to pass? Is she progressively dilating and contracting effectively? Is she fever-free and prepared to push?

Skeletal Shortcomings

Sometimes labor progresses perfectly, but it turns out that the mother's pelvis is just too small for a vaginal delivery. In the most extreme cases, we can predict this problem; for example, dwarves or women with deformed pelvises from severe trauma are unlikely to have successful vaginal deliveries. Excessively obese women may also struggle with this because of the extra soft tissue lining their pelvises. For the majority of women, there is no way to predict whether their pelvis is adequate for the task A diagnosis that the pelvis is too small is made only after labor has stalled and there is no other explanation for it, such as the baby's position or inadequate contractions. A diagnosis could be made anywhere from twenty minutes to thirty-six hours after labor commences and is resolved by performing a C-section.

Problems with Contractions

Ineffective and/or infrequent uterine contractions can lead to a stalled labor, which may require medication and ultimately could lead to a C-section. Conversely, a patient can experience *precipitous labor,* in which the contractions come too frequently and last

NONSCIENTIFIC ASSESSMENTS

When I was a resident, the labor and delivery ward had an inconspicuous marker five feet from the ground, just inside the entrance. This was an easy way to assess whether a patient was under five feet tall, in which case we'd immediately prepare for a caesarian section (and this was in the days of the 3 percent C-section rate). Being less than five feet tall doubles the chances of having a C-section because the shorter the woman, the narrower her skeleton. Shoe size is another simple indicator of how big a woman's pelvis is—a shoe size of 5 or smaller is a pretty sure sign of a petite frame and a small pelvis.

too long. In *precipitous labor,* there are more than six contractions in ten minutes and/or the contractions last more than ninety seconds. The problem with this type of labor is that the baby never has time to recover from the contractions and the fetal monitor may show Type II decelerations. In this case, either you deliver quickly, you are given medication to slow contractions, or you have to have a C-section to spare the baby's health.

Occasionally, precipitous labor is the result of an excess dose of Pitocin, which results in what is called *hyperstimulation* (see page 217). Although this complication is a needless one caused by the medical team, the good news is that the doctor can quickly fix it by stopping the drugs, giving the baby a chance to relax.

Problems with the Cervix

Sometimes the cervix refuses to dilate, a condition called *cervical stenosis.* This can happen to anyone, though the risk rises with multiple cervical procedures like abortions or cone biopsies. There is no way to make a resistant cervix open, so this results in a C-section.

Fever During Labor

Fevers sometimes happen during long labors, though doctors don't always know why. Obstetricians assume that a fever during labor is due to labor (and not, say, the flu), and therefore the most likely cause is an infectious process going on inside the uterus, known medically as *chorioamnionitis*. After the water breaks and the uterus starts contracting, bacteria can climb up there and cause an infection.

As a woman in labor develops a fever, the baby's temperature passively rises with hers, leading to a raised heart rate in the baby, called *fetal tachycardia*. Tachycardia usually precedes any visible symptoms in the mother, such as a fever. Therefore, doctors become concerned about uterine infection at a fetal heart rate exceeding 180 beats per minute, and most obstetricians suggest a C-section if the baby's heart rate remains high.

Obstetricians try to avoid giving the feverish mother antibiotics because it can obscure tests done on the baby after delivery, called a *sepsis workup*. Instead, after delivery, the uterus, placenta, and maternal blood are cultured for infection, as are the baby's nasal secretions, blood, urine, and spinal fluid (yes, that means a spinal tap). However, because it can take two or three days for the culture results to come in, most doctors prefer to preemptively treat the baby with IV antibiotics. A baby who tests negative for all infections, can go right home with Mom, and the antibiotics are discontinued; if lab results show that there is an infection of some kind, the baby already has a three-day head start on treatment.

If the mother is on antibiotics during labor—perhaps for a preexisting health condition such as a heart problem—the baby's sepsis workup will be flawed because of the antibiotics in the bloodstream. Such results may lead to a full course of IV antibiotics once the baby is delivered because the baby's infection-free status cannot be conclusively determined. Depending on the baby's health and evolving protocols, this treatment can take anywhere from three to ten days.

Significant Preexisting Health Issues

There are women with health issues that require preventive medical intervention. For example, patients who are susceptible to infection, due to a significant heart problem or a new prosthetic device like a synthetic joint, need to take antibiotics in anticipation of labor when a lot of bacteria will enter their bloodstreams. The general idea is to kill bugs in the blood before they can cause serious problems to the mother. Prophylactic antibiotics are administered when the patient is about eight centimeters dilated or two hours before delivery. Some women's health problems can be significant enough to make any attempt at labor unnecessarily risky. Significant kidney or blood problems, for example, can pose such a threat to the life of both mother and child that the obstetrician recommends a scheduled C-section.

Vaginal Birth After Caesarian Section (VBACS)

A caesarian section leaves a scar on the wall of the uterus that is like a fault line—meaning it is weaker than the rest of the organ. Under the stress of labor, the chances of the uterus rupturing are higher after a C-section, and they are intolerably high for patients with anything other than the most standard C-section incision. For example, women who have had extensive fibroid surgery in which the uterine wall has been completely transected are not eligible for vaginal deliveries. Uterine rupture is a life-threatening situation

PLAYING WITH FIRE

I once had a patient who badly wanted a vaginal birth following a previous caesarian section, but she had been in a nonprogressing prodromal labor pattern for hours, and we agreed that if she didn't deliver by a certain time we'd have to go for another C-section. I had just walked into her hospital room to check on her when she said, "Oh! Something just ripped!" It was clear from examining her that her uterus had just ruptured because the baby's head, which had been in the pelvis, disappeared back up into the abdomen. We didn't even have time for an anesthesiologist—instead, I injected local Novocain on the skin and made a quick incision into the uterus, hastily delivering the baby. Though patient and child were perfectly fine in this situation, the lesson here is that a VBACS is risky, even in a hospital setting.

that can lead to a blood transfusion, significant surgery, a hysterectomy and, on rare occasions, death.

For women who delivered abdominally (via a caesarian section) in the past, there are many specific factors that can affect their risk of uterine rupture and, therefore, their chances for a safe vaginal delivery. Most of these factors have to do with why these patients received a C-section in the first place. For example, was it because the baby was a breech presentation or because the mother is four feet, seven inches tall and labor stalled? In the former case, a vertex presentation this time around might make a vaginal delivery reason-

---

AN OBSTETRICIAN'S EDITORIAL ON VBACS

Obstetrical cripple is a nontechnical phrase that dates back to obstetricians in the 1960s and 1970s. It reflected the widely held belief that once a woman had had a C-section, she would always have to have one for subsequent pregnancies. Of course, the word *cripple* implied that this woman was somehow not fully functional.

By the 1980s, the Vaginal Birth After Caesarian Section (VBACS) movement was starting to gather steam. Various interests took up the cause of giving women who had previously had C-sections the chance at vaginal deliveries. Insurance companies were especially supportive of the VBACS trend, because C-sections are much more expensive than vaginal births. At the time, the numbers suggested that only 0.5 percent of VBACS cases actually ruptured their uteruses in labor—meaning 199 unnecessary C-sections out of every 200 births.

Even at the height of fervent VBACS support, the C-section rate still hovered at around 40 percent for patients who had had previous C-sections. Further, with a new body of accumulated data, it became clear that the chance of uterine rupture was not 0.5 percent of VBACS cases, as had been concluded previously, but rather 2 to 5 percent. This certainly took a little wind out of the movement's sails. Another factor detrimental to the VBACS movement was that it seemed that some women simply preferred to have a C-section. A VBACS patient of mine asked, "Why didn't you let me have a section again? I didn't like this at all."

able. In the latter case, labor is likely to stall again, putting a dangerous strain on the woman's uterus. When it comes to things that do not change from pregnancy to pregnancy—like the size of the maternal pelvis—a vaginal delivery may never be in the cards.

For a woman who's had a previous caesarian section, spontaneous labor is a requirement for a vaginal delivery. A cold induction (inducing labor in a woman with no contractions or cervical changes) increases the risk of a ruptured uterus by ten to twenty times; doctors do not really know why this is the case, but statistics show a clear relationship between an induction and a ruptured uterus. Even women with effaced, dilated cervixes who are not in active labor face a five- to ten-times increased risk of uterine rupture if they are given medication to start their contractions. Using medication to augment a labor that's already in progress does not appear to increase the risk of uterine rupture, but a VBACS is most often successful and relatively safe when labor progresses naturally and efficiently.

One final, and essential, factor in determining whether a patient can have a vaginal birth after a C-section is whether the hospital is appropriately equipped to handle a VBACS. Because the chance for rupture is relatively high and dangerous with VBACS patients, ACOG requires that at all times the hospital's obstetrical team be capable of executing a caesarian section within thirty minutes of an emergency.

HEROIC MEASURES OR NEEDLESS RISK?

In the 1980s, at the height of VBACS fever, apocryphal tales surfaced of women desperate for vaginal deliveries, despite their previous C-sections. I remember hearing the story of a woman who was delivering at a regional hospital that did not meet the ACOG emergency C-section requirement. So she sat in the parking lot until she felt rectal pressure, which indicates the baby is in the pelvis and it's too late for a C-section. Whether this is true or urban legend, it is a bit like Russian roulette. Don't play with your own life and the life of your unborn child just to achieve your desired labor esthetic.

WHEN DO WE INDUCE?

- If your water breaks, but you don't go into labor
- If you're at term and the baby's not growing
- If you have a hypertensive disorder
- If you have any deteriorating medical condition
- If it is in the best interests of you and your baby to deliver pronto
- If you are one week past your due date

Inducing Labor

An induction is when doctors attempt to initiate the labor process. When there's a medical reason the baby needs to be delivered, most commonly because it is late, then the induction is *indicated.* An induction is *elective* when doctor and patient decide to induce for nonmedical reasons. In both cases, inductions are not 100 percent successful. If there's a medical reason that requires the baby to be delivered, a failed induction most often culminates in a caesarian section.

Although an induction may start a little differently than normal labor, the process tends to be very similar. First, the patient is admitted into Labor and Delivery, where she gets an IV, preliminary blood work, and a baseline fetal heart rate. Enemas used to be standard because they stimulate prostaglandins, cause contractions, and make delivery more esthetic and less stinky. They are not routine anymore; however, for women who have been constipated for a while, an enema at this point might make for a more comfortable labor. If you want one, ask for it.

If the membranes are still intact, most obstetricians suggest rupturing them—a procedure called an *amniotomy* (see page 175) to make an induction more effective. Not only does rupturing the membranes stimulate the mother's body to produce oxytocin , but it also helps to dilate the cervix.

Then the obstetrician evaluates multiple characteristics of the cervix: Is it firm or soft? What is its position? How effaced and dilated is it? These measurements, in combination with the baby's station, are boiled down to a number between 1 and 10—6 is a good score. This number becomes one of many factors that help determine how to proceed with an induction and predict whether it's likely to be successful. That said, labor is never predictable; some women with bad scores end up delivering soon thereafter, while others with excellent scores end up having C-sections.

Women with other compromising factors, such as a hypertensive disorder, and a zero score on their cervical evaluation will likely be encouraged to have a C-section instead of attempting an induction. But if everything about the pregnancy has been perfect, her doctor might go all out trying to induce. It's important to remember that indicated inductions are happening for a health reason; the more significant the indication, the sooner the doctor will want to move to a C-section.

Most obstetricians commence inductions with prostaglandins if the cervix is undilated and uneffaced. These come in several forms, but are usually put in the vagina or taken orally. Prostaglandins may not always stimulate active labor, but they reliably prime the cervix, softening it so that the next steps in the induction stand a better chance of success.

If the cervix is already dilated (more than two centimeters) but the contractions are weak, the obstetrician may skip the prostaglandins and go right to Pitocin (synthetic oxytocin). This bioidentical pituitary hormone is naturally released at many stages of labor: in response to the cervix dilating, when the membranes rupture, and with nipple stimulation as the baby breast-feeds. When the uterus is contracting ineffectively, added Pitocin can kick labor into a higher gear.

Pitocin is given intravenously at a very slow drip and increased slowly until the dose produces effective contractions. Each hospital has its own protocol for how, when, and by how much to up the dose. When the amount of Pitocin is high enough to spur stronger contractions, it can feel like a dramatic, painful shift in labor.

The biggest thing that can go wrong with an induction is over-stimulation. Even though the medication is gradually increased, the body can suddenly respond with contractions a minute apart, which is not good for the baby. Type II decelerations in the baby's heart rate are often a result of too much stimulus. If this occurs, the doctor will stop the induction by ceasing all medication. Once the contractions slow and the baby recovers, the obstetrician will recommend either another attempt at induction or a C-section, depending on the specific circumstances.

Inducing an Overdue Pregnancy

The placenta is a miracle, but it's not built to last more than nine months. The problem with an overdue pregnancy is that the placenta may start to deteriorate, delivering a diminishing supply of oxygen to the baby.

For this reason, obstetricians are very interested in accurately assessing whether their patients are overdue and, if so, by how much. They accurately predict overdue pregnancies two-thirds of the time and are most accurate with patients they have seen from the earliest point in pregnancy. Before sixteen weeks' gestation, all

IT'S *NOT* THE PITOCIN

I hear a lot of women describe their experience with Pitocin like this: "I was doing just fine. My contractions were every seven minutes, and I was on top of them. Then they gave me that horrible Pitocin, and the contractions were every two minutes and I couldn't stand it. The Pitocin was so awful, I needed an epidural." Here's the thing: Pitocin doesn't make labor more painful. In fact, when it's just the Pitocin causing contractions, they're not that bad. It's when Pitocin successfully gets you into real, efficient, active labor that it hurts. Prodromal or dysfunctional labor may give you the illusion of being in control, but this is because you are not in real, progressive labor. Most women find that active labor is really, seriously painful. It's not the drugs in your IV that are doing it to you. Pitocin is not your enemy; it's your friend. Without it, the C-section rate would likely approach 80 percent.

fetuses are about the same size, so obstetricians can diagnose the gestational age within a few days on either side. If a woman is already twenty weeks' pregnant when she sees her doctor for the first time, her due date will be less precise.

Overdue babies face a number of risks. About one-third of the time, the due date is inaccurate despite the obstetrician's best efforts, and the baby is not actually overdue. In another third of these cases, the overdue baby simply continues to grow and mature. This means the suture lines in the skull begin to fuse, and the skull becomes harder. A seven-pound baby at forty-two weeks' gestation is much more difficult to deliver than a seven-pound baby at thirty-eight weeks; it's like the difference between delivering a cantaloupe and delivering a bowling ball.

The final third of overdue babies lose weight as the placenta deteriorates. This condition is called *postmaturity,* which can be just as serious as prematurity. These babies have simply been in the uterus too long, and they emerge looking a little scrawny and wizened. They have long hair and fingernails, and their skin can peel. If these are the only problems, the baby will get past them after a bath and a haircut; the real concern with postmaturity is that it can cause permanent harm through lack of oxygen to the baby and can ultimately lead to stillbirth if and when the support systems for the baby deteriorate to the point of not functioning.

Thirty years ago, obstetricians waited until forty-four weeks to induce a post–due date pregnancy, but the rate of stillbirths was unacceptable. Today, perinatologists suggest that postdate pregnant women should be delivered at forty-one weeks. Unfortunately, inducing more women earlier means more C-sections, because not every induction is successful.

Elective Inductions

An elective induction is usually done when there is a concern that, for whatever reason, the patient may not be able to get to the hospital in time. This most often applies to women on their second or third child, because their labors are much faster, and it therefore makes sense to preempt the possibility of having a baby on the way

SOCIAL INDUCTIONS

Elective inductions have also been called *social inductions*, because they are sometimes done for utterly nonmedical reasons. For example, I had a patient whose husband was working in Alaska and flew home on weekends. She was forty weeks along and begged for me to induce her on the weekend when her husband was around. I figured that was a good argument for induction and obliged. I had another patient who wanted to be induced because the end of the month was approaching and she did not like the birthstone for the following month. It's not up to me, her obstetrician, to decide whether this is a good reason or not, only whether it's medically safe. Because she was less than a week from her due date, I saw no reason not to give her the birth day she wanted. I've induced labor for tax purposes and to make sure the child was the youngest person in his grade as opposed to oldest. As long as the patient is less than one week from her due date, it's at least her second child, and her cervix is favorable, an induction is fairly safe, so I don't quibble.

to the hospital. But a scheduled induction can be logistically necessary, as well. For example, if a patient one week shy of her due date living two hours away from the hospital turns out to be dilated four centimeters at her routine OB exam, she is likely to be sent directly to the hospital to be induced rather than sent home to wait and see what happens, especially if her last labor was short. Sometimes an elective induction makes sense because of the child care arrangements required for the patients' other children. Whatever the reason, elective inductions certainly serve a purpose and are justifiable in certain circumstances. If getting to the hospital is a concern of yours for whatever reason, discuss a scheduled induction with your obstetrician.

CHAPTER 11

Delivery

*A*fter nine months, your baby is ready to come out one way or another. The two paths available are either through your vagina or through your abdomen, and each has its pros and cons. It's like taking the scenic route versus the highway; it really doesn't matter as long as you and your baby get through it safe and sound.

Vaginal Delivery

When the baby is ready to be delivered and the doctor tells you it's time, it can be surprisingly hard to focus on pushing, especially if you have had an epidural. To help guide you, the nurse or doctor presses where you should be pushing, toward the back wall of the vagina. Some patients aren't much helped by this; others can't push without it. During this time the nurse may also pour mineral oil or lubricant into the vaginal opening and massage the perineum to stretch the vagina and reduce lacerations.

If you're looking in a mirror while you're pushing, you may notice your rectum dilate. This happens as the baby's head descends farther and butts up against it. Soon, the labia will separate a little with every push. Everyone in the room will be looking at your crotch to see the first glimpse of the baby's head, which is referred to as seeing *caput*. At the end of the contraction, the head often slides back up into the vagina. This makes for a very slow, arduous process—hence, the name *labor.*

At some point shortly after caput, the obstetrical team prepares you for the delivery. Exactly how they do this depends on the hospital—each institution has its own standard operating procedures. It used to be that most women were rushed to the delivery room at this point, but most hospitals are now equipped with what are called labor/birthing rooms, which have beds with hidden stirrups that adjust to accommodate a semirecumbent position. After caput, the nurse or doctor is likely to clean the external vaginal area and maybe slide some sterile drapes under your bottom. There's no way to sterilize the baby's entrance into the world, but we like to get it as clean as possible. Caput is also the time when a pediatrician is called in for the delivery if there is a reason to do so, such as a fetal heart irregularity, meconium in the amniotic fluid, or a previously identified problem with the baby that could require immediate attention. In a perfectly normal, uneventful delivery, there is an obstetrician or midwife, a nurse, and the patient's partner in the room, as well as a doula, if the patient has elected to have one.

A WORD ABOUT FATHERS

Sometimes expectant fathers are reluctant to be in the delivery room. I had a patient whose husband kept saying, "I don't know about going into the delivery room. It grosses me out." My answer was, "Okay, you don't have to look!" No one's asking either patient or husband to see anything he or she doesn't want to see. It might help for the father to focus on his wife's face and on holding her hand. Say, "Whatever you need, I'll get it." Husbands often come out to the nurses' station to report, "My wife thinks her epidural is wearing off" or "My wife needs to go to the bathroom." Your partner is your advocate and supporter. And although it's natural for him to balk at what can be unpleasant and icky, involving the father in childbirth ensures he won't feel like a third wheel.

HOW MANY IS TOO MANY IN THE DELIVERY ROOM?

Some women like the idea of having any and all family members—their own and their husband's parents, siblings, and so on—present for the birth of their child. If you feel this way, then go ahead and invite them all. First, consider this: Having a lot of people makes for a crowded and tumultuous delivery room; furthermore, try to imagine how you'll feel about your brother or father-in-law being present for all the blood, feces, and vaginal display typical of a normal delivery. If this thought makes you uncomfortable, perhaps only your partner should be present at the birth; some people feel that delivery is the time when a couple becomes a family, so only those three people need to be there.

The next stage of delivery after caput is *crowning*, which is when the widest diameter of the baby's head has gone under the pubic bone and through the pelvic outlet, so that one-third to one-half of the head is out during contractions. To maintain control of the head, the obstetrician feels through the soft tissue of the perineum for the protuberance of the baby's chin. She helps to maneuver it out and over the perineum. Her other hand sits on the top of the baby's head. Once the obstetrician has the baby's head in her hands, she will instruct you to stop pushing.

Good vaginal deliveries happen in a controlled manner. The pressure should be even and gradual on the baby's skull, so there's less trauma to the brain. Control is essential to limit lacerations to the mother as well.

Once the baby's head is completely out and free, it naturally turns sideways to align with the shoulders, a process called *restitution*. The obstetrician uses *external rotation* to continue that motion to bring the baby's shoulders vertical in the maternal pelvis so the baby faces the mother's inner thigh. This is the optimal position to deliver the shoulders because it allows the obstetrician the greatest maneuverability.

Before delivering the shoulders, however, the doctor feels around the neck to check for the umbilical cord, which gets wrapped around the baby's neck in 10 percent of deliveries. If the cord is loose enough around the neck, the doctor might simply pull it over the baby's head to get it out of the way. If it's tight around the neck, the patient has to try not to push while the doctor clamps the cord and cuts it so the delivery can continue. Doctors try to keep the baby in place in such cases to avoid rupturing the cord, which would bleed profusely, at the baby's expense.

After the head is out and any issues with the cord have been taken care of, the obstetrician uses what looks like a small turkey baster to remove the mucus from the nose and mouth before the baby takes the first breath. Because the chest is still encased in the maternal pelvis, the pressure squeezes much of the mucus out. This is especially important if there was meconium in the amniotic fluid.

At this point, the deliverer should have one hand on each of the baby's cheeks and should be facing the same direction as the baby. The doctor then gently pulls down to release the top shoulder from under the mother's pubic bone, then pulls up to get the other shoulder. She puts her hand on the back of the baby's neck, slides the other hand down the baby's back, grabs the baby's buttocks, and flips the baby out onto the mother's belly. Now everyone's excited! Everybody coos over the baby. The nurse towels the baby off so he can have a good cry and clear all the mucus. The obstetrician clamps the cord twice so that the blood doesn't leak out as it is cut—a step often ceremoniously completed by the father

While the baby is being evaluated, suctioned, and placed in your arms, the obstetrician has to worry about the placenta. There is a specialized layer in the uterus called the *decidua basalis* that is designed to make the placenta highly peelable; this layer is like the paper side of a sticker. The placenta is just a glob of glands that should have already separated somewhat from the wall of the uterus immediately following delivery. As the uterus contracts, it separates itself from the placenta. Once it's completely unattached, there is usually a gush of blood and the uterus changes shape.

Most obstetricians wait five to ten minutes for this to happen naturally before commencing some uterine massage. Some gently pull the cord and push on the uterus, though they shouldn't pull too hard; if it breaks, the doctor has to go in manually for the placenta.

Less than 1 percent of the time, the placenta refuses to come out. After about fifteen minutes, obstetricians call this a *retained placenta,* and it requires evaluation. Even if the placenta has been only partially expelled at this point, it's important to make sure the entire placenta is removed, because any tissue left behind will eventually become infected and could cause hemorrhaging.

One approach to emptying the uterus is the *manual removal of the placenta,* whereby the obstetrician puts her whole hand in the uterus and attempts to peel the placenta off the uterine wall. If the epidural has worn off, the patient needs more medication for this procedure. If she didn't have an epidural, she requires general anesthesia. Another approach would be to use a *horse curette,* which is like a long, hollow tablespoon used to gently scrape the placenta off the uterine wall.

Less than 10 percent of retained placentas (as in, occurring in less than 0.1 percent of overall deliveries) are due to a missing dedicua basalis. In these cases, the placenta grows directly into the wall of the uterus, called a *placenta accreta,* or even through the entire thickness of the uterus, called a *placenta percreta.*

A good sonographer should always find a potential placenta accreta on a routine sonogram at some point in the second half of the pregnancy. The risks of the condition increase with a previous caesarian section, the number of children, and the mother's age. Placenta percretas can burrow into neighboring organs like the bowel or the bladder; therefore, once the condition is diagnosed during pregnancy, the obstetrician is likely to encourage a scheduled C-section with a team of specialists on hand because it is virtually impossible to remove a placenta that's become part of the uterine wall without extensive blood loss. The obstetrician would also discuss the high probability that if the bleeding cannot be stopped, the patient will require a hysterectomy. Although doctors prefer to avoid having to remove the uterus, they will do it to save your life.

Operative Vaginal Techniques

Operative vaginal techniques can be used to shorten the second stage of labor. They can also come in handy when the caput is visible but the mother is simply exhausted and can't continue. Finally, these are called for when there's a fetal heart irregularity that mandates getting the baby out immediately. Your delivery depends on your doctor and the technique with which she is most experienced.

Vacuum Extractor

This is a relatively easy approach to a tough delivery, usually for a stalled labor where the baby is relatively close to the vaginal opening. It does not require much skill—it basically just involves using a rubber cup, applied to the top of the baby's head, to literally suck the baby out.

The major advantage of a vacuum extractor is that it does not require an experienced practitioner; obstetricians who have limited forceps experience frequently train with a vacuum extractor instead. It's almost impossible to pull too hard, because the seal between the vacuum and the baby's head breaks before any damage can be done (although the fontanelles should be avoided). The downside is that this can lead to a huge swelling on top of the baby's head; therefore, it shouldn't be attempted more than twice.

SCANT ALTERNATIVES TO A HYSTERECTOMY

Unfortunately, in the event of an accreta, the only possible alternative to a hysterectomy is to cut the cord at the cervix and then keep the woman under watch in the hospital, where she's relatively safe in the event of infection or hemorrhage. It can take weeks for the placenta to deteriorate and come out on its own. It's also possible to make a surgical attempt to remove the accreta; once you manipulate it, if bleeding commences there is no way to stop it except to remove the organ. Only twice in my career have I seen an accreta that did not result in a hysterectomy.

Forceps

While forceps are among the oldest obstetrical devices, they have extremely limited application these days: only 3 to 5 percent of deliveries involve forceps. Obstetricians today typically use forceps only for *low* and *outlet* forceps deliveries. Both outlet and low forceps deliveries are called for when the mother can't push anymore or when she's not progressing past caput. The doctor might also use forceps to deliver immediately because of concern for the baby's well-being. Some doctors use forceps to control deliveries, claiming that they protect the baby's head from the soft tissue at the vaginal opening.

Low forceps are used when the baby's head is completely in the pelvis, meaning it is visible when you separate the labia. This means that the widest part of the baby's head is far past the narrow ischial spines—the equivalent of being at least at +1 station. These situations call for a little traction to pull the baby down another inch below the pubic bone and then extend the head.

Outlet forceps are used when caput is visible, and their use involves no pulling on the baby's head whatsoever. The procedure is designed to simply extend the baby's chin over the perineum.

The prerequisites for good application of forceps are critical to a successful outcome. These include adequate anesthesia, as forceps are an additional item in the pelvis and are painful to the mother. Even in superemergent situations, most obstetricians at least give their patient a pudendal block (see page 189) if there isn't an epidural already in place. Second, the person applying the forceps has to be experienced with the device and in determining the position of the baby's head.

In the hands of an expert, low and outlet forceps deliveries are probably better controlled than those that use the vacuum extractor, but finding an expert in this outdated art can be difficult. It's important that the forceps blades be placed appropriately on the baby's head; they're supposed to slip in away from the eye, past the ear, and hook under the baby's cheekbone. There's a knack to putting them on that should make the two pieces fit together easily and snugly against the baby's head.

Obstetricians also used to use forceps to deliver babies from even higher up in the maternal pelvis, called mid- and high-forceps deliveries. Midforceps are for babies at zero station, and high forceps are for babies who are not even at zero station. However, midforceps are only rarely used and high forceps are unknown in modern obstetrics because C-sections are so much safer now.

Fundal Pressure

A vaginal delivery technique called *fundal pressure* involves pushing down on the baby through the mother's abdomen. The concept of fundal pressure does not appear in any textbook and is not taught in any medical school class; it is one of obstetrics' biggest secrets. The risks are poorly understood because this technique is not documented. In other words, if a patient's uterus ruptures during fundal pressure, her records would be unlikely to show that fundal pressure was used. For these reasons, this technique should be used only rarely in the United States. However, it seems to continue to crop up in delivery rooms across the country. The frustration of seeing a woman stalled in pushing drives many doctors, nurses, and doulas to resort to fundal pressure.

Fundal pressure was (and is, in some places) most often used in situations where the mother can't or won't push. For example, forty years ago, women in labor were sometimes heavily sedated so the baby's head would be right at the opening, but they would not be able to push. To get the baby out, the obstetrician would use her arm to push down from the top of the uterus. This method is also used

---

YOU HAVE TO PUSH

I know an obstetrical nurse who was in the Peace Corps several decades ago. In the village where she served, some of the upper-crust women felt it was beneath them to push during labor. In delivery, these women would lie on their backs while the midwife would squat on the belly facing the woman's head, just above the uterus and, in a sliding motion, push the baby out with her butt. This technique was likely aided by poor maternal nutrition during pregnancy, which resulted in small babies.

when a caesarian section is not an option due to lack of resources, although this is probably not an issue in the developed world.

These days, women tend to be awake and alert during labor, with bigger, healthier babies. A doula or nurse might try fundal pressure if the patient has pushed as hard as she can for an hour or two and the head is right at the vaginal opening. Although this may be effective in certain circumstances, it's important to recognize that maybe there's a good reason the baby is not coming through, such as especially broad shoulders that could lead to shoulder dystocia if too much pressure is applied (see page 204). The point is that fundal pressure can be a tool in the delivery room, but it should be used gently and sparingly.

Caesarian Sections

It's true that most of the time when doctors recommend a caesarian section, the chances are still pretty good that you would have a safe, healthy baby vaginally. But let's say the odds of something bad happening suddenly increase from 1 to 10 percent. That's a significant and unnecessary health risk. These days, it's rare that obstetricians wait to discuss a C-section until it's a life-or-death situation; obstetricians try to prevent things from reaching an emergency situation

TRUST YOUR DOCTOR

A caesarian section can be a cure-all for anything that could possibly go wrong vaginally. The fact that it's a simple solution makes some patients nervous that the doctor is too quick to suggest it when another doctor might press on with a vaginal delivery. If you've trusted your doctor for nine months of pregnancy, delivery is not the time to question her judgment. She may have to make decisions quickly, based on the most immediate circumstances and your entire pregnancy history. Competent doctors only want what's best for their patients, and more and more frequently that seems to be a C-section.

LIKELY CANDIDATES FOR A SCHEDULED C-SECTION

Some women are very likely to have a scheduled caesarian section. These include those to whom any of the following apply:

- An abnormal presentation, such as a breech

- A placenta previa

- A previous classical C-section

- A previous extensive myomectomy

- A contracted pelvis from a previous trauma or a medical event

- Very small stature

- Multiple gestations of triplets or more; also likely for twins

by weighing the pros and cons and recommending a C-section when both mother and baby are likely to have a safer, healthier outcome.

Of all C-sections that were not scheduled for medical reasons, the vast majority are called for when labor stalls—such as when the baby won't descend. Only 2 percent of C-sections during labor were performed because of a nonreassuring fetal heart rate pattern.

Forty years ago, forceps were often used in cases that now call for a C-section. In 1968, the C-section rate was 3 percent. At that same time, the forceps rate was 60 percent, and the majority of these cases involved midforceps, which are rarely used anymore. These numbers have been reversed. Today, American obstetricians deliver 40 percent of babies via C-section and use low or outlet forceps in less than 5 percent of deliveries. This is not only because forceps are often more traumatic, but also because babies have gotten bigger and medical testing has become more sensitive and varied. Today, we are much better at monitoring everything about the pregnancy, from where the placenta is in the uterus to how the baby is doing before and during labor. Twenty-first-century obstetrics dictates very strict criteria for what constitutes a healthy labor, and once you depart from those guidelines the obstetrician must consider taking action.

The Procedure

If you're scheduling a caesarian section, you cannot eat anything the day of the procedure. However, you can take a shower, shave your legs, do your nails, brush your teeth, and tell your whole family that the big day has come. Once you get to the hospital, you'll be admitted and put on the fetal monitor. A nurse will start an IV and may or may not draw some blood for tests.

The next step is for you to meet your anesthesiologist for your epidural, which is done in the same way as for a vaginal delivery (see page 183). For a caesarian section, however, you receive more medication because you don't have to push and really don't need to or want to feel anything. Most anesthesiologists usually give more anesthetic and proportionally less narcotic. This sort of epidural may make it difficult or even impossible for you to move your legs, and you will be numb higher up on your body than with the normal epidural. After the epidural is in, the anesthesiologist tells you to

PARTNERS IN THE SECTION ROOM

Having the father or partner witness the caesarian section became standard within the last fifteen years, as C-sections became more common. Although today doctors try to make the experience of a C-section as close to that of a vaginal delivery as they can, it's impossible to remove the surgical element. C-sections, like most surgeries, require two doctors (the obstetrician and usually a resident or staff member), which means there are a lot of hands going back and forth and a lot of blood. Abdominal surgery is not something the partner has to see; he is simply there to support the mom. Coaches who are having trouble stomaching the blood in the delivery room should simply sit down, put their head between their legs if they feel dizzy, and relax. The coach is not there to witness the procedure, but to support the mom.

SPONGE COUNT

One of the first things many patients notice in the operating room is that someone is counting out loud. This is the scrub nurse doing the *sponge and instrument count* with the circulating nurse. Every tool, sponge, pad, and anything else that could be used in the surgery is counted and recounted, to ensure accuracy. A count is done again after surgery. Should the postoperative count not match the preoperative count, the patient is X-rayed for the missing item. Luckily, every sponge and lap pad used in an operating room has a radio-opaque line in it that readily appears in X-rays. If no sponge is revealed by the X-ray, then we can rest assured it's not still inside the patient. If the X-ray shows a forgotten sponge in the patient's body, we have to reopen her abdomen to get it.

lie down. The nurse then puts a catheter in your bladder and possibly trims your pubic hair just above the pubic bone, where the incision will be, so that when the hair grows back, the scar will be hidden. Of course, if you opt for Brazilian waxes, the scar may remain visible.

After all these preparations are complete, you are taken to an operating room, if you're not already there. While you're waiting for the epidural to take effect, it's a good time to meet everyone in the room. In fact, new federal guidelines meant to protect patients' privacy suggest that everyone in the operating room should be pointed out to you. Of course, in an emergency this protocol is usually set aside.

There should be five people there (six, if you count your partner). Of course, there's your obstetrician and the anesthesiologist whom you already met. There should also be a *scrub technician* or *scrub nurse,* who is in charge of the surgical instruments. Then there's the *circulating nurse,* who is not sterile and is therefore responsible for fetching things for the other members of the surgical team, who *are* sterile. Finally, the *first assistant* is there to help the doctor. This person should be at least a resident, a staff obstetrician, or a *trained surgical assistant.*

At this point, you are lying on your back. The table should be tilted a degree or two, or the nurse will put a little pillow under your hip so the uterus does not rest on the aorta, compromising the baby's blood supply. Your belly is washed with antiseptic while the anesthesiologist wraps your arm with a blood pressure cuff, sticks EKG monitor pads on your chest, and puts the pulse oximeter on your finger to monitor your vital signs. You may get some nasal oxygen to ensure good supplies for you and the baby. Your partner sits up by your head and most likely you'll be chatting about what you're going to name the baby.

The nurse sets up a little curtain so that you and your partner are screened from the incision. This is not only to avoid the problem of the fainting father (see sidebar), but also to prevent any germs or unwanted material from getting into the incision. For example, if the coach throws up, that mess needs to be kept away from the open belly. The screen also protects the parents from any splattering blood and bodily fluids.

Sterile technique is the guiding principle of all operating rooms. Surgeons don their hats and masks before washing their hands and arms for ten minutes. Once scrubbed, the surgeon cannot touch anything that is not also sterile, not even to scratch his or her own nose. The nurse helps the surgeon to don the gloves and gown. Meanwhile, sterile drapes are placed around the patient's abdomen, leaving an open square where the incision will be. Everything that touches the patient below the screen is sterile.

CLASSIC ISN'T ALWAYS BETTER

The first caesarian incision was done through a vertical incision at the top of the uterus. The problem with this was that it cut through the thickest part of the uterine muscle, creating a weakness in the organ. In future pregnancies, these women were often advised to schedule a C-section before their due dates because once the uterus reaches a critical size, it may split. This type of incision is rarely done these days, especially since it eliminates the possibility of a vaginal birth in the future.

After the patient is draped, the surgeons are ready, and the coach is seated next to the mother, the ten-minute process of delivering the baby begins. The obstetrician makes a transverse incision in the crease where the bottom of the belly joins the top of the pubis. This is not only cosmetic but medically optimal. It's a relatively thin part of the abdomen. Afterward, when you sit up, the abdominal wall weighs on the incision and keeps it closed.

The incision cuts through the skin and the uterus horizontally. The abdominal wall is cut vertically to avoid severing the muscles, which are then stretched apart. All the incisions tend to be six to eight inches long. *Cautery,* the process of burning small capillaries, is often used to control the bleeding, so you may smell something reminiscent of barbecue.

If the patient's water has not broken already, the obstetrician ruptures the membranes and places a hand inside the incision, where the baby's head is most often located. She puts her hand under the head, and the first assistant applies pressure to the top of the uterus, pushing the baby down. The obstetrician's hand is like a slide on which the baby's head can enter the world. The obstetrician puts her hands on either side of the head and delivers the shoulders, followed by the rest of the baby without difficulty. The obstetrician then clamps the cord and shows the baby to both parents.

The baby is then placed in a warming unit to be dried off and have

EMERGENCY C-SECTIONS

With a scheduled caesarian section, patients and medical team alike are calm, prepared, and well-rested. In an emergency, things could happen more quickly and corners might be cut, depending on what the problem is. For example, if the patient ruptures her uterus, there might not even be time for anesthesia. On one occasion I operated in my street clothes with a nurse pouring Betadine on the mother's belly ahead of a quick, one-knife incision. We delivered a healthy baby, got the mother some anesthesia, put on our sterile attire, and evaluated the situation. Even though the process was not ideal, everything turned out fine, which is the best you can hope for with labor and delivery.

the mucus suctioned out of her mouth while a pediatrician evaluates her. The pediatrician then reports to the parents, usually saying something like, "I just saw your baby. Congratulations, she's perfect." If there's a medical issue with the child, the pediatrician might show her to the parents and then take the baby to a neonatal unit.

After this, the placenta is delivered much in the same way as the baby, by squeezing the top of the uterus through the abdominal wall. The obstetrician may clean out the inside of the uterus with a sponge, then sew it closed with dissolving sutures. It's a good idea for the doctor to take this opportunity to look at the mother's tubes and ovaries to make sure they're normal. Then the obstetrician washes out the belly, making sure there is no residual blood anywhere, and sews the abdomen closed with several layers of sutures.

A BRIEF HISTORY OF THE CAESARIAN SECTION

There's no evidence that Julius Caesar was born by caesarian section, although the name is probably a reflection of the law during his day that you had to cut into the belly of a mother who had died in childbirth to try to save the child. Despite these arguably well-intentioned beginnings, for thousands of years after their invention, caesarian sections were a death sentence for the mother. This includes the birth of Edward VI, when King Henry VIII instructed his physicians to perform a C-section on his wife Jane Seymour in the hopes of securing a male heir. They did deliver a boy, but Jane Seymour died about two days later of blood loss and/or infection.

To doctors hundreds of years ago, the incised uterus resembled a dilated cervix, since both are essentially holes in the uterus. They assumed it would close on its own, so they would only suture the skin, leaving the mother to slowly bleed to death internally. Then, in a remote silver-mining town in Nevada in the 1880s, the local surgeon had an unanticipated breakthrough with a woman stalled for days in labor. He delivered her baby via C-section, but he was not well versed in the obstetrical practices of his day, and he stitched up her uterus with the material he had on hand—silver wire. The woman got better, and according to legend she even had another child.

Still, up until 1945, in the United States there were no IV fluids, no antibiotics, and no blood banks, which made any kind of surgery far more dangerous than it is today. Women would labor for days, develop fever, and become delirious before their doctors considered performing a C-section because the procedure carried a 15 to 20 percent fatality rate. This led to two obstetrical approaches, one for the Catholic doctors and patients, and one for everyone else. The Catholic method was to perform the C-section to save the baby, even though this put the mother's life at great risk. Non-Catholic doctors would use destructive forceps to crush the baby's skull and save the mother.

These days, there are no destructive forceps in labor and delivery and a C-section carries no greater risk than a vaginal delivery. Babies and mothers are equal human beings in the eyes of the obstetrician and the law. A vaginal delivery has a higher rate of lacerations and trauma of the vagina and rectum, which can lead to fecal incontinence and bladder dropping. An abdominal delivery requires a longer hospital stay and carries a higher risk of abdominal infection and injury to internal organs. But the fatality rate is the same. While C-sections get a bad rap in the popular press, they are a necessary, lifesaving tool of obstetrics.

Most obstetricians use either staples or subcuticular sutures for the skin, although some still use old-fashioned mattress sutures. These all work equally well; however, subcuticular sutures are probably the most esthetic and the simplest because there's no removal required. Staples and mattress stitches have to be removed four to six days later.

The Newborn Baby

Whether delivered vaginally or by C-section, as soon as he's out in the air, the baby is likely to be cold. Try to keep the little tyke against your skin, which is closer to its familiar environment of warm water. The baby used to be a passive traveler and didn't need

> ## NEWBORNS HAVE IT TOUGH
>
> If you've had extensive labor, your baby might have a swollen face, an oblong head, or some bruising. This is nothing to worry about. Your baby's cosmetic issues will dissipate within two days.

to expend any calories to keep warm. These are the first moments in which the baby tries to control his own body temperature. Right after delivery, the baby's temperature frequently drops below normal, and hypothermia (low body temperature) makes pediatricians very nervous.

If the baby is pink, crying, and/or breast-feeding, it could be thirty minutes or more before the pediatric staff evaluates him to make sure he's warming up. If the baby is blue and cold, the medical team might rush him to a warmer in the nursery, which slowly brings the baby back to a normal body temperature.

The Apgar Score

The anesthesiologist Marie Apgar developed a method to determine the level of medical attention that a newborn requires. She sought to quantify the qualities that suggest health. In other words, a baby who isn't looking so great might need a neonatal evaluation, but a pink, crying, lusty, breathing, heart-beating, strong baby is almost definitely perfectly healthy. These qualities are scored by the nurse at one minute and again at five minutes. This is a way for doctors to determine that the newborn baby is healthy and feeling good.

A perfect *Apgar score* is 10, and most babies do better than a 6. All newborns are a little blue since they've been living on much lower oxygen levels. As soon as they take a breath, their bodies turn pinker, but it can take up to an hour for hands and feet to lose their blueness. A pediatrician is usually called if the Apgar score is lower than 6. Meanwhile, the nurse, parents, and/or doctor will tickle the baby's feet, rub the back, and make sure there's no mucus in the nose or mouth. Just breathing in oxygen for a few minutes can perk

BREAKING DOWN THE APGAR

Heartbeat: 2 Points
Over 100 beats per minute: 2 points Under 100 beats per minute: 1 point Zero heartbeat: 0 points
Color: 2 Points
The whole body is pink: 2 points The extremities are blue: 1 point The whole body is blue: 0 points
Crying: 2 Points
A lusty cry: 2 points A weak "eh": 1 point No cry: 0 points
Breathing Effort: 2 Points
Easily breathing: 2 points Signs of respiratory effort: 1 point No breathing: 0 points
Tone: 2 Points
Scrunched-up body: 2 points Reaction to touching: 1 point Floppy baby: 0 points

> ## CORD BLOOD AGAIN
>
> While you're playing with the baby, the umbilical cord, which looks like a rope of blue veins, is hanging out of your vagina between your legs. This is an appropriate time for the obstetrician to collect cord blood, if you have requested it in order to store your baby's stem cells. To do this, the doctor inserts a needle, hooks it up to a bag provided by the cord-blood company, and fills it up. There may be some paperwork to complete. The company is then called to pick up the blood. Hospitals require the collection of a little cord blood to do an antibody screen, syphilis test, or other analysis because this is the first chance to test the baby's blood.

the baby right up. By the time the pediatrician arrives, nine out of ten times the baby is already fine.

Unattended Deliveries

If, by some unlikely chance you are having an incredibly precipitous labor and cannot get to the hospital, try to have someone with you. Ask that person to call the obstetrician and/or hospital. A labor and delivery doctor can walk you through the delivery. If you think you have some time, call the local police or fire department, whose personnel should be trained in emergency medical care and might be able to get to you even if you can't get to the hospital.

Once you feel rectal pressure, have someone in position to catch the baby. Don't do anything fancy. Unread newspapers are nearly sterile, so put those or some clean towels under your bottom. Remember to keep the baby's head lower than the body, so as the baby comes out the mucus drains from the nose and mouth. Make sure the baby has an airway to breath through by wiping the mouth and nose, and keep the infant warm. Don't bother with the placenta or cord, and get to a hospital so you and your baby can get the proper postpartum care.

CHAPTER 12

Postpartum

Yay! The baby is born and is perfect, you're bonding, and it's all wonderful! So many people wrongly think that the show is now over, but recovering from pregnancy is a process that can take weeks to months. In fact, it never ends.

Once the placenta is out, the obstetrician evaluates the mother's perineum for any lacerations, abrasions, or injury. Often, there are at least a few minor tears to sew up, which is done under local anesthesia in the absence of an epidural.

After delivery, the uterus continues contracting to expel all its contents and stanch the blood flow. Obstetricians help this process along by massaging the uterus through the abdominal wall. Many women expect discomfort to end at delivery, but uterine massage hurts. Women with epidurals often request more medication.

Meanwhile, you're holding the baby and making calls from a mobile phone. Friends and relatives are excited to hear crying in the background. When the doctor is done stitching up any lacerations, your legs are put down and your sheets and gown are changed; you're feeling great and maybe even hungry. Slowly the epidural wears off, and you can try breast-feeding and urinating. In some hospitals, you'll be moved from a delivery room to a postpartum room, at which point you will likely go to sleep and the doctor will go home.

The six weeks that follow all this excitement are called the *puerperium* or *postpartum* period. At the end of this time, your uterus and vagina have reached their new normal states. You look as well as you're going to look without any effort such as diet or exercise. You're no longer pregnant, but that doesn't mean you're symptom-free.

Newborns experience an *awake-alert period* for the first hour after delivery, which is a great time to try breast-feeding (see "The Role of Breast-feeding"). After that, babies go to sleep for almost the entire first day of life. They've been through a lot and probably have a very bad headache. They are spending huge amounts of energy on things you used to do for them: breathing, temperature regulation, digestion, and so on. There are all sorts of new stimuli, such as light, noise, smells, tastes, and being rubbed with irritating towels. In this first day, babies lose approximately 10 percent of their birth weight due to all the extra calories they're burning.

Health Risks and Nuisances

Regardless of how labor and delivery go, there are some continuing, important medical concerns to stay on top of in the period immediately following birth. In this time when you are supposed to be adjusting to your new role as mother, emotional issues can become as important as physical ones.

HOME FOR THE PUERPERIUM

It may seem daunting that all the things in this chapter happen to you at home, with your baby. These things—hemorrhoids, breast-feeding, catching up on sleep, and so forth—used to get taken care of in the hospital, where the postpartum patient stayed for ten days. Everything healed before you went home, so that all the rare things that could go wrong and all the minor nuisances of new motherhood would occur where you had immediate help on hand. Now you take care of it yourself.

IF YOU HEMORRHAGED PREVIOUSLY

There are studies that suggest the prostaglandin Cytotec dramatically lowers the risk of postpartum hemorrhage when taken immediately after delivery. If you have had a previous postpartum hemorrhage or uterine atony, or if you're having twins or a huge baby, your obstetrician is likely to use medication proactively.

Postpartum Hemorrhage

At delivery, the whole uterine lining is shed, exposing arteries where the placenta used to be. Normally, continuing uterine contractions squeeze these vessels shut. *Uterine atony* is when the organ is distended and flaccid, allowing the exposed arteries to continue bleeding. Unchecked, this complication can lead to dangerous postpartum hemorrhaging. Your risk of uterine atony rises if the organ is distorted by fibroids or has been taxed with a long labor, a large pregnancy, or multiple babies. Many previous pregnancies also heighten the risk of hemorrhage, since the uterus is tired from all the prior gestations.

In the first hour after delivery, your doctor will manually stimulate the uterus to induce contractions and is also likely to administer medication to force the uterus to contract more effectively. Pitocin can be given in much higher doses to the postpartum woman because the doctor does not have to worry about the flow of blood to the baby anymore. Ergotamine is a medication that can be used only after labor because it causes sustained, significant contractions that would be very bad for the baby. It's also possible to inject Pitocin or prostaglandins right into the uterus, which can trigger very strong contractions.

After the immediate postpartum period, the nurse should continue to check on your postpartum uterus and show you how to check it yourself. It should be firm and accompanied by light bleeding. When the bladder is empty, the uterus should be at or below the navel and feel like an unripe cantaloupe. If you're doing well, the nurse may check on you as infrequently as once every few hours.

THE ROLE OF BREAST-FEEDING

Remember how nipple stimulation can lead to contractions (see page 125)? Well, nipple stimulation is useful not only for bringing on labor, but also for helping the uterus contract and prevent blood loss after delivery. When a newborn is placed at the mother's breast shortly after childbirth, the mother's body reflexively releases oxytocin, helping the uterus contract. This little trick of nature was a huge help to our earliest ancestors, who immediately placed newborns at their breasts, thereby avoiding bleeding to death.

If, however, the uterus starts to fill with blood it will feel like a bag of Jell-O and expand above the navel. A full bladder can raise the uterus and impede contractions, so it's important to make an effort to pee. If urinating doesn't work, the nurse will massage and squeeze the uterus until it's below the navel again. To reiterate, this process is painful.

When a postpartum woman continues to hemorrhage in spite of medication, she faces limited options. Her obstetrician might look for missed lacerations around and above the vagina. The obstetrician might use a curette to double-check for pieces of placenta or try putting one hand in the vagina and one hand on the top of the abdomen for a bimanual massage. If things don't look up quickly, it's time for surgery and a blood transfusion.

If you're heading to the operating room because of postpartum hemorrhage, your treatment depends on the hospital's protocols and who is doing the surgery. There are four approaches to this situation:

1. The most traditional method is called *hypogastric artery ligation,* whereby the doctor sutures (ties closed) some of the major vessels to the uterus. The idea is that reducing blood flow also reduces blood loss.

2. Another method is to pack the uterine cavity with gauze, which compresses the walls of the uterus and stops the bleeding.

3. A newer technique is to use large sutures to compress the entire organ.

4. When all else fails, the patient may require a hysterectomy to save her life.

It's possible to suffer a *delayed postpartum hemorrhage* seven to ten days after delivery. During pregnancy, the uterus develops major blood vessels to the placental site; once the placenta is out, this area should shrink into a scarlike patch. If the placental site doesn't heal properly, the clot (that is, the wet scab) that forms over it can become dislodged, and the blood pours out of all those large vessels. This is called *subinvolution of the placental site*, and while it's extremely rare (a fraction of 1 percent), there's no way of predicting whom it might strike. If you are bleeding continuously and copiously at home, you should call your doctor or go to an emergency room right away.

Depression

You're exhausted, your breasts hurt, your bottom hurts, you're thirty pounds overweight, you still look pregnant, and you have a crying baby in the next room who will not stop. Does this sound like a happy

NO ONE WANTS TO TAKE YOUR UTERUS

After a C-section, my patient's uterus refused to contract. I was already right there, in the abdomen, and I still could not stop the bleeding. I massaged and massaged, gave her six units of blood, and massaged some more. Finally the bleeding slowed, and it was only then that I remembered that this woman was 47; she had had an egg donor and was six months away from menopause. If it had been possible to ask her, she might have preferred a simple hysterectomy to a five-hour operation. Believe me, most doctors do not want to remove your uterus for no good reason—you'd sue our pants off. We do this only in the absence of other, better, lifesaving options.

BEEN DEPRESSED BEFORE?

If you have a history of any psychiatric problems, particularly depression, the postpartum period is a high-risk time for you. You should talk with your obstetrician and psychiatrist about warning signs and possibly about medication. If you've had a previous experience specifically with postpartum depression, your psychiatrist should be available right after delivery and/or should start prophylactic antidepressants. I have seen patients pop their first antidepressant as I delivered the placenta.

place to you? Additionally, you've just gone abruptly from producing a huge amount of euphoric hormones to relatively few. All this means that it is normal and completely expected that you might be a little bummed out. This condition is referred to as the *baby blues*, which is a euphemism for mild *postpartum depression*.

Postpartum depression ranges from the baby blues to persistent sadness to suicidal thoughts to psychotic delusional behavior. Because melancholy can rapidly and unexpectedly progress from persistent sadness to a more serious condition, early intervention is very important. Ask your partner, family, coach, and best friends to look out for your emotional well-being during these six

LISTEN TO BROOKE SHIELDS (*NOT* TOM CRUISE!)

I once received a phone call from a concerned husband whose wife (my patient) had locked him out of their apartment and was claiming that people were out to get her. She was in the apartment, alone, with the baby, claiming there were plots to murder her. A local psychiatric hospital admitted her for evaluation and treatment, and she's been fine ever since. I had a patient with postpartum depression who said that from the moment the placenta was delivered, it felt like "a curtain coming down." Postpartum depression is a real problem for some women that deserves attention and treatment.

weeks. Depression is dangerous for the mother and therefore dangerous for the baby. Being sad makes having a baby no fun, and this tends to make a depressed mom less attentive to her child's needs.

The number one contributing factor to postpartum depression is sleep deprivation, which will make the sanest person crazy in a short period of time. Sleep is as essential to the body as food and water, even though science does not completely understand why. If you're a little moody, irritable, or teary, you might find that resting and sleeping more is enough to raise your mood.

It can be harder than you think to sleep after having a baby— you just want to look at him and play with him and make everything around him perfect. The adrenaline immediately following birth can keep women up for a whole twenty-four hours, which is not the way to kick off a postpartum experience. To an obstetrician, a woman with a one-week-old infant and a really tidy house can mean trouble, because unless her partner is a neat freak or they have a maid, it's a sure sign she's not sleeping. Ironically, once you are sleep deprived, it can become easier and easier to skip sleeping, just as an anorexic person can breeze through the day on one cracker with spray butter. It's even possible to get to a place where you haven't slept for so long that you can't sleep at all. If this is the case, it's time to see a mental health professional.

If left untreated, depression can spiral out of control. If you feel that life is not worth living, if there's a sense of doom about everything, if you can't seem to sleep, if you think harmful thoughts, please call somebody. Medication can be extremely effective in treating and/or preventing postpartum depression, and early intervention can make an amazingly positive difference. Do not ignore worsening depression, and if you feel as if you are becoming entrenched in sadness, share your concern with someone close to you who can help monitor your mood and suggest professional help when and if warranted.

Vaginal Discharge

Postpartum vaginal discharge, called *lochia,* is especially plentiful and stinky. Lochia is heavier for women with vaginal deliveries, because during a C-section the obstetrician will often clean out the uterus with a sponge. Lochia is thick liquid that changes appearance throughout the postpartum period. It starts as *lochia rubra* (that is, with blood), then it turns yellow, then white, as the lining of the uterus sheds completely. Within six weeks you should be back to close-to-normal secretions.

Lochia in the first postpartum day is surprisingly heavy, probably about two to three times your heaviest period. All the lining of the uterus (the *decidua*) sheds as the uterus contracts in what are called *afterbirth pains*. These are most likely to strike when you're breast-feeding, due to the corollary increase in oxytocin, which leads to uterine contractions; it's worth noting that afterbirth pains get worse with each pregnancy.

Lochia slows down in fits and starts. If you feel as if you're expelling much more fluid all of a sudden, consider the entire twenty-four-hour period. There may be a gush first thing in the morning because the lochia collects in the vagina while you sleep and then it all falls out when you stand up. This can look like you're hemorrhaging, but the discharged fluid ceases in one gush. Overall volume is much more important than an isolated incident. You may also notice blood clots in your lochia, which are perfectly normal and not a cause for concern.

Weight Loss

The morning after delivery, you will have lost anywhere from ten to fifteen pounds. You're thinking: But I gained thirty-five! True, you may have some dieting ahead of you. There's simply no way to safely manage a pregnancy so that you're the same weight and shape when you leave the hospital after giving birth. The human body is programmed to store food for the future in case of a famine, so a certain percentage of the calories you consume are, by default, made into fat and stored on your hips. In addition to weight gain, the abdominal wall itself is stretched and stays that way for two weeks as the skin and muscles shrink. It takes most women three to six months or more to lose the bulk of their pregnancy weight, though some never take all of it off.

FORGET MADONNA, TOO

Forget about looking like Demi Moore after three kids unless you have a personal trainer, a specialty chef, a maid, and the need to look fantastic for your career. Your body is likely to stay in a slightly different shape after you have a child. Even Scarlett O'Hara never got back to her prepregnant sixteen-inch waist. Set realistic goals for yourself regarding how many pounds and inches you can lose, and in what time frame.

If you feel up to it, you can try light exercise about two weeks after delivery. You should not do sit-ups, but you can start to tone your abdomen by lying on your back and just lifting your head off the floor. When this is comfortable, try to also lift your shoulders. Using light upper-body free weights or doing leg lifts should be fine. Avoid putting pressure on your perineum by staying away from high-impact activities (that is, those in which both feet are off the ground) and weight lifting for at least four weeks. Don't do anything that makes you grunt or groan, which often is the result of pressing down on your pelvic floor as you try to lift something heavy.

Vaginal Delivery Issues

If you have a baby the traditional way, your postpartum recovery revolves around your crotch—there may be issues about everything from the top of your pubic hair, in between your legs, and up to your tailbone. Luckily, none of these postpartum problems are dangerous.

Urinary Tract Problems

Shortly after you deliver, your nurse will start asking you whether you've urinated, which may no longer be the easy task it once was. After a vaginal delivery, the urethra and bladder weep; their walls are swollen and there's microscopic bleeding. A baby's skull has

GETTING SOME OUTSIDE HELP WITH THE BABY: AN OBSTETRICIAN'S EDITORIAL

Many new mothers have a relative who is available and willing to help care for the newborn in the days following childbirth. If you're fortunate enough to have more than one willing volunteer, try to choose someone *nonjudgmental, nonthreatening,* and *reassuring.* You want a person to take the pressure out of being all alone with the newborn baby so you can have a well-deserved physical and mental health break. Avoid having someone around who will criticize your methods or insist on using her own. You don't want to be lying in bed wondering if your stubborn Great Aunt Sue is going to feed the baby *her* way or according to your instructions.

Relatives are cheap but tricky. If your mother is bossy and rules the roost, she can be more of a disturbance than a help. Mothers-in-law can be even worse. The ideal helper/relative is someone who says, "Tell me what you want me to do." Sometimes you just want someone to do the laundry or watch the baby while you take a nap. These relatively simple tasks can be glorious gifts when you're recovering from childbirth and adjusting to caring for a newborn.

Of course, if you don't have a relative you can—or want to—call on, you can also hire a baby nurse. Baby nurses are wonderful: They've got experience and they work for you, so there's no question about who's calling the shots. Of course, not every woman can afford a baby nurse. If you, like most, are in this category, try to accept the generosity of people who offer you help, unless you don't trust or don't like the person offering. It can be hard to accept aid, but a newborn is a constant, unrelenting responsibility and everyone needs a break now and then.

been ramming your bladder and urethra for six to eight hours. The trauma can lead to temporary *atony of the bladder;* in other words, the bladder just can't contract.

You'll probably be parched after delivery, but take it easy on the water. It's best to drink gradually but constantly. This allows your bladder some time to recognize that it's filling up and possibly respond.

If you're having trouble initiating a stream, be patient. A nurse is likely to hand you a little squeeze bottle filled with warm water (called a *perineum bottle,* or *peri-bottle* for short). I learned about these lifesavers in my own postpartum experience. A peri-bottle produces a jet of water that you can use to soothe and clean your vulva, in the process stimulating urination. Warm water on your crotch or running over your hands can help you get a stream of urine going, and afterward you can use the peri-bottle instead of rubbing the area with dry toilet paper. Spritz your crotch and then pat with toilet paper to avoid irritating the area.

If you struggle to pee and can't, you will likely feel the pain of *urinary retention* and an overly distended bladder. If six hours or so go by, or you're uncomfortable because you still haven't been able to urinate, a nurse will relieve you with a catheter. You will try again later, and eventually peeing in the toilet happens. In less than 1 percent of deliveries, women go home with a catheter that they continue to use for a week or so.

Whenever a catheter is used, the risk of a urinary tract infection escalates. If you had a catheter a few times following delivery, try drinking some cranberry juice to preempt an infection. For women who have had several catheter insertions and removals, prophylactic antibiotics may be a good idea.

On the other end of the spectrum, some women can't *hold* their urine postpartum; it just dribbles out. Although it's frightening to lose control of your urinary function, these deficits are almost always temporary and don't mean that you'll have to use a catheter or a diaper for the rest of your life. As your bladder heals from the birth experience, tone and continence are overwhelmingly likely to return. But avoiding urinary incontinence is a good reason to *always* do your Kegel exercises—pee, stop peeing, pee, stop peeing, and so on, to improve the muscles that control your bladder.

Peeing Problems

Peeing can present a unique problem to the postpartum patient because urine is acidic and stings lacerations. This can be harder than you think to manage, because vaginal delivery tends to alter

FISTULAS

A *fistula* is a hole between the bladder and the vagina (or the vagina and the rectum) that is created in prolonged labor, when the baby's head squeezes against the mother's pelvis for hours to days, cutting off the blood supply to the tissue between. After delivery, that patch rots, creating a hole (that is, the fistula). This is a huge health issue in developing countries; some places in Africa are especially notorious for high fistula rates. There are stories about women who walk for weeks to get their fistulas surgically corrected. For a woman with access to health care, fistulas are not a concern.

the entire vulva, at least for a little while. Patients often like to tell me about their postpartum urinary streams. Sometimes, they spray or go in a different direction or just do "funny things." For the most part, this self-corrects within a couple of weeks. Before you've learned your new urinary bent, be sure to lean forward when you sit on the toilet so the urine bypasses any stitches. Diluting it by being well hydrated can help with the burning, too. If you're breast-feeding, you're likely to be thirsty all the time anyway, because breast milk requires a lot of water. So drink up and pee with caution.

Bottom Problems

Once the epidural wears off, most women are bothered by hemorrhoids and vaginal lacerations. The entire vaginal and rectal area is bruised and swollen. For the first postpartum twenty-four hours, applying ice helps to prevent swelling. After that, warm soaks help to drain any swelling that might have happened anyway. These are not medically mandatory treatments, but they may make you feel better.

Before you leave the hospital, it can be a good idea to use a mirror to look at your perineum so that you know how it is supposed to look. If you're lucky, it will look surprisingly unharmed relative to the discomfort it's causing. Taking a peek right when you get home may help later, should you suspect an infected laceration or episiotomy. If you feel that you're more uncomfortable than you should be a week after being home, take another look at your perineum. If it's gaping or very red, or there's pus in or around the episiotomy, speak to your doctor.

The postpartum perineum is a prime place for infection, because the vagina is wide open, it's got a few lacerations, and there are lots of bacteria around. Be on the lookout for *foul-smelling lochia, uterine tenderness,* or a fever. The problem with relying on foul-smelling lochia to identify a possible infection is that all lochia stinks; therefore, to catch a burgeoning infection, you have to distinguish between normal stinky lochia and foul-smelling lochia, which should be even smellier. If the latter describes your condition, take your temperature. An infection can take root anywhere along the path of pregnancy, including the uterus. Try pressing against your uterus—does it hurt more than it did yesterday? If yes, or if you have a fever, call your doctor. A postpartum infection can be readily treated with oral antibiotics and you can probably continue breast-feeding.

There are many ways to prevent infection in the postpartum period. Soaking your bottom in warm water and hydrogen peroxide can relieve discomfort and kill bacteria. Neosporin is great—try applying it to any laceration or abrasion. Witch hazel pads can help cool stitches and hemorrhoids, making them more bearable. For more pain relief, try Novocain ointments and sprays. My recommended postpartum recipe to help with "bottom troubles" calls for

SITZ BATHS

A sitz bath is a little basin designed to sit on the rim of a toilet and hook up to the sink faucet to provide a flow of warm water over your bottom and into the bowl. You can also add a dash of hydrogen peroxide to the basin to prevent infection. Many women swear by the sitz bath, but others find the pressure of sitting over a hole uncomfortable and prefer the handheld showerhead. I've visited postpartum patients in the hospital who don't want to get out of the shower because the warm water is so soothing.

a menstrual pad covered with a witch hazel swab (Tucks), smothered in Novocain ointment. Wear this concoction in your panties for pain relief and infection prevention.

Another simple way to pamper your bottom is to invest in a small, inflatable inner tube to sit on. Play around with the amount of air you need in the tube for maximum comfort; some women prefer to be as high off their bottoms as possible, while others need just a little pressure relief.

Within two weeks of childbirth, your bottom should feel 90 percent better. There may be occasional twinges or problems with bowel movements that take another month or so to correct themselves. At the end of six weeks, you should have no problems whatsoever with urinary or bowel function. Sex may be another issue.

Intimacy

Traditionally, obstetricians recommended that their patients avoid sex for the postpartum period. Of course, if you've had no episiotomy, you're not bleeding, you're feeling great, you're in the mood, and it's been at least three weeks since delivery, go for it! However, there are many reasons why sex in the six weeks after having a baby might not top your list of priorities. The most antilibidinous thing in the world is fatigue, which you're likely to have from feeding the baby every three hours. Breast-feeding in particular can kill your desire for sex, because it limits hormone production. *Prolactin,* the hormone that stimulates milk production, inhibits ovulation and the hormones that are made by ovulation

CONTRACEPTION

Unless you're ready to face another pregnancy within six weeks of delivery, practice contraception. If you're not breast-feeding, use contraception. If you're breast-feeding, use contraception. You can use progesterone-only birth control pills that do not suppress lactation or, of course, condoms.

(estrogen and progesterone), which make the vagina moist and resilient. Thus, the vagina will be somewhat dry and inhospitable, which may cause or coincide with a lowered libido. Most women have gained some weight and are still uncomfortable in the first weeks following delivery, and let's not forget the smelly lochia! None of these conditions are particularly conducive to physical intimacy, and many women don't feel at their sexiest.

Very rarely, the vagina can heal in such a way that it's too tight for vaginal intercourse. Sometimes the episiotomy leads to a scar that won't stretch or give, in which case the obstetrician can perform a very minor revision of the episiotomy. Although the procedure requires anesthesia, it takes only five minutes to recut the episiotomy, remove the scar tissue, loosen the vaginal opening a little, and make sex more comfortable. If it's been ten weeks postpartum, and you are still having trouble with vaginal intercourse, speak to your doctor.

Skeletal Issues

Vaginal deliveries can stress the pelvis to the point where bones break, though this is very rare. As the baby's head enters the birth canal, it can crack the mother's coccyx, or tailbone. This is unpredictable, and doctors don't really know why or how frequently it happens. Usually we discover it in the postpartum period if the mother complains of severe low back pain, although in many cases these cracks heal without being diagnosed.

SIZE MATTERS

Rather than become too small, most vaginas are a little bigger after a vaginal delivery. A doctor I know would assure the husbands that he'd snugly stitch up their wives' vaginas. Once a husband became infuriated with him, shouting, "Do you think I married my wife's vagina?" Then there are husbands who say, "Throw another stitch in there for me, Doc." Either way, to maintain vaginal tone and urinary function, *practice your Kegel exercises.*

Separation of the pubic symphysis is more serious and more rare. This is when the front of the mother's pelvis, which is usually connected by cartilage, comes apart. In addition to suffering extreme pain, women who experience this complication cannot walk, especially backward. Separation of the pubic symphysis is more likely to happen after a long, arduous labor, although it can occur after any vaginal delivery. Women unfortunate enough to experience this complication are in for weeks in a wheelchair and at physical therapy; however, these gaps heal within eight weeks.

Caesarian Section Issues

The postpartum period is somewhat different after a caesarian section. Instead of trauma to your crotch, you've had an abdominal operation. There's more blood loss during the procedure, though less bleeding postpartum. Discomfort centers on the abdomen as opposed to the perineum. This pain is somewhat mitigated by a little extra morphine injection in the epidural catheter just before it is removed postoperatively. This provides relief for up to twenty-four hours after the C-section, so by the time it wears off, the worst pain is gone. Women who have had a C-section usually spend an extra day or two in the hospital, which may sound unappealing but can provide some much-needed time to begin establishing a schedule with the newborn.

Urinary and Bowel Function

Because it's surgery, everyone gets a urinary catheter for a C-section. Some doctors leave it in for the twenty-four hours afterward, so the patient doesn't have to worry about getting out of bed until the next morning.

Once the patient has urinated on her own, the medical team turns its attention to her bowel function, which is an issue with all abdominal surgery. Opening the abdominal cavity unavoidably leaves air behind, which temporarily paralyzes the intestines. Additionally, removing the contents of the uterus decompresses the abdominal cavity. The extra space fills up with distended loops of bowel.

Until the intestines are definitely functioning again, a patient cannot eat. Farting is considered the universal sign of healthy bowel function, because it means the intestines successfully pushed the gas along and out of your body. Passing gas can happen on the first or second day after surgery, although there are women who take days to resume normal bowel function.

After you pass gas, pee, stabilize your vital signs, go twenty-four hours without a fever, and your blood levels stabilize, you go home. When you leave the hospital has little to do with medical management and everything to do with your health insurance. Most HMOs will not pay for an extra day without a significant reason.

Incision Risks

It used to be that a woman who had had a C-section spent two weeks in the hospital, during which time medical personnel could monitor all the rare but dangerous complications that might arise. Now it's up to the patient to stay on top of these things herself.

Most often, the caesarian incision is covered with *steristrips* (little tapes) to help it heal attractively. Sometimes the incision becomes *infected* or *separated.* A full wound separation without an infection, or a *dehissence,* could be due to a collection of fluid (called a *seroma*) or a blood clot (called a *hemotoma*) keeping the wound from healing. *Dehissences* are rarely painful, but they require drainage and irrigation.

Wound infections are rare and are accompanied by some obvious symptoms. First, the incision grows noticeably more tender. Fever and redness around the incision are other symptoms. Some infections lead to a preponderance of pus that may split the wound open. In this case, drainage, irrigation, and antibiotics may be called for. Wound infections can also happen under the skin's surface, and these are usually treated with antibiotics only. When treating these infections with antibiotics, many doctors use a marker to draw an outline around the red blotch of infection so that the patient can judge the effectiveness of the antibiotics by examining this outline on the following days. If the redness is within the outline, the antibiotics are working, if it exceeds the line, it's possible that the infec-

IT HAPPENS

The only evisceration I've handled was with a patient who was supposed to go home the next day. I was in the hospital, making rounds at two in the morning, and she was up smoking. She was a drug addict, which increased her risk factors but also meant she was especially eager to get out of the hospital. We agreed on removing her stitches a little early, so she could leave first thing in the morning. So I took out the stitches and, lo and behold, she eviscerated. The good news was that this didn't happen while she was home alone. The bad part was that I had to get the attending surgeon out of bed at 2 A.M. to repair the incision. The patient was fine when she left the hospital a week later.

tion is being caused by aggressive bacteria that may require hospitalization to treat. Even less serious wound infections or separations can require several trips to your doctor and a home care regimen of cleaning and irrigating the infected site.

Another extremely unlikely possibility is that the abdominal wall could split open, an event called an *evisceration*. Much as the name suggests, an open abdomen results in exposed intestines. An evisceration is much less likely with the latest sutures and a bikiniline incision. Women most at risk for this complication are those who suffer from malnourishment, drug addiction, or a history of poor wound healing, as well as those who are HIV positive or have compromised health. If you are at home in the days following your caesarian section, and you feel a tear and look down to see loops of intestine, call 911 immediately and cover your intestines with a wet towel. Keeping the intestines moist is of paramount importance.

Breast-Feeding

Milk comes into the breasts about thirty-six to forty-eight hours after delivery, and the breasts get big and swollen. As for its consistency, don't expect cow's milk. Human milk looks watery, but don't let that fool you: It's the perfect food for the baby. It's chock-full of everything your infant needs: protein, water, glucose, fat, and antibodies. Furthermore, as the baby grows, the properties of the milk change to accommodate the shifting needs of the child.

Some women get militant about breast-feeding, and although their attitudes may appear fanatical, the health benefits of this practice support their strong feelings. Studies suggest that breast-fed babies have lower incidences of allergies, asthma, heart disease, and diabetes. It could be that these results are exaggerated or are the result of other factors, but it seems undeniable that humans thrive on human milk. If only it were that simple to deliver the milk to the baby.

Getting Started

A new mom's first breast-feeding experience does not always go smoothly. Ideally, a nurse or a doula helps the new mother learn how to accomplish this. First, tickle the baby's cheek to get him to open his mouth. Then shove as much breast as you can into the baby's mouth, which stimulates the hard palate's sucking reflex. Not only the nipple, but often the whole areola is often required. Eventually, the baby closes his mouth and realizes . . . Wow! Milk!

BABY FORMULA'S UNFAIR BAD RAP

In the 1950s, some baby formula companies ran huge advertising campaigns in developing countries to market formula to impoverished women. In an effort to get the women hooked, some companies distributed free samples (some still do), which lasted until the mother's milk dried up. The mothers would then have to go out and buy some formula, and if they couldn't afford it they would dilute the formula they still had with water that was not always sterile. Kids who were fed this way were set up for electrolyte imbalances, malnutrition, and diarrhea. These health problems became associated with formula, and soon bottle-feeding caught a bad rap. Of course, if you follow the instructions, you nullify these risks.

The best time to attempt breast-feeding is in the hour after the baby is born, during the awake-alert period. This is a good time to try to imprint this behavior, which is a learned experience for the baby as well as the mother. This sets you up for an easier time with it in the postpartum future.

Additionally, the liquid the breast expels in the first twelve to twenty-four hours after delivery is not really milk but something more watery, which is called *colostrum*. This fluid is chock-full of the mother's antibodies, so the baby gets some immunity to a spectrum of infections. Even a couple of mouthfuls can be very beneficial to the baby's health.

In spite of all the benefits attributed to breast milk, many women are understandably exhausted right after birth and may not be in the mood to attempt breast-feeding. Even if you really don't feel like it, this is a good time to push yourself because teaching your baby to breast-feed later can be like walking between the raindrops. She may be too hungry and therefore won't breast-feed because she's crying and upset, or she may be more interested in sleeping, and who wants to wake her up to try breast-feeding?

Different lactation experts have different recommendations regarding how to conduct the first breast-feeding session. Some say to try five minutes on each breast and work up from there to avoid any painful nipple problems. Others say that the nipples remain unharmed if you know the right technique—for example, it's very important to get the whole areola in the baby's mouth so he's not just ineffectively and painfully nibbling on your nipple. There are lactation helpers in every hospital, and there are even people who come to your home to instruct privately; call for help if you need it.

Minimizing Discomfort

Breast-feeding can be uncomfortable for some women. American women in particular tend to suffer from nipple problems because their breasts are very seldom exposed to the air or sun, making them extra delicate. A chomping baby can lead to sore, cracked, bleeding nipples. Bacteria on the skin can enter the breast through a duct and cause an infection called *mastitis*, which is readily treated with antibiotics. Look out for a hard, red lump (called an *abscess*) or red streaks on the breast, both of which are signs of mastitis. It's important to remember that any breast problems can also cause a fever, usually one out of proportion to the severity of the problem. In other words, a temperature of 103 degrees Fahrenheit is not uncommon with mastitis, but this condition is nothing to be alarmed about.

To avoid nipple problems, it's smart to prepare your breasts throughout pregnancy (as advised in Chapter 3). Experts recommend a variety of ways to toughen the nipples, including sunbathing nude, scrubbing them with a washcloth, and simply exposing them to air as much as possible. You should also keep them supple with vitamin E or cocoa butter cream throughout pregnancy. Don't wash your nipples before breast-feeding, which may dry them out; dab them with a damp cloth if you want to.

When you're breast-feeding, it's important to keep the milk flowing. If you skip a feeding or decide to wean early, you continue to produce milk, which can lead to *engorgement,* or an excess of milk in the breast. This causes discomort and can lead to fever. Engorgement is also a danger if a duct becomes plugged. The only

SOME ADVICE ON BREAST-FEEDING

I often suggest to patients that they approach breast-feeding with good intentions and low expectations. I've seen the most amazingly pessimistic mothers be very successful with breast-feeding and the most positive ones have incredible troubles. The latter end up surfing the Web for advice, pumping all the time to bottle-feed, and crying a lot. If, after two days of trying, your breasts are engorged, your nipples are bleeding, and you break into a sweat two hours before an attempt, it may be time to reconsider. There's a limit to how important breast-feeding is. You are not a mammary gland but a full human mother. Not breast-feeding your baby will not ruin your relationship with her or damage her in any way. When breast-feeding becomes destructive, desist and move on.

Like I did.

thing to do about it is to get the milk out of the breast (by means of either the baby or a pump) and get production going in a more consistent way. For example, if one breast is always engorged, you may have to commence feedings on that side—an empty breast is less likely to pose problems. If the breast is becoming engorged because the flow of milk is inefficient, hot compresses and warm showers may be of use to dilate the main ducts, allowing the milk to flow more freely.

When to Wean

I admit that it looks ridiculous to me when I see a four-year-old unbuttoning his mother's blouse. That said, some families think extended breast-feeding (until four or five years of age and beyond) is very positive for the physical and emotional health of their children. Because there are so many factors to consider— the child's preferences, the mother's schedule, socioeconomic factors, cultural forces, and so forth—it's impossible to say that any one age is the right age at which to wean. As far as physical health, children cannot be breast-fed exclusively for more than six months of life, though pediatricians recommend breast-feeding for at least that long. After that, the baby's diet must include solid foods, with or without breast milk. There is no established medical reason to continue breast-feeding after six months, though some activists and organizations suggest otherwise. As for breast-feeding into early childhood, there is no consensus about the relative health benefits of extensive breast-feeding. Similarly, the long-term mental health impact is also hard to know—that is, no one knows how it will impact the future emotional life of a young boy to recall suckling at his mother's breast well into childhood.

Nursing Frequency and Duration

When it comes to the frequency of breast-feeding, most pediatricians recommend *demand feeding*, which means that when the baby cries, you feed him (as opposed to *scheduled feedings*, which follow a preset time frame). You can still exert some control over the schedule. After about six weeks of demand feeding, start to increase the time between nursing, which will likely lead the baby to eat more at each session. Slowly stretch the feeding intervals, waiting an hour and fifteen minutes between feedings for a few days, then an hour and a half for a few days, and so on.

Pumping Breast Milk

Many women who work use pumps to store a supply of milk in the fridge or freezer, although not every woman can make enough milk to have extra on hand. Breast milk lasts a few days in the refrigerator and a month in the freezer. It takes about half an hour to empty both breasts. Some workplaces have breast-feeding rooms with professional-grade equipment where moms can pump and store; however, this accommodation is pretty extraordinary. If your office doesn't offer a special breast-feeding room, you can still pump at work with a portable, rented pump—perhaps in the bathroom or another place where you can have a little privacy.

Another reason to pump may be because you have to temporarily take medication that shouldn't get to the baby through breast milk, in which case you must continue pumping to maintain milk production while you give the baby formula. This process of expressing breast milk and then throwing it away is often called *pump and dump,* and it is useful for any period of time when you want to maintain lactation but aren't able to breast-feed.

Is It Birth Control?

While it's true that lactation suppresses ovulation, it does not do so completely. A woman who is breast-feeding exclusively, meaning that she does not supplement with formula, is 90 percent protected against pregnancy. However, even within this group, ovulation can resume within six weeks of delivery—this happens 7 percent of the time. Generally speaking, the less you breast-feed, the more likely you are to be ovulating. Further, once you get a period, even if you are breast-feeding exclusively, you're probably fertile. Because

WHAT TO DO WITH THE OVERFLOW

If you make a huge amount of milk, consider donating to a human milk bank. I had a patient who donated her extra milk to a cancer hospital for babies whose mothers couldn't make milk. There are regional milk banks, or check whether your local hospital accepts it.

breast-feeding is not 100 percent effective as a contraceptive, do not rely on it for birth control. Unless you're ready to be pregnant again, use a backup method (see page 252).

Weaning

When you're ready to wean your baby, you can do so gradually or go cold turkey. In the first case, you simply drop one feeding each day or so. The all-at-once plan requires a tight bra, which you should put on and sleep in for about twenty-four hours to restrict milk production. Some women swear by cabbage leaves on the breast—this is an old wives' tale that seems to work for inexplicable reasons. It's also important to avoid all stimulation of the nipples when you're weaning, so as not to invite milk production. If you decide to use the cold-turkey method, keep in mind that weaning, slow or fast, can lead to enlarged, swollen, hard, and uncomfortable breasts, which may last for several days. An over-the-counter pain medication or anti-inflammatory should help relieve the discomfort.

BREAST SURGERY AND BREAST-FEEDING

Breast implants typically do not pose a problem in breast-feeding. Usually, the implant pushes the nipple out, making it easier for the baby to latch onto. In breast reductions, however, some milk ducts may be severed when the tissue is rearranged. The more ducts that are severed, the less milk gets to the baby and the more likely you are to suffer breast engorgement and infection, as all the severed ducts produce milk that has nowhere to go.

What If You're Bottle-Feeding?

The major advantage of bottle-feeding is that you, the mother, are no longer the food source for the baby. This means that anyone at any time can feed the child. For women who don't make enough milk, formula can be the only way to make sure the baby is getting enough to eat. And for those who cannot breast-feed due to health or personal issues, formula is obviously essential.

Beyond the fact that formula does not offer the health benefits of human breast milk (mentioned previously), the drawbacks include expense and convenience. Breast milk is free; formula is not. Feeding your baby by bottle requires you to carry lots more stuff with you when you go out: Formula, bottles, and nipples are all essential for bottle-feeding, while the breast-feeding mom needs only her breasts. And, of course, when the baby wakes up in the middle of the night for a feeding, it's a lot easier to simply put her at your breast than to have to get to the kitchen and warm up a bottle.

Like many other aspects of pregnancy, you should not let the breast-feeding versus bottle-feeding option drive you crazy. If you cannot breast-feed for one reason or another, your child will still thrive with formula.

CHAPTER 13

Myths of Obstetrics

*O*f course, pregnancy, labor, and delivery are all incredibly important, emotional, personal events—so much so that expecting moms can bump medical concerns and their own physical well-being from their top priorities. When the quest for the perfect pregnancy or an idealistic labor "experience" becomes too important, it can compromise rational health decisions. Before deciding, for example, to have a baby at home, ask yourself whether your child is likely to benefit from that decision (the evidence suggests not). Be realistic and flexible about what you expect; just because parenting can be wonderful, doesn't mean pregnancy, labor, and delivery will be. Most of the misconceptions about human reproduction arise from this disconnect between romantic notions and actual facts about the event.

Common Pregnancy Myths

1. Pregnancy has been overmedicalized. It's a natural thing; you don't need a doctor.

On the one hand, having babies is a natural event. Every species must reproduce or face extinction. On the other hand, *natural* does not always mean safe. Kidney stones and arthritis are both natural, but not desirable, and medicine helps reduce the health risks and physical discomfort associated with them. The same is true of pregnancy. The human female is not well built for delivering babies.

Medical science has worked for centuries on making childbirth more comfortable and safe, and while hospitals may not be esthetically pleasing, they do tend to keep you alive.

At the turn of the last century in New York City, one in a hundred childbirths resulted in a maternal death. Childbirth is the leading cause of death among women under 30 in Afghanistan *today*. While nearly 7 percent of Afghani women who enjoy a perfectly *natural* pregnancy will die, that number is only 0.007 percent in the United States. In other words, modern obstetrics reduces your risk of dying by one thousand times. Your obstetrician has many tools at her disposal to anticipate, prevent, detect, and treat all the complications of pregnancy, labor, and delivery. Creating a partnership with your doctor should make you feel comfortable about entrusting yourself to her care and will make your pregnancy and delivery safe and healthy.

2.An unmedicated labor is the best kind of birth for me and my baby.

In the 1960s and 1970s, before the advent of regional anesthesia and before the booming popularity of Lamaze and natural childbirth, women in labor were given heavy doses of narcotic sedation

EVEN PUKING CAN KILL

Charlotte Brontë, the author of *Jane Eyre*, was the last surviving child of a pastor in England. On a tour of the Brontë homestead in England, I learned that Charlotte had died from an obstetrical complication. As an obstetrician, this drove me crazy. What exactly killed her? It took weeks for me to find the precise cause of her death. In the end, I learned that it was morning sickness. She started throwing up and didn't stop. She grew weaker and weaker over a protracted period of extreme malaise; she was sick long enough to have had time to send letters and see visitors on her deathbed. She passed away in her fourth month of pregnancy from dehydration and an electrolyte imbalance. Were she alive today, her doctor would have put her on an IV, given her a couple of liters of fluid, and sent her home.

to relieve their pain. These drugs crossed the placenta and resulted in some sleepy, drugged newborns who failed to breathe right away. While it sounds frightening, these babies did not suffer any health ramifications. We rarely use narcotics in labor anymore, but those sleepy babies are likely to be part of the reason pain medication has a bad rap.

The most common pain relief in labor is the epidural, and it has helped many women not only with their pain but with the overall efficiency and health of labor. On the plus side, epidurals relax the vagina for delivery, which translates into less resistance (and trauma) to the baby's head. The cervix tends to dilate more quickly with an epidural. Further, the regional anesthesia given in an epidural makes it possible for the mother to communicate with her doctor during the delivery. Unlike unmedicated women who are expending all their energy getting through their extreme pain, women who have epidurals are more responsive to directions to push or stop pushing, making the delivery more controlled. Some experts suggest that the incidence of postpartum depression is lower among women who had pain relief during labor and that as many as 7 percent of women who skip epidurals experience symptoms of posttraumatic stress disorder. Finally—and for some, most importantly—the medication in the epidural does not cross the placenta or get to the baby.

IF IT'S GOOD ENOUGH FOR THE QUEEN . . .

When general anesthesia was first introduced, Queen Victoria of England had already had several children. The queen was no fool and signed herself up for anesthesia in labor as soon as it became available. This became the subject of national theological debate. Many claimed labor was supposed to be painful; it was Eve's eternal punishment for handing Adam the apple. It was broadly stated that pain relief during labor was simply "unnatural." Needless to say, Queen Victoria did not buy it and opted for anesthetic for all of her subsequent childbirth experiences.

The main risk with epidurals is that the mother's blood pressure might drop and decrease blood flow to the baby. This risk, however, has been virtually eliminated by advances in epidural technique (page 185), and a competent anesthesiologist and medical team will take plenty of precautions.

3. Any *medication is bad for the baby!*

There are drugs that have a very high risk of causing birth defects if taken anytime during pregnancy. For instance, medication for epilepsy carries a significant risk of cleft palate. Doctors try to minimize that risk by prescribing the safest medication available; however, with epilepsy, there is still up to a 3 percent chance of the baby developing a cleft palate as a result of the drugs. Without them, though, the woman would be risking nine months of seizures, which can be devastating for her and the baby. There's the considerable risk of physical harm in falling down and thrashing around, and seizures cut off oxygen to the fetus, ultimately contributing to brain damage. It's much easier to healthfully address a known risk instead. There is a risk/benefit ratio for any decision in pregnancy.

So don't be "heroic" for your baby by avoiding treatment for a tooth abscess or some other kind of infection. If you need antibiotics to treat an ailment when you're not pregnant, chances are you need them when you are pregnant. Remember that many illnesses do not

YOUR HEALTH IS VERY IMPORTANT

A pregnant patient suffered through a very high fever (103 to 104 degrees Fahrenheit) from a virus. She didn't call me because she thought I'd "make her take something." She would have refused Tylenol. A week later she reported the event, and many months later her baby was born with an extreme learning disability, which very likely was caused by her high temperature. If you develop a medical issue in pregnancy, you are not doing anyone any favors by suffering in silence.

seem life threatening to us today because we can effectively treat them before they progress very far.

4. Hospitals are hotbeds of dangerous infections, so it's better to have a baby at home.

If you think it's nice to douse your bed in blood, fluids, and feces, then, yes, home deliveries are nice. Similarly, people who hate needles, antiseptic hospitals, and doctors might be more psychologically comfortable envisioning childbirth at home rather than in a medical setting. But there is a price for this comfort. Babies can get into trouble, and your house is unlikely to be equipped with fetal monitors, resuscitative equipment, or pediatric specialists. If the mother hemorrhages in labor, having a blood bank and an operating room down the hall can make the difference between life and death. All I'm saying is have your baby at the hospital.

Many women fear infection in a hospital setting. This is the only real increased risk in a hospital, and medical personnel do every-

NATURE DOESN'T ALWAYS GET IT RIGHT

Water births are particularly trendy right now for nonscientific reasons. Patients of mine have used the birth experience of porpoises as a reason for their own water births, even though porpoises are mammals that happen to live in the ocean. However, even baby porpoises drown when they occasionally swim for the bottom instead of the surface. Porpoises are also born tail first, while humans are born head first. So the porpoise doesn't need to breathe until the whole body is out. While many midwives claim that there is a reflex that prevents the human baby from breathing until she hits the air, there are plenty of instincts I wouldn't depend on. Some midwives wait for a contraction to push the baby's body out, while the kid's head is still underwater—this is putting the child at risk of drowning as well as exposing her to all sorts of fecal matter floating in the water. Perhaps there are good rationales for water births, but don't try to convince your obstetrician with the porpoise explanation.

thing they can to minimize it. The obstetrical unit in a hospital is strictly segregated from the other departments to protect women and their babies from infections. In addition, the nursery rules about cleanliness are extraordinarily strict, and the nursery staff is periodically cultured for bacteria. Finally, because the vast majority of dangerous bacteria are likely to be right in the mother's vagina, infection via this route becomes more of a risk factor in home deliveries because the mother is not always tested or treated for bacteria beforehand. This mitigates the tangible advantage of home births.

The risk of an infection in a hospital setting is still far lower than that of complications associated with a home delivery. The unique risks of a home delivery are too many to list here, but they mainly revolve around the inability to respond to a real emergency in a timely fashion.

There are ways to handle an alternative birth without increased risks. For example, a birthing center that's part of a hospital offers as safe a delivery as possible.

5. Women have been having babies for millennia, mostly without medical help. All this testing and medicine is excessive.

The *vast* majority of the time, if you do nothing whatsoever to aid your pregnancy, you and the baby will be just fine. Most obstetrical care aims at addressing easy issues like birth weight, nutrition, and vitamins, but the small percentage that deals with life-threatening developments, such as gestational diabetes, hypertensive disorders, and birth defects, justifies all the extra tests and possible intervention. Don't get me wrong, no matter how well managed your health care, bad things can happen. But in the proper setting, the effect of those complications can be managed, treated, or, best of all, prevented.

Considering that women have been dying for millennia from childbirth, it's quite an accomplishment that today it is a relatively safe event. In nature there is a high mortality rate associated with reproduction—the percentage of early attrition among many species would be simply intolerable to us. Consider that most other animals produce litters to guarantee the survival of at least a few individuals.

It's important to consider that the human female has evolved rather poorly to tolerate birth. When humans started walking on two feet instead of four, our skeletons had to become lighter so that our legs alone could carry us. This included a narrowing of the pelvis, which made it a very tight fit for the human skull. Shed any illusions you have about your great-great-grandmothers popping out five kids like it was nothing—childbirth has always been dangerous.

6. The more weight you gain, the better.

The average weight gain during pregnancy in the United States is thirty-five pounds. According to the March of Dimes, the calculated optimal weight gain is somewhere between twenty-two and twenty-seven pounds. If everything you eat is nutritionally valuable, you can have a wonderful pregnancy with a twenty-five-pound weight gain. Those other ten pounds are the Twinkie factor—putting mayonnaise on your sandwich to get the chicken down or having a cookie with your milk. In my opinion, these are the things that make life worth living. If you want to exert more control over your daily nutrition, you can keep your weight gain to twenty-five pounds.

Obstetricians don't get that worried about excessive weight gain if it is gradual. But your doctor will pay attention to a patient who is *not* gaining, because her baby could be nutritionally shortchanged.

MEDICAL ADVANCES CANNOT BE OVERESTIMATED

A pregnant patient of mine was reading *War and Peace*, in which one of the characters dies in childbirth. She exclaimed to me, "But, my God, the book doesn't say anything more about it! What could have happened?" Dying in childbirth was such a common occurrence before the twentieth century, it didn't warrant much explanation. Conversely, today, a maternal death is a catastrophe that is examined and reexamined by the entire medical team.

YOU'RE PREGNANT! EAT SOMETHING!

A pregnant patient with an eating disorder just could not bring herself to eat. In spite of all our efforts, she had gained only about five pounds by the eighth month. She would say to me, "I'm doing the best I can." At thirty-six weeks, the sonogram revealed that the baby was barely alive. We admitted her and did an emergency C-section on a four-and-a-half-pound baby who looked like a child of famine and died shortly from malnutrition. In contrast, a bulimic patient of mine navigated her pregnancy successfully, with some compromises. We agreed, at her therapist's recommendation, that she would have three square meals a day, in which she consumed all her recommended nutrition. In the middle of the afternoon, hours after lunch, she would eat a Snickers bar and throw it up. Granted, this approach to maternal nutrition is not ideal or orthodox, but this woman had a healthy child.

7. You must avoid hair dye, nail polish, swimming pools, waxing . . .

Because obstetricians are so frightened of giving advice that might later be construed as harmful, they often err on the side of extreme caution. Also, it's often easier for them to simply tell you not to do something than to thoughtfully discuss the options.

For example, women have been advised by their physicians to avoid things as innocuous as swimming after the seventh month of pregnancy. One male doctor told his more pregnant patients to stay out of the water because being immersed would make it difficult to notice if their water broke. When you pee in the pool, do you notice? The only real danger with water recreation is in the bathtub, where you're off balance. If you're going to do something that involves slippery porcelain, get a safety bar, have your partner help you, and try not to slip, but the water itself is very safe. Getting in and out of an empty bathtub is the most dangerous part.

With that in mind, you should still try to avoid most environmental hazards in the first twelve weeks of pregnancy. The first trimester is when organogenesis takes place, whereby one cell

QUESTIONABLE HAIR DYE

There was an article twenty years ago about a certain black hair dye that utilized coal tar to produce blue-black hair. When scientists put this coal tar on albino rabbits that are bred to be especially sensitive to their environment, a few got skin cancer. So the extrapolation was that all hair dyes must cause birth defects. This is pretty far from established medical doctrine. The active ingredient in most hair dyes is hydrogen peroxide (H_2O_2), an antiseptic that you would use on a cut, even while pregnant. Nothing about hair dye has ever been implicated in a pregnancy complication—and the same goes for nail polish and waxing. And that coal tar dye is no longer available.

grows into all the body's organs, and while the slightest environmental disturbance might not cause any harm, it's far less likely to do so later on. That's why the rules get laxer as you get closer to your due date.

8. You should not have sex for six weeks prior to your due date.

This is probably the most negative of all the myths. Sex is wonderful for childbirth. It keeps the vagina dilated and relaxed, allowing for easier pelvic exams. Celibate pregnant women tend to have congested and swollen vaginas. Sexually active women are easier to examine and have easier labors.

9. Your sex life is over.

Maybe. The effects of pregnancy on libido are impossible to predict or explain. Some women are averse to sex in pregnancy, while others have never more been more horny. Likewise, there are plenty of men who can't get enough of their pregnant wives. There's something voluptuous, Rubenesque, and fabulous about a pregnant woman that is so erotic to some men that they would have sex twice a day if they could. Then there are husbands who cannot touch their wives when they are pregnant, because they are afraid of hurting

SEX IS LIKE RIDING A BIKE

I knew a man who said that after he and his wife got through their first year of being parents, he suddenly looked at her and felt as if it was their first date all over again. It may take time, but it will happen. One day, you're going to look at your partner and say, "Oh, yeah, *that* person. I really like having sex with him." And you will, and it will be great.

the baby. Unless your man has razor blades on the tip of his penis, this is simply not possible.

Labor and delivery add a few new elements to the mix. You have a newborn, maybe you've put on a lot of weight, your hemorrhoids could be acting up, and most likely you haven't been getting much sleep—these are the most common, legitimate reasons for postpartum celibacy. Breast-feeding can also deaden libido by cutting off the production of estrogen and progesterone. However, most women are physically able to have sex at four weeks past delivery, and some are ready at two. The recovery time depends on many variables, notably the size of the baby—a six-pound baby does less harm to the vagina than a nine-pound baby. Of course, lifestyle factors also play a role. For example, a woman who has a full-time nurse, housekeeper, and nanny is likely to be interested in sex much sooner than one who has to do all the work herself, because the former is simply better rested. A woman who's just had her third kid and has no help at all may never be interested in sex again!

10. Bed rest is a proven way to help an unstable pregnancy.

Bed rest is one obstetrician's tool that lacks any scientific evidence for its efficacy. Many obstetricians still prescribe bed rest when a patient stains or bleeds because logic dictates that it is better for her and the child, because (1) she uses less oxygen, theoretically maximizing blood flow to the baby; (2) she's horizontal, so her cervix remains untaxed from standing or jumping; and (3) she isn't burning many calories for herself, so all possible nutrition is arguably going to the baby. In spite of these rational explanations, studies have shown that total bed rest has been of little help when it comes to preventing miscarriages and premature labor (but it may help a growth-delayed baby).

Although science does not support the benefit of bed rest in every instance, it is surely never a good idea to overdo physical activity. A woman who passes up her doctor's suggestion to take it easy is rarely consoled by the fact that her miscarriage was probably scientifically inevitable, and she might feel better knowing the medical team did everything they could to support the pregnancy. Although it doesn't make a statistical difference over a large population, bed rest may help on a case-by-case basis.

As with everything in pregnancy, do not become obsessed with bed rest. Although prolonged repose does not harm the baby, it can have negative effects on the mother's well-being, including diminished cardiac health, muscle atrophy, and a slower metabolism. For these reasons, obstetricians recommend bed rest as infrequently as possible, and they increasingly couple this regimen with a bed-friendly exercise program.

11. You glow when you're pregnant.

Maybe. Some women never look as good as when they're pregnant. They have beautiful pink cheeks, a gleam in their eyes, extra energy, and translucent skin. Larger breasts are also a shapely addition to some smaller frames. For some women, their radiance may simply be the result of sleeping more than they have in years. Women who are delighted to be pregnant tend to smile more and therefore look better. Hormones and increased blood flow probably alter the appearance of pregnant women, too, but no one knows exactly how or why some women look better while others look worse.

Conversely, some women look their worst during pregnancy. Their noses seem to get bigger, their skin is sallow, and they have stretch marks everywhere—often these women don't feel great, which doesn't help them look any better. In addition, women with large breasts to begin with may end up with a chest so large it's no longer flattering.

My opinion is that it's preferable to look your worst during pregnancy over looking your best. After all, who wants to think, "I was never as beautiful as when I was pregnant"? Pregnancy is a finite part of your whole life. Isn't it better to look good the rest of the time?

12. Motherhood is an instinct.

Maybe, but in many cases we have clearly diminished our instinctive capabilities in favor of intellectual ability. Take breast-feeding, for example. Today, there are lactation consultants, hospital classes, and institutions all devoted to breast-feeding. This is because many women struggle to get the hang of it at first, perhaps because we've lost the instinctual ability to execute this basic task. So when it comes to breast-feeding or any other responsibility of motherhood, don't be afraid to seek some extra guidance. Think of information as a tool to be used at your discretion.

WHAT ABOUT PARENTING BOOKS?

A couple I knew personally underwent seven in vitro fertilization cycles (at costs approximating $7,000 per cycle) before getting pregnant. I asked the mother what she and her husband were reading on child rearing, and she said, "We're gonna fly by the seat of our pants." There are experts out there who have studied all of the ins and outs of the early years of motherhood and can give you the best advice on every aspect of parenting, from soothing a colicky baby to weaning, toilet training, and how to teach verbal and motor skills. Although not every bit of parenting advice you'll find in a book or on a website is going to be useful, consider the information you can glean from these sources as food for thought. This "expert" advice is not Holy Writ, and you certainly don't have to follow every instruction. (You don't *have* to do everything we tell you, either.) There are many good ways to handle motherhood, and the more you familiarize yourself with some of them, the more options you'll have.

13. Caesarian sections are more dangerous to the mother.

Today, the mortality rate from caesarian section is no different from that with a vaginal delivery. It's important to remember that no matter how perfect your obstetrical care, complications can always develop. Very few of them are fatal; a handful come with some health risks.

Each route to motherhood has pros and cons. Caesarian sections carry a greater risk of wound infection and require longer hospital stays. However, there is no doubt that a simple caesarian section is much safer than a very involved (e.g., midforceps) operative vaginal delivery. Complications unique to vaginal deliveries include lacerations of the mother's bladder and/or rectum and shoulder dystocia, which can cause partial nerve damage to the shoulders and arms of the baby (see page 204). There are also future health concerns with vaginal deliveries that do not exist with caesarians, such as fecal and urinary incontinence—significant quality-of-life issues that may be avoided, or at least delayed, when a woman delivers via a C-section. As a longtime obstetrician, I cannot overestimate the value of being able to offer safe C-sections to all my patients.

Conclusion

March 31, 1976

At 3 A.M. a contraction woke me up. I looked at the clock and went back to sleep. About seven minutes later, another contraction jerked me awake, and while it was uncomfortable, it wasn't enough to keep me from falling back to sleep.

At about 7 A.M., I had to pee, and on the way to the bathroom my water broke. That's when my husband, Richard, woke up, looked at me with a towel between my legs, and said, "What's going on?"

I told him my water had broken, but I curtly reminded him that we were going to stay home as long as possible. That was the plan, and I was going to shower. Richard called the obstetrician.

I was in the shower when I had my first post-water-breaking contraction. It was blinding, and there was nothing to hold onto—just a blur of white tile. When it was over, I tried to wash my hair. Another contraction hit me three minutes later, and then another one right away. After that, I gave up.

I came out of the bathroom very wet, mostly still dirty, with soapy hair. I sat down at my makeup table with the intention of doing my hair. Richard asked, "Well, if we're staying home, do I have time to take a shower?"

Richard's normal fifteen-minute shower seemed to take five hours. When he got out, I was still just as he'd left me, slumped over at the makeup table, stark naked and totally wet. I said, "I think we have to go to the hospital. I betcha I'm fully dilated."

He said, wagging a finger, "I'm supposed to keep you home as long as possible." A string of expletives flowed from my mouth, culminating in, "Shut up and get me dressed."

He managed to find me a bra, a jumper, and some flip-flops, but no panties. We went downstairs past the entire building staff, where

I hid myself in the lobby until Richard got a cab with a very nervous driver. I think I heard him whimpering in between my moaning.

I don't remember getting to the hospital, or the elevator, or anything until we walked into labor and delivery. I grabbed the first resident I saw and growled, "Check me! Check me!" I was sure the excruciating pain meant that I was already fully dilated.

From there we went to the labor room and someone got me into a hospital gown. All the while I was moaning, groaning, and carrying on. Let me remind you that thirty-two years ago, epidurals were brand new, so their availability was spotty—the two guys who could do them at my hospital were not available that morning. And no one was going to give me anything else for pain until my doctor showed up. When he finally arrived, he examined me and reported that I was four centimeters dilated.

I said, "Four centimeters! Are you crazy?! Stretch me! Make it six! Do something!" So he asked the nurse to give me an enema. I sat up and screamed, "No enema. I don't want an enema! Give me Demerol. I don't want an enema. I want another doctor." Everyone laughed at me.

Next thing I'm hearing is the head nurse saying, "Hold it. Hold it." I guess they were already done putting the enema in, and someone instructed me to hold my cheeks together and get to the toilet, which was five steps away. I got there, dragging my husband with me. (This is not typical of other labors I've seen.) I sat on the toilet bowl and held onto Richard for dear life.

An enema is unpleasant under any circumstances, but when there's a baby in your uterus and fluid in your rectum, it's excruciating and confusing. I had no idea what was going to come out of my body. In my case, that twenty minutes was just the longest, most thorough bowel movement of my entire life. At some point, I bit Richard's stomach.

Afterward, I got back into bed and the nurse started an IV. My doctor reexamined me and reported that I was six centimeters dilated. This seemed impossibly slow, but at least he finally agreed to give me some Demerol. While the nurse administered the pain-relieving drug, I noticed she also gave me Pitocin to increase my contractions.

I can't say that I loved the Demerol. I was blissfully asleep when I wasn't in pain. That was three great minutes, and then the contraction would wake me up. First, I'd be disoriented, then there were another thirty seconds of total wakefulness and pain before it would wane. I'd say that the Demerol helped for the first ten seconds and last ten seconds of each contraction; the middle part was horrible. Richard timed my contractions for me, and the entire time I was awake I'd ask him how many seconds had passed. He'd intone something like, "Ten seconds . . ." and I'd say, "What do you *mean*, ten seconds? Oh my God! Oh my God!" Then I'd ask again, "What is it now?"

It was like I was seeing God when he would finally announce "Forty seconds." This meant the contraction was at its peak, and it would be over in less time than it had been going on. That was a split second of absolute joy.

When I wasn't asking for the seconds, I was pleading for more Demerol.

This went on for two hours—two hours of counting every second of the contraction, two hours of asking for more Demerol. Then I was fully dilated.

I pushed and I pushed for what must have been an entire half hour. During the pushing phase, nearly every woman in labor asks every person in the room who can see her vagina, "Do you see anything? Do you see anything?!" When I asked the four people present, two heads went side to side and two heads went top to bottom.

The doctor and the head nurse said no. Richard and the resident said yes. I grabbed Richard and said, "Richard, you're the only one I trust. What do you see when I have a contraction? You're the only one. Look me in the eye, tell me what you see."

He said, "I don't know, Carol, I think I see a little wisp of hair."

I said, "That's it. Forceps delivery. I want to have a forceps delivery. I believe in resident education, and I think the resident should do it. Where's the anesthesiologist?" As they wheeled me to the delivery room, I told my husband to bond with the baby, because I was going to sleep.

I don't remember anything other than the anesthesiologist, whom I grabbed by the waist and demanded anesthesia from. I snatched the mask out of her hand and then I was asleep. The next day, she came by my room to show me the black-and-blue imprint of my five fingers on her flank.

The favorite anesthesia among obstetricians at the time was cyclopropane because it put patients to sleep in five seconds, and they could be awakened just as fast. Unfortunately, cyclopropane is highly explosive. In fact, on March 31, 1976, they were removing all of it from labor and delivery rooms because it was so dangerous. I was one of the last patients at my hospital to be given this fast-acting gas.

When I woke up briefly in the delivery room, a nurse asked, "So? What did you think?"

"Adopt."

Index